D0675328

# NEW TESTAMENT MESSAGE

*A Biblical-Theological Commentary*

Wilfrid Harrington, O.P. and Donald Senior, C.P.
EDITORS

*New Testament Message, Volume 5*

# LUKE

Eugene LaVerdiere, S.S.S.

A Michael Glazier Book
THE LITURGICAL PRESS
Collegeville, Minnesota

## ABOUT THE AUTHOR

Eugene LaVerdiere, Blessed Sacrament Father, is an Associate Professor of New Testament Theology at the Jesuit School of Theology in Chicago. After his ordination in 1964, he received a S.T.L. from the University of Fribourg (1965) and S.S.L. from the Pontifical Biblical Institute (1967) and he was accepted as an Eleve Titulaire of the Ecole Biblique de Jerusalem (1968). In 1977 he received a Ph.D. from the University of Chicago. Father LaVerdiere is well known as a writer and lecturer in the United States and several foreign countries.

A Michael Glazier Book

*published by*

THE LITURGICAL PRESS

7       8       9

**Library of Congress Cataloging-in-Publication Data**

LaVerdiere, Eugene.
    Luke / Eugene LaVerdiere
        p.     cm. — (New Testament message ; v. 5)
    "A Michael Glazier book."
    Reprint. Originally published: Dublin : Veritas Publications, c1980.
    Includes bibliographical references.
    ISBN 0-8146-5128-3
    1. Bible N.T. Luke—Commentaries. I. Title. II. Series.
BS2595.3.L38    1990
226.4'07—dc20                    90-41519
                                          CIP

*To my parents*
*Gladys and Laurier*
*in gratitude for*
*life abundantly given*
*and*
*faith generously shared*

# Contents

# EDITORS' PREFACE

*New Testament Message* is a commentary series designed
to bring the best of biblical scholarship to a wide audience.
Anyone who is sensitive to the mood of the church today is
aware of a deep craving for the Word of God. This interest
in reading and praying the scriptures is not confined to a
religious elite. The desire to strengthen one's faith and to
mature in prayer has brought Christians of all types and all
ages to discover the beauty of the biblical message. Our age
has also been heir to an avalanche of biblical scholarship.
Recent archaeological finds, new manuscript evidence, and
the increasing volume of specialized studies on the Bible
have made possible a much more profound penetration of
the biblical message. But the flood of information and its
technical nature keeps much of this scholarship out of the
hands of the Christian who is eager to learn but is not a
specialist. *New Testament Message* is a response to this
need.

The subtitle of the series is significant: "A Biblical-
Theological Commentary." Each volume in the series, while
drawing on up-to-date scholarship, concentrates on bringing to the fore in understandable terms the specific message of each biblical author. The essay-format (rather than
a word-by-word commentary) helps the reader savor the
beauty and power of the biblical message and, at the same
time, understand the sensitive task of responsible biblical
interpretation.

A distinctive feature of the series is the amount of space
given to the "neglected" New Testament writings, such as
Colossians, James, Jude, the Pastoral Letters, the Letters

of Peter and John. These briefer biblical books make a
significant but often overlooked contribution to the richness
of the New Testament. By assigning larger than normal
coverage to these books, the series hopes to give these parts
of Scripture the attention they deserve.

Because *New Testament Message* is aimed at the entire
English speaking world, it is a collaborative effort of international proportions. The twenty-two contributors represent biblical scholarship in North America, Ireland, Britain
and Australia. Each of the contributors is a recognized
expert in his or her field, has published widely, and has been
chosen because of a proven ability to communicate at a
popular level. And, while all of the contributors are Roman
Catholic, their work is addressed to the Christian community as a whole. The New Testament is the patrimony
of all Christians.It is the hope of all concerned with this
series that it will bring a fuller appreciation of God's saving
Word to his people.

Wilfrid Harrington, O.P.
Donald Senior, C.P.

# INTRODUCTION

LUKE'S GOSPEL is a literary and pastoral interpretation of the story of Jesus, the Son of Adam, the Son of God (Lk 3:38). As the first of Luke's two volumes to Theophilus, it concerns all that Jesus began to do and teach until the day he was taken up to heaven after instructing the apostles he had chosen through the Holy Spirit (Acts 1:1-2). As such it provides the background necessary for the second volume, which concerns the witness which the apostles gave in Jerusalem, throughout Judea and Samaria, and which they brought to the end of the earth, once the Holy Spirit had come upon them (Acts 1:8).

In modern times, the two volumes are ordinarily referred to as Luke-Acts, a designation which recognizes their unity and indicates that they should be viewed as one literary work. For the gospel, this means that 24:53 is not the end of the story, as it would be in Mark, Matthew and John, but only the signal for a short intermission. For Acts, it means that 1:1 is not an absolute beginning but the resumption of Luke's narrative of the sequence of events fulfilled in our midst (Lk 1:1-3).

Taken together, Luke's two volumes constitute by far the longest work in the New Testament. This material observation, however, which indicates that Luke had a great deal to share, says quite little about the scope of Luke's achievement. Like Mark's gospel which came before it,

Matthew's gospel which was its near contemporary, and John's gospel which reached its definitive form somewhat later, Luke-Acts represented a new literary genre, which has points of comparison in and out of the New Testament but which cannot be reduced to any of these. In relation to the other gospels, the very existence of Acts makes this quite plain. In relation to the Old Testament, which Luke knew through the Septuagint, and the literary forms of Greek literature, familiar to him at least from his cultural environment if not from formal education, the christian events in which Luke participated provided an extremely creative literary crucible.

To appreciate Luke's achievement, a description of the christian context out of which the narrative was written and which it addressed is very helpful. Narratives are written with special readers in mind, and unless we have some sense of who these are, we miss much of the story's intention, even if our concern extends beyond the narrative's original addressees. Accordingly, this introduction begins with a consideration of the Lukan communities.

For modern readers, who stand far removed from New Testament times, it is equally helpful to have a synthesis of Luke's message. Such a synthesis, whose form in commentaries and special studies is usually discursive, never replaces the narrative itself, but it does alert us to its major themes and to the hierarchy of their importance in relation to Luke's intended readers. The second part of the introduction is consequently devoted to a synthesis of Luke's message to the Lukan communities.

Like Luke's readers, who were provided with a brief preface (Lk 1:1-4), we also need a statement of the objectives and methods which inspire and guide our interpretation in this commentary. It then becomes possible to situate this contribution to the *New Testament Message* with regard to other Lukan commentaries, whose objectives and methods are different, and to see how it complements these and needs to be complemented by them. Accordingly, the concluding part of the introduction presents the commentary's objectives and methods in addressing twentieth century Theophilus.

## The Lukan Communities

Luke does not describe the readers for which Luke-Acts was intended. But then few creative writers do. The people who fill Luke's narrative lived earlier in the first century, and the concluding events of Acts antedate his writing by approximately one quarter of a century. His addressees belonged to a new generation of Christians, Christianity's third generation.

Nevertheless, the primary source for describing Luke's first readers remains Luke-Acts itself. The Lukan narrative not only recorded and interpreted events long past but spoke them to Christians living at a new time and in a new social setting. In light of this second aspect of Luke-Acts, we must assume that the events were presented not only as they affected their original participants but also from the point of view of their relevance to Luke's readers as he perceived them. In scientific work, the study of the readers which a narrative presupposes follows the study of the narrative itself. In presenting this work, however, it is possible to begin with the addressees and to leave their life context open for verification by an examination of the author's message.

The intended readers of Luke-Acts were Christians who lived in the ninth decade of the first century. Like the Matthean community, these Christians had been nourished by Mark's account of the beginning of the gospel of Jesus Christ, the Son of God (Mk 1:1) and by a collection of sayings of Jesus which scholars call Q, the first letter of the German word for source, *Quelle*. Although we have no literary record of this collection, much of it can be retrieved by a comparative study of Luke and Matthew. Unlike the Matthean community, Luke's readers had even earlier roots in the communities sprung from the Pauline missions which we know so well from the corpus of Pauline letters and from Luke's own Acts of the Apostles.

Paul's apostolic appeals for attitudes and behavior consistent with the christian story had presupposed the gospel story, just as the Old Testament prophets had presupposed the *Torah*. It had not, however, dispensed with the need to formulate the story in writing. In a time of crisis (*circa* 70 a.d.), which saw the destruction of Jerusalem and its temple, Mark responded to this need, and his work acquired enormous authority in communities as diverse as those of Matthew and Luke. However, with the passing of this crisis and the rise of new crises, Mark proved no longer adequate for the Lukan and Matthean communities. A new time with different needs and fresh challenges called for new accounts of the gospel. Luke and Matthew responded to the needs of their respective communities by reinterpreting Mark in creative and vastly expanded gospel syntheses. In doing so, they enriched their narratives with the sayings of Jesus handed down in Q and showed how these applied concretely to various christian settings.

With their origins in the Pauline missions, Luke's readers were quite different from those of Matthew, who had a long tradition in Judaism and had had a close association with the synagogue. Recently thrust out of Judaism, Matthew's jewish christian community had taken on the gentile mission. Still suffering from exclusion from the synagogue, it was threatened by absorption into a gentile world with which it had little experience. Matthew's gospel would help it to maintain its christian identity in these difficult circumstances. The historical and social context it addressed, however, made it little suited to Luke's readers, who were not jewish but gentile, and whose problems stemmed precisely from being gentile Christians in circumstances which challenged a faith and a way of life which they had come to take for granted. Just as Matthew would write a gospel for jewish christian communities,

Luke would write a narrative specifically aimed at gentile christian communities.

Luke's gentile readers lived in communities radiating from Antioch, the political and cultural capital of the Roman province of Syria and one of the great formative centers of early Christianity. The same city and the region which surrounded it was home for the Matthean community. For Matthew's jewish christian community, however, Antioch was a home away from home, a home in the diaspora in which they were now called to sink permanent roots. The Lukan communities, on the other hand, were not diaspora communities. As gentile Christians, Antioch and other Greco-Roman cities had provided a true home for them practically from the beginning. After the persecutions which had propelled hellenistic jewish Christians into their midst, it had taken very little time before the communities acquired a clearly gentile stamp. Their stance toward Jerusalem was consequently quite different from that of the Matthean community.

The Lukan communities had seen the center of Christianity shift from Jerusalem, the religious capital of Judaism, northwards to Antioch, and for a long time they had been able to assume this transfer as a normal development. With Christianity's rapid spread through the empire, however, and the emergence of a very significant community at Rome, the imperial capital, Antioch, which was but a provincial capital, saw its dominant position in Christianity relativized. Jerusalem's christian dominance was past. Rome's loomed in the future. Times were changing for Antiochene Christianity and for all the communities born of its missionary outreach.

Born of a mission to Antioch and of missions from Antioch, the Lukan communities also had a profoundly missionary character. They were missionary communities first by reason of their origins in the mission of another community and second by reason of their own active missionary stance. Unlike some of the other churches, they had not received Christianity through Jews from the diaspora who met Christians while on pilgrimage to Jerusalem and carried the christian message home with them at their return. Having benefitted from the mission, the Lukan communities saw mission as the normal way for spreading the gospel. Just as others had reached out to them, they saw themselves as needing to reach out to others. Luke's readers thus belonged to missionary communities in both the passive and the active sense of the term.

The Lukan communities were also urban communities, living and developing in hellenistic cities whose sphere of influence dominated the countryside. Their main experience was consequently with the city, its public buildings, temples, theatres, market places, arenas, wealthy homes, palaces, crowded hovels, and with the sea routes and Roman roads which joined city to city. Their world was filled with visitors from other cities and lands as well as from the countryside, with administrators, tax collectors, soldiers and mariners, with a cosmopolitan blend of religious and mercantile associations, and with a proliferation of cults old and new which thrived alongside of the official imperial religion. Living in the city, they viewed their christian mission primarily in terms of the city. The urban setting of the Lukan communities had a profound effect on Luke-Acts, which interpreted the traditional christian story for the urban context and directed its message to the needs of city dwellers.

In their origins, the Lukan communities must have been influenced by the general apocalyptic ferment which surrounded Christianity's early development and which resurfaced during the seventh decade with the First Jewish War and the destruction of Jerusalem. Mark's gospel had addressed the tendency to interpret these events as evidence of the approaching end. Insisting that the end was not yet, he had reasserted the demands of the christian mission which had to be pursued even in the midst of seemingly overwhelming difficulties.

At the time of Luke's writing, however, the apocalyptic tide had once again ebbed and its challenge had slipped into the past. Involved in a history which had brought them far from their origins, the Lukan communities' basic challenge was that of their own unfolding history. As they continued to develop, could their christian life and commitment meet the test of a world which was culturally Greek and politically Roman? At first they had been but little people, peering into that world from the stance of the lowly. But now that their numbers increasingly included the more influential, they found themselves in growing contact. Could their Christianity survive such a confrontation? Would they be absorbed by the world to which they were sent? Resisting absorption, would they be crushed by it? The situation at Luke's writing did not appear promising.

Judging from the account of Luke-Acts, the Lukan communities were troubled by problems from within and persecutions from without. The internal problems affected doubtless many aspects of life. From Luke's repeated treatment of behavior at table fellowship, the sharing of goods, reconciliation, and the exercise of leadership, we may assume that these four areas stood out among the others as major concerns. The external problems came from persecutions on various fronts. While it is difficult to define the nature and extent of these persecutions, Luke-Acts' preoccupation with them shows that they were viewed as significant threats and that they were related to the politics of the Roman Empire and Christianity's former association with Judaism.

For decades, Christians had been able to present themselves as a licit religion by reason of their origins in Judaism which Romans accepted as licit. As the gentile christian communities moved further and further away from Judaism, however, and as they grew in influence, their claim to licitness became increasingly precarious. When difficulties arose, they could easily be marked as followers of a superstition which disturbed the good order of the Roman Empire.

The combined impact of the communities' internal and external problems resulted in a severe loss of christian identity, raised serious doubts about their faith and weakened dedication to the apostolic mission. Long removed from the Judaism from which they had sprung, separated from Jesus' death-resurrection by over half a century, and immersed in the gentile world, had they lost their way? Did the problems which now affected them indicate that they had moved too far from their jewish origins, from the context of Jesus' teaching, and from the events of his life, death and resurrection? At best, the lines of continuity seemed dangerously thin.

Such was the situation out of which Luke wrote and which he addressed. His readers were gentile Christians living in the first century's ninth decade in communities associated with Antioch and missions from Antioch. These communities were also urban communities with a history of dedicated commitment to the christian mission. Sprung from the Pauline mission to the Gentiles, they had later been strengthened and enriched by gospel accounts such as that of Mark as well as by the sayings of Jesus. The communities were now confronted by the problems of their own historical development and success. Difficulties arose from within and from without. Having travelled a great distance from Christianity's origins, the very basis of christian life as they lived it and of the christian mission as they exercised it was brought into question. Clearly there was need for a new gospel synthesis which would help them to understand and meet the situation. It came in the form of Luke-Acts.

## The Message of St. Luke

Luke's message to Theophilus is as complex as the situation he meant to address. At the same time, like any creative work of genius, it is very simple, and its simplicity accounts in large part for its success as a classical work of christian literature and its inclusion of the New Testament along with other expressions of the inspired word. The challenge is for us to uncover its simplicity without destroying its complexity.

Luke's work is pastoral in intent, narrative in form, historical in conceptual design and theological in inspiration. In view of these four interpenetrating aspects, it would be inappropriate to limit his message to history alone or even to its theological themes. Too much would be left out. In the following presentation, I shall consequently try to respect Luke's synthesis of pastoral, narrative, historical and theological concerns.

## PASTORAL INTENT

In the last verse of the gospel's preface (Lk 1:1-4), Luke says that his intention in writing was to reassure his readers with regard to the truth of matters concerning which they were already informed. Since, unlike the remainder of the gospel, the preface speaks directly and explicitly of the readers' concerns, the work's pastoral intent could not be clearer. Luke-Acts was written to meet the needs of Christians who no longer recognized the solid foundations of the christian life in which they had been catechized and as they had understood and lived it. Its purpose was not so much to speak new things but to present old things in a new way, old things which the readers knew from the very sources and traditions Luke used in his work. For the truth of the old to be clear, it had to be reinterpreted for the readers' new circumstances.

Bolstered in their christian faith and identity, the Lukan communities would then be able to pursue the mission which Jesus had given his apostles prior to the ascension (Acts 1:2,8). Such was Luke's pastoral intent as it emerges from a secondary preface at the head of Acts in which Luke personally summarizes the gospel (Acts 1:1-2) and from a fresh statement of the events which occurred between Jesus' resurrection and the ascension (Acts 1:3-14). Like Luke 1:1-4, Acts' preface stands back from the narrative and speaks explicitly to the reader. In Acts 1:8, however, it is Jesus the risen Lord who speaks in a narrative which flows without break from the opening prefatory verses. Through this device, Luke invests the program of Acts and the story of how things came to be as the readers knew them with the authority of Jesus himself. Luke the interpreter of the gospel thus steps aside to allow Jesus the risen Lord to speak as interpreter.

At the end of the gospel in the resurrection narratives, Jesus had already been introduced as the interpreter of events which the disciples of Emmaus and the apostolic community did not understand (Lk 24:13-35, 36-53). From the risen Lord's role in Acts 1:3-14 and the relationship of these verses to Acts 1:1-2, it becomes clear that even in the gospel the things that Jesus did and said were meant to lead Luke's readers to the truth concerning their catechesis. This applies of course to Jesus' interpretation of the events which surrounded his passion-resurrection but also to the entire story leading up to it, as we see from the Lord's response to the Emmaus disciples' lack of understanding concerning Jesus' whole story (Lk 24:19b-24, 25-27). Luke's references to Jesus as Lord throughout the gospel were clearly by design.

Luke's pastoral intent in presenting the gospel was consequently fulfilled primarily through the person, acts and message of the risen Lord. In much of the gospel as in Acts 1:8, the risen Lord addresses the Lukan communities pastorally and far more effectively than Luke would have done had he maintained the direct address form of the preface. It follows that to appreciate the pastoral nature of Luke's gospel we must interpret it as speaking to the current situation in the Lukan communities and not merely in relation to historical events long past. The way Luke translated the setting of rural events into urban contexts

similar to those of his readers, as for example in the mul-
tiplication of loaves and fishes (Lk 9:10-17), provides
independent support for this observation.

Luke's pastoral intent was also fulfilled through others
who interpreted Jesus' life and message, as we see from
the role of the two men in the tomb and of the women who
visited it after the resurrection (Lk 24:1-11). However,
since the validity of their message was in question (Lk
24:11), it had to be grounded in the Lord's own teaching,
as we see from Lk 24:13-35, 36-53, where the risen Lord
takes up their message and interprets it according to the
scriptures. The Lord's teaching also provided the basis
for that of Peter and Paul, whose story takes up much of
Acts, as well as for other prophetic teachers (Acts 13:1-3)
and the elders (Acts 14:23) which Paul appointed to lead
the communities after his departure.

Like the events in which the Lukan communities had
been catechized, the scriptures also were misunderstood.
Luke brings the scriptures to bear on the life of his readers
through the authentic interpretation of the risen Lord who
showed how they were fulfilled. The risen Lord interprets
the events of Jesus' historical life and of the passion-
resurrection as well as the scriptures. He shows how the
events fulfilled in the midst of Luke's readers (Lk 1:1) were
according to the life and teaching of Jesus and how that life
and teaching were according to the scriptures.

## NARRATIVE FORM

Luke could have carried out his pastoral intent to bring
his readers to a renewed understanding of matters concerning which they had already been informed in a number
of ways. He chose to write a narrative. As he indicates in
Lk 1:1, many had employed this form before him. Close to
the traditional form which was already familiar to the
troubled Lukan communities, his narrative was more

likely to be accepted and to achieve its pastoral goals than would have been the case with an entirely new form.

Narrative is to literature what story-telling is to the spoken word. It communicates by presenting the story in such a way that the readers enter the story and discover that it is their own. To accomplish this effectively, the narrative must evoke the readers' life context even as it presents events which occurred quite independently of their involvement. For this to occur, the events must be told in their concreteness and particularlity and with great attention to specific details, as though they were absolutely unique. Through the use of evocative language which engages the imagination, the concreteness of narrative is what opens it to new incarnations in a multiplicity of contexts, each of which is limited and concrete. A good narrative's universal relevance springs from its very particularity. Such is the paradox of narrative.

A master of narrative form, Luke employed it to great effect in addressing his readers. After nineteen hundred years, all who in some way share the life context of his first readers continue to be drawn into his narrative and to be nourished pastorally by his account. In Luke-Acts, narrative form is not only the servant of pastoral communication but its inseparable ally.

One of the more striking features of Luke's narrative art is the highly polished character of its individual episodes. Consider, for example, the account of Jesus' remaining behind in Jerusalem (Lk 2:41-52), his inaugural presentation in the Nazareth synagogue (Lk 4:16-30), and his encounter with the lawyer who wanted to know how he could inherit eternal life (Lk 10:25-37). Consider also the Zacchaeus and Emmaus accounts (Lk 19:1-10, 24:13-35), literary gems which fill the imagination and quicken the spirit. In each of these stories and so many others, the setting is very graphically presented, the personages are sharply delineated and their stance with regard to one another is highly dramatic. With a few deft literary strokes, the background becomes so clear that little dialogue is required. There is no need for long and heavy discourses. A short exchange, a saying, a brief discourse suffice to engage the reader and communicate the message.

Several of Luke's short narratives, notably that which concludes the prologue (Lk 2:41-52) and that which introduces Jesus' mission in Galilee (Lk 4:16-30) evoke the whole story of Jesus from the beginning to the ascension even as they narrate a particular episode. Through this technique, which can be termed programmatic or proleptic, Luke showed his readers how a story transcended itself and invited them to see how it spoke of their situation as well. Grieving and searching with Mary and Joseph, they heard a message which, like Mary and Joseph, they needed to hear. With the Jews in the Nazareth synagogue, they heard Jesus' call to rally in solidarity with him in his mission to others rather than confine his mission to themselves.

The narrator's role in Lukan stories is particularly important. With the exception of Jesus, the risen Lord, Luke's narrator always knows more than the personages in the story, and he shares some of this information with the readers. As privileged participants in the story, the readers consequently know how a situation which is problematic to the story's personages should be resolved but not how in fact it will be resolved for them. A measure of tension is thus built up in the readers. Engaged in the story and gifted with special knowledge, the readers little by little learn how the story's personages arrive at the knowledge which they themselves already have but whose truth and implications they need to discover (Lk 1:4). As they come to understand the personages' situation in the story, the story brings them to a new understanding of their own situation.

A clear example of this is found in the Emmaus story, where the two disciples do not know that the person who has joined them on the journey is actually Jesus (Lk 24:15-16) and that upon arriving at Emmaus Jesus merely acted as if he intended to go further (Lk 24:28). Informed that the visitor (Lk 24:18) was Jesus (Lk 24:15) and that Jesus had no intention of going further, the reader follows the story's unfolding to its joyous resolution when the disciples finally recognize Jesus who had accepted their invitation to remain with them (Lk 24:29-31). As privileged participants, the readers had already felt the irony of the disciples' retelling of the gospel story as bad news (Lk 24:19b-24). Unrecognizing, the disciples had been telling Jesus in effect how terrible it was that he was dead. Jesus himself then shows them the truth concerning the matters which they already knew but had badly misinterpreted. By using vocabulary associated with the readers' eucharistic assembly (Lk 24:30), the narrator also makes it very plain that the disciples' story is their own. With their lack of understanding removed, the readers are then inspired to take up the mission and to share their experience of the gospel with others (Lk 24:32-33), only to find that others had already discovered the truth concerning the Lord's resurrection (Lk 24:34).

Luke's individual stories, satisfying as they may be, were not meant to stand on their own but to contribute to a much longer narrative, to the part of the gospel into which they were inserted, to the gospel as a whole and to all of Luke-Acts. They are but pericopes, segments of a narrative synthesis in which the whole is greater than the sum of its parts. As theological and pastoral statements, they are consequently limited. They need to be complemented by other accounts and appreciated from the vantage point of Luke-Acts as a whole. For example, although the Emmaus story (Lk 24:13-35) appears quite luminous as an individual unit, we miss much of its message unless we pay close attention to the visits to the tomb which precede it (Lk 24:1-12). Unless we see how it is complemented by Lk 24:36-53, we also risk viewing it as a far more comprehensive message than Luke intended. And, of course, we must situate it within the function which Lk 24:1-53 plays as the gospel's climactic chapter and the point of transition to Acts.

One of Luke's devices for linking pericopes into more comprehensive units and maintaining awareness of the gospel's overall message is his use of summaries, of which there are several kinds. Some summaries are presented by the narrator. Functionally, some of these introduce major sections of the gospel as in Lk 4:14-15, which provides a capsule statement of Jesus' activities in Lk 4:16-44 and, through this major unit, of all that is presented in Lk 5:1-9:50. Later, Lk 9:51 serves as an introduction for the journey narrative which ends only with Lk 24:53. Some of the summaries have a concluding function (Lk 1:80, 2:40, 52; 24:52-53). Others are both concluding and transitional (Lk 19:47-48; 21:37-38). As in Acts (see 1:14; 2:42-47; 4:32-35; 5:12-16; 19:21-22; 28:30-31), all of these summaries contribute to the gospel's structural design.

Within the major sections of the gospel, further divisions are indicated by the accounts concerning the disciples, who were called (Lk 5:1-11), constituted as the Twelve (Lk 6:12-16), included women (Lk 8:1-3), and were sent on mission (Lk 9:1-6). New stages in the great journey to Jerusalem are indicated by some of the narrator's references to it (Lk 10:38; 13:22 and 17:11).

Other summaries draw on the scriptures to present a major personage's role in history. For John the Baptist, we have Lk 3:4-6 (Is 40:3-5); for Jesus, Lk 4:18-19 (Is 61:1-2; 58:6); and for the apostolic community, Acts 2:17-21 (Joel 2:28-32). In the case of Jesus and the apostolic community, these scriptural summaries are not presented by the narrator but by Jesus himself and by Peter, who speaks for the whole community.

In addition, there are the canticles, such as those of Mary (Lk 1:46-55), Zechariah (Lk 1:68-79), the heavenly host (Lk 2:14) and Simeon (Lk 2:29-32, 34-35), and the prayers as in Lk 10:21-22; 11:2-4 and Acts 4:24-30, all of which serve a summarizing function. Nor should we forget the discourses, in which Jesus sums up the prophetic nature of Christianity's ethical stance (Lk 6:20-49) or addresses the needs of Luke's readers (Lk 22:14-38), following the conventions of hellenistic historiography for farewell discourses (see also Acts 20:17-35). Through such discourses and the apostolic discourses of Acts, Luke provides important summaries of his gospel message which enable the readers to grasp Luke-Acts as a comprehensive narrative synthesis of the events fulfilled in our midst.

To fulfill its pastoral purpose, Luke's narrative had to be read not once but many times. No one could have grasped the implications of Mary's *Magnificat* without having read the story of Acts. The account of a journey to Jerusalem in which Jesus was lost at Passover but found in the temple on the third day and in which Jesus announced that it was necessary for him to be with his Father (Lk 2:41-51) becomes clear only in Lk 9:51—24:53.

The first reading invites readers to ponder the events (Lk 2:19), to keep them in their hearts (Lk 2:51), and to wonder at them (Lk 24:12) as their meaning is gradually disclosed in the narrative's unfolding. Without such openness, attentive pondering and wonder, much of the narrative would remain forever opaque. With the understanding eventually provided by the whole story, a second reading then proves much more meaningful, and this second reading itself constitutes a new vantage point for a third reading, and so on. With each reading of Luke-Acts, the narrative is consequently ever new. The narrative techniques Luke employed indicate that he himself expected that Luke-Acts would be read and reread, and that the readers' growth in understanding the gospel would walk hand in hand with growth in their own self-understanding.

## HISTORICAL DESIGN

Pastoral by intent and narrative in form, Luke-Acts is also historical in conceptual design. This means above all that Luke conceived and presented Luke-Acts as a work of christian history. If others had done this before him, their work is no longer extant. From our standpoint, Luke gave Christianity and the world a new literary genre, that of christian history, and he himself was the first christian historian, one who approached the gospel from a historical point of view and history from a gospel point of view.

Not that Luke followed the strict chronological sequence of events as they had actually unfolded and as a modern historian would lay them out. In this sense, Luke-Acts is historical only in its broadest outlines. Rather, Luke had a clear plan of christian history, and this plan or conceptual design shaped his writing of the gospel narrative at every point.

While staying relatively close to the order established by Mark and others, Luke did not hesitate to transform events and juxtapose them in new ways to bring out their historical significance. Significance was primary, strict chronology quite secondary, with regard both to events in the life of Jesus and to historical events of a more general nature. Note, for example, how the extraordinary catch of fish, a post-Easter event in John 21:1-14, and Mark's account of Jesus' teaching a large crowd by the sea (Mk 4:1-2), an event which comes after the call of the first disciples (Mk 1:16-20), were inserted into the account of the call of Peter and his companions in Lk 5:1-11. Note also how a Roman census which could have occurred only later was inserted into the account of Jesus' birth (Lk 2:1-2) to show its relationship to the world of Rome and its provinces and provide the grounds for Mary and Joseph's journey to Bethlehem.

Luke's historical design responded to the pastoral needs of the Lukan communities, for whom the lines of continuity from Christianity's beginnings in the events of Jesus' life to their own troubled situation had become unclear. Its expression in narrative form, the normal form for historical writing, also served his pastoral intent.

Through his historical narrative, readers would see themselves in relation to christian history, appropriate that history as their own, and discover the solid grounds of those matters in which they had been catechized.

The clearest indication we have that Luke viewed his narrative as a history comes from his two prefatory statements (Lk 1:1-4; Acts 1:1-2), whose form corresponds to the primary and secondary prefaces long employed by hellenistic historians. These prefaces leave no doubt that Luke wanted his readers to approach Luke-Acts as a hellenistic historical narrative. From the content of the prefaces, it is equally clear that he wanted them to see how such a narrative could be at the service of the gospel tradition. This dual perspective, with its marriage of hellenistic historical writing and the christian gospel would enable them to see how the gospel could be at home in hellenistic culture as well as how hellenistic culture could thrive in a world infused with the gospel.

In writing his christian history, Luke also took great pains to situate events in human history. We see this, for example, in the introductions of Jesus' birth narrative (Lk 2:1-5) and of John the Baptist's ministry (Lk 3:1-2), but also whenever the christian story intersected with Roman officials and institutions, particularly in the passion narrative and in Acts. Readers would thus be able to view their own history as part of the much broader history of the Roman empire, and the history of the empire would be viewed in relation to the transcendent values of the gospel. This too was pastorally significant for communities who saw themselves threatened by persecution.

From a *chronological* point of view, Luke's historical design is universal, reaching back to creation, looking forward to the fulfillment of time at the Lord's return, and embracing everything in between.

History has a beginning which coincides with the creation of the first human being. This focus on ultimate origins stands out most clearly in the genealogy of Jesus, whose family record goes back to the son of Adam, the son of God (Lk 3:23-38). For history to begin in the act of creation means that its origins lie in God himself. In relation to history, God is both Father and the Lord of heaven and earth (Lk 10:21). These two titles also characterize God's relationship to the entire course of history, and as Jesus' prayer demonstrates this is how those who participate in history should respond to him (Lk 10:21-22; 11:2-4).

History also has an ending. Unlike its origins, however, this ending is not absolute. It consists rather in the full manifestation of the kingdom (Lk 17:20) with the coming of the Son of man in glory (Lk 17:24; 18:8; Acts 1:11). There are other endings, of course, each of which marks a new historical beginning. Luke speaks of these as being with the Father (Lk 2:49), being in paradise (Lk 23:43) and being received in heaven (Acts 3:21). They consist in an exodus (Lk 9:31), an ascension (Lk 9:51), a committing of one's spirit into the Father's hands (Lk 23:46) or to the Lord Jesus (Acts 7:59) and an entry into glory (Lk 24:26). Among all of these expressions, Jesus' ascension into heaven, which forms the conclusion of the gospel (Lk 24:50-53) and is again found in the introduction to Acts (1:9), is especially significant. Luke presents it as an image of history's definitive end. Jesus, who was taken up into heaven will be seen returning in the same way (Acts 1:11).

History thus begins and ends in God's creative presence. This dual focus on the beginning and the end affects all intervening events, which are seen in relation to both their origins and their destiny. History is seen as flowing out of the past, unfolding its implications as it moves through time. The past thus helps us to understand historical events and to place them in context. History is also seen as drawn to the future, ever in tension towards its fulfillment. Each event thus encloses a secret and a promise of future disclosure and fulfillment. Thus it is that the preface describes the entire narrative as dealing with the events fulfilled in our midst (Lk 1:1).

In this view, events spring from what God has done in history and how human beings responded as well as from an inner necessity which moves them toward what God will do. Since this necessity calls for a human response and collaboration, we can call it a prophetic necessity. One of the most important ways of expressing this necessity is through the term *dei*, meaning "it is necessary," which appears some forty times in Luke-Acts.

As we might expect, Luke's bipolar view of history, with its origins and destiny, contributed to the gospel narrative's structure. The prologue, which presents the entire gospel in miniature, begins with a presentation of Jesus' origins (Lk 1:5—2:40) and ends with a narrative statement of his destiny (Lk 2:41-52). Conceived as the Father's Son through the Holy Spirit, Jesus must (*dei*) return to his Father. His ultimate origins and his ultimate destiny coincide. The account of Jesus' ministry follows the same pattern. Filled with the Spirit and manifested as the Father's beloved Son (Lk 3:21-22), Jesus' Galilean ministry focuses on his mission's unfolding in relation to its origins (Lk 4:14—9:50). The great journey narrative takes up the mission from the point of view of his destined return to the Father at the ascension (Lk 9:51-24:53). At the same time, the narrative shows how the Church's origins and destiny are related to those of Jesus.

In Luke's design, history includes three major eras. First there was the era of the Law and the prophets which was epitomized by John the Baptist, the prophet who called Israel to fidelity to the Law and prepared the way for the Lord's first advent. Second there was the era of Jesus, whose historical life, death, resurrection and ascension fulfilled the hopes of Israel and opened God's covenant to all mankind. Third there was the era of the Church, which continued the mission of Jesus to the end of the earth and prepared the way for the Lord's second and definitive advent at the fulfillment of time.

Each of these eras is distinct from the others. The era of Jesus is a new manifestation of God's presence in history.

So also the era of the Church. Neither of these can be accounted for by what God has already accomplished in and through history. There was a certain continuity between the eras but it came from outside of history, from the Word and Spirit of God. All three eras spell out the history of God's Word, how it came to John as it had come to Israel before him, was manifested by Jesus and continued to spread and develop through the life and mission of the Church. Continuity also came through the Holy Spirit, whose creative energy enabled salvation history to transcend its inherent discontinuities and enabled the Word to bridge the chasms which divided the eras.

From a *geographical* point of view, Luke-Acts can be described as a tale of three cities, in which Luke did all he could to show that what appeared to be the worst of times was indeed the best of times.

The first city is Jerusalem, where Luke's first volume begins and ends and where his second volume also begins. It is at Jerusalem that the revelation preparatory to Jesus' life takes place (Lk 1:5-25) and at Jerusalem that his destiny would unfold and be fulfilled (Lk 2:41-52; 22:1—24:53). Jerusalem was the object of Jesus' journey (Lk 9:51; 13:22; 17:11; 19:11,28,41), the city of his final teaching (Lk 19:47—21:38) and of his passover into glory (Lk 22:1—23:49), as well as the city of Pentecost and the formative days of Christianity (Acts 1:3—5:42).

In Jerusalem, Luke focused above all on the temple, the place of divine manifestation (Lk 1:5-25) and prophetic revelation (Lk 2:25-35), the locus of Jesus' final preaching (Lk 19:47-21:38), and the image of the Father's heavenly dwelling (Lk 2:41-52). When Jesus ascended to his Father, his disciples returned to the temple (Lk 24:50-53), and the Jerusalem community continued to frequent it daily after Pentecost (Acts 2:42-47). It was also there that Peter first proclaimed the gospel after Pentecost (Acts 3:11-26).

For Luke's readers, it was important to see clearly how their origins were associated with Jerusalem and the temple, but it was equally necessary to see how and why they had moved so far away from these. Jesus' sorrowful announcement that Jerusalem and its temple would be destroyed (Lk 19:41-44; 21:5-6, 20-24) has already been fulfilled. Jerusalem had not recognized the time of its visitation (Lk 19:44) and its temple had been made a den of robbers (Lk 19:45-46). Jerusalem had persecuted the Christians (Lk 21:12) just as it had betrayed and murdered the Righteous One (Acts 7:52), the king who came in the name of the Lord (Lk 19:38). Historically the great persecution against the Church in Jerusalem is what led to Christianity's movement out of Jerusalem and as far as Antioch (Acts 8:1-3; 11:19).

Before the persecution, however, the risen Lord had told the apostles and the others assembled with them that they were to stay in the city until they were clothed with power from on high (Lk 24:49; Acts 1:4) and that they were then to preach repentance and forgiveness of sins to all nations beginning with Jerusalem (Lk 24:47; Acts 1:8). Blessing them at the ascension, which took place on the heights of Olivet overlooking Jerusalem (Lk 24:50-51; Acts 1:12), Jesus fulfilled the promise made to Abraham that all the families of the earth would be blessed in his posterity (Acts 3:17-26).

The message was clear. Christianity's diffusion among the Gentiles may have been occasioned by persecution at Jerusalem, but its true foundations lay in the commission of the risen Lord and his ascension blessing. The Jerusalem experience itself had demanded that Christianity move beyond its jewish origins in Jerusalem.

Later, the Jerusalem Church explicitly approved Christianity's outreach to Gentiles (Acts 11:1, 18, 20-23) and recognized that Gentiles should not be subject to jewish circumcision and the prescriptions of the Mosaic Law (Acts 15:1-35). Gentile Christianity's continuity with Jerusalem's judaeo-christian community was undeniable. Its way of life outside of Judaism had been fully backed by the Jerusalem community's authority.

The second city in Luke's tale of three cities is Antioch, first mentioned in connection with internal community problems at Jerusalem as the city of Nicolaus, a gentile convert from Judaism and the seventh of seven appointed for special service (Acts 6:5). The story which follows shows how, as a result of persecution, the word of God spread from Jerusalem through Judaea and Samaria (Acts 8:1-3) and as far as Phoenicia, Cyprus and Antioch (Acts 11:19-26), where the disciples were first called Christians (Acts 11:26).

Antioch soon became a center of missionary activity. Inspired while gathered for the liturgy, the Antiochene community sent Barnabas and Paul on their first mission (Acts 13:1-3). Upon completing that mission, the two returned to Antioch and reported on their success with the Gentiles to the community which had sent them (Acts 14:24-28). It is also from there that Paul embarked on even more extensive missions (Acts 15:36-41; 18:18-23), which eventually brought him as far as Rome (Acts 19:21-22; 28:14b-16). The experience of Antioch and its missionary activity proved decisive for Christianity's opening up to the Gentiles (Acts 11:20; 13:44-49; 14:1, 27; 15:1-35) and for the founding of the gentile communities for which Luke wrote.

Terrible as the early persecutions at Jerusalem had been, had they not occasioned Christianity's coming to Antioch? The missions from Antioch also had been filled with persecution, but had they not led to the establishment of the gentile communities to which some of Luke's addressees now belonged (Acts 13:44-52; 14:4-7, 19-20; 17:5-10, 13-14)? Persecution had unwittingly served the universal mission which the Lord had announced. Through the persecution and rejection narratives, Luke showed his readers that the persecutions they now experienced were no reason to abandon the mission. In ways yet hidden, persecutions might actually be serving their missions to others as they had served the mission to them.

In Jesus' life, the Samaritan experience provided a good model. When the Samaritans rejected Jesus because he was going to Jerusalem, the disciples reacted violently, only to be rebuked by Jesus (Lk 9:51-56), who later told a story about a Samaritan who proved to be a true neighbor and one to be imitated (Lk 10:29-37). Later the Samaritan mission proved to be a huge success (Acts 8:4-25). Nor should they forget the experience of Paul, whose story filled the early history of their communities. Had not Saul the persecutor become a zealous apostle? Had not the persecution he suffered at the hands of Roman authorities brought him to Rome for further fruitful preaching and teaching? Together, all of these examples strongly suggested that those who now persecuted the Lukan communities might yet receive the word and join them in the christian mission.

The third city is Rome, the imperial capital, whose Caesar could order a census of the whole world (Lk 2:1). For Luke, Rome was an ideal symbol for all nations (Lk 24:47) and the end of the earth (Acts 1:8), and it is with Paul's arrival and preaching at Rome that his second volume ends (Acts 28:14-31). Unlike the other cities to which Paul brought his gospel message, however, Rome had already been evangelized. When Paul arrived, he was met and welcomed by Rome's christian community (Acts 28:15-16). The same had been true of Antioch where Paul was introduced to the community by Barnabas (Acts 11:25-26). Consequently, Rome was not included among the communities of the Antiochene mission.

Just as Antioch's relationship to Jerusalem had had to be clarified, so also its relationship to Rome. This would be done through the great Pauline journey (Acts 19:21-28:31) which shows how Antioch's apostle came to Rome as a result of persecution just as Jerusalem Christians had earlier come to Antioch. In his journey to Rome, Paul would first go to Jerusalem (Acts 19:21), thus establishing a link between Jerusalem and Roman Christianity. Clearly,

Luke's tale of three cities is not three independent tales but one tale which embraces all three in a history whose scope is geographically, as well as chronologically, universal.

With regard to Rome, Luke also had to reassure his readers that the position of Christians vis-a-vis Rome and Roman law was unassailable. This preoccupation first surfaces in the story of Jesus' birth, where Mary and Joseph respected the decree of Caesar Augustus and the imperial decree itself is what brought them to Bethlehem for Jesus' birth in the city of David (Lk 2:1-5). In his life, Jesus declared that the faith of a centurion was superior to any he had met in Israel and he cured that centurion's servant (Lk 7:1-10). On another occasion, Jesus staunchly affirmed that what was Caesar's should be given to him (Lk 20:20-26). As Jesus died, another centurion glorified God with the confession that Jesus surely was an innocent man (Lk 23:47), an innocence already recognized by both Pilate and Herod (Lk 23:13-15).

At Philippi, a Roman colony (Acts 16:12), Paul and Silas accepted imprisonment by Roman magistrates (Acts 16:19-24), did not flee when they could have in the aftermath of an earthquake (Acts 16:25-34), and caused no little consternation upon declaring that they were Roman citizens with the rights of Roman citizens (Acts 16:37-38). Respecting the law, they also had rights under the law. Later in an incident at Corinth, Paul was declared innocent by a Roman proconsul (Acts 18:12-17). Still later his rights under the law would again be acknowledged by the town clerk of Ephesus (Acts 19:35-40).

At Jerusalem, the commander of the temple garrison twice rescued Paul from the mob (Acts 21:30-35; 23:10). Again Paul's rights as a Roman were respected (Acts 22:24-29). Unlike the commander, he was even a citizen by birth (Acts 22:28). Thwarting a plot against Paul, the commander sent him to the Roman governor at Caesarea with a letter attesting to his innocence (Acts 23:23-30).

Claiming the right to be tried before the imperial bench at Caesarea (Acts 25:10) and later appealing to Caesar (Acts 25:11), Paul was sent to Rome, although he was found innocent by both Festus the governor (Acts 25:25-27) and Agrippa the king (Acts 26:30-32). So it is that Paul came to Rome through an appeal to Caesar and was able to preach unhindered with the protection of Roman law (Acts 28:30-31).

Beginning with Jesus' life and through the years of Christianity's development in the Pauline communities, Christians were not outlaws. They had always respected Rome, Rome had protected them, and they had clear rights in Roman law. Under attacks which impugned their origins, Luke's readers could appeal to this history, know themselves innocent and again claim their rights without fear.

From a *personal* point of view, Luke's historical narrative focuses primarily on four people: John the Baptist, the last prophet of the old Israel, who prepared the Lord's coming; Jesus, in whom the Lord came and who established a new Israel with the Twelve as its foundation; Simon Peter, the first of the Twelve and a rock of strength for the apostolic Church; and Saul Paul, the prophetic missionary to the end of the earth who appointed elders to lead the Church's far flung communities. All four, John, Jesus, Peter and Paul, played distinctive personal roles in what Luke presented as a history of salvation.

In Luke, John the Baptist is primarily John the prophet. Filled with the Holy Spirit from his mother's womb (Lk 1:15) at his first encounter with Jesus (Lk 1:44), the word of God came to him in the wilderness of the Jordan region where he preached a baptism of repentance in preparation for the Lord's coming (Lk 3:2-4). The greatest of those born of women (Lk 7:28), John fulfilled Israel's hopes for Elijah's return (Lk 1:17; 7:27), epitomized the era of the Law and the prophets, and brought it to a close (Lk 16:16) with the baptism of Jesus (Lk 3:21). Insisting that being a son of Abraham was not a matter of one's human origins

(Lk 3:8), John's message even prepared the way for Christianity's opening to the Gentiles. For all his greatness, however, John was not the Christ. His baptism was only in water. The Messiah's baptism would be in God's creative Spirit and with the fire of Pentecost (Lk 3:15-16).

Like John, Jesus also was a prophet, but not as John's successor. The Holy Spirit came upon him not during his baptism by John but after it while he was at prayer (Lk 3:21-22). Mightier than John (Lk 3:16), he had been conceived by the Holy Spirit (Lk 1:35), and it is through him that John had been filled with the Spirit while in his mother's womb (Lk 1:15,44). Jesus was called the Son of the Most High (Lk 1:32), the Son of God (Lk 1:35). He was a king. He was given the throne of his father David (Lk 1:32b), but as the events of the passion would reveal and ensure, his kingdom would have no end (Lk 1:33). Through the passion-resurrection-ascension, he fulfilled his mission as a Savior, a redeemer king. Suffering the passion, he was the Christ, a messianic king. Glorified, he reigns as Lord over all peoples (see Lk 2:11, 29-32, 24:41, 26,44). When finally his reign will be actualized in history with the fulfillment of the times of the Gentiles (Lk 21:24; see Acts 3:21), he will return in glory (Acts 1:11). For Luke, Jesus' advent, life and exodus constituted the second and central era of salvation history.

Jesus was a prophet like Moses (Acts 3:22; 7:37) through whom God gave the Law and entered into a covenant with Israel. In Jesus, however, the law, or Moses, and the prophets were fulfilled (Lk 4:18-21; 16:17; 24:27, 44), and the good news of the kingdom of God was proclaimed (Lk 16:16). As the Christ, he established a new covenant which, unlike the old Mosaic covenant, was in his own blood (Lk 22:20). More than a prophet, he accepted to suffer the passion and entered into his glory (Lk 24:26). In his ascension, he fulfilled the promise made to Abraham that all peoples would be blessed in his posterity (Lk 24:50-51; Acts 3:21, 25).

In the baptism of his passion (Lk 12:50), Jesus kindled a fire that would spread upon the earth (Lk 12:49), driven by the power of a mighty wind from on high (Lk 24:49; Acts 2:2). John had announced that the Christ would baptize with the Holy Spirit and with fire (Lk 3:16). The risen Lord confirmed that the apostolic community would indeed be baptized with the Spirit (Acts 1:5,8). The promise was fulfilled at Pentecost when, ignited by the Holy Spirit, the apostolic community began to speak with tongues that transcended every language and nationality (Acts 2:3-11).

Simon, whom Jesus named Peter (Lk 6:14) is the third major personage in Luke's historical narrative. The first of those whom Jesus called (Lk 5:1-11), a rock of strength for the Twelve (Lk 6:12-16), he was also the first to whom the risen Lord appeared (Lk 23:34). Although he denied Jesus during the passion (Lk 22:34, 54-62), thanks to Jesus' prayer he turned again to strengthen his brothers (Lk 22:31-32), played a critical role in the days which followed Jesus' ascension (Acts 1:15-26) and became the apostolic community's spokesman on Pentecost (Acts 2:14-40). Through this carefully drawn statement of Peter's role in Jesus' story and in earliest Christianity, Luke presented Peter as Christianity's most basic personal link with the era of Jesus. His knowledge of Jesus, experience of the risen Lord and proclamation of the gospel would be normative for all who followed him in the third and final era of salvation history. Luke thus assured his readers of continuity between the era of Jesus and that of the Church.

To extend this continuity to their Pauline communities, however, he also had to show how Paul and his missions were related to Peter. There can be no question that for Luke Paul was *the* apostle to the Gentiles. To legitimate Paul's work and the missionary communities which sprang from it, Luke developed Paul's link to Jerusalem Christianity, which gave him full approval, as we have already seen. Beyond this, however, he showed how, like Peter, Paul also had been blessed with an appearance of the risen Lord (Acts 9:1-9) and how Paul's message closely paralleled that of Peter (Acts 13:16-41; see Acts 2:14-40; 3:12-26; 4:8-12; 5:29-32). Even more fundamentally, he laid great emphasis on Peter's role in opening the mission to the Gentiles (Acts 10:1-11:18). When Paul proclaimed the gospel to Gentiles (Acts 13:44-48), he thus acted on a firm precedent established by Peter.

Luke's readers had no reason to hesitate about the legitimacy of their gentile Christianity. It had indeed sprung from Paul's missions, but it had normative roots in the work of Peter, which was ultimately grounded in the life of Jesus and which had been announced and prepared by John the Baptist. In every case, and from every point of view, it was also according to the scriptures. Heirs to this tradition and enlightened by the scriptures, it was now for them to further Christianity's movement toward its final destiny.

## THEOLOGICAL INSPIRATION

Luke's message is not only pastoral in intent, narrative in form and historical in design. It is also profoundly theological in inspiration. In light of its stated purpose in the prefaces and from the role of the risen Lord and of the scriptures in that purpose's realization. Luke-Acts must be approached as a work of pastoral theology. In view of its narrative form and overall development, which presupposes a theological appreciation of the events in Jesus' story and of the story's relationship to its readers, Luke-Acts is a work of narrative theology. Its historical design, which contributed so much to shaping the narrative, also requires that we view Luke-Acts as a work of historical theology. Stripped of its theological perspective, very little would remain of Luke-Acts, and its pastoral intention, narrative form and historical design would be unrecognizable.

From the very beginning of this exposition, we thus have been exploring Luke's theology, and many of its major themes have already been surfaced. In this final section on the gospel's message, we need only show how its historical design, narrative form and pastoral intent function together in one theologically inspired synthesis and how that synthesis is brought to bear on a number of major life issues in the christian communities.

A christian historical theology could have been written in a number of ways. Luke could have written a work analogous to the Law, with its epic story of human origins, divine covenants and liberation. In various ways, the first five books of the Old Testament did provide inspiration for Luke's writing. He could also have written a wisdom history and followed the sapiential patterns for historical writing which are well exemplified in Israel's collection of wisdom literature. Like the Law, but not so markedly, wisdom literature also influenced Luke in a number of ways. Luke's most basic theological inspiration, however, came not from the Law and wisdom literature but from prophetic writing. Luke's historical theology is primarily prophetic, and every other approach to historical writing in the biblical tradition is secondary.

The prophetic nature of Luke's historical theology rests on far more than his interest in Israel's prophets and how their message had been and was being fulfilled. Nor does it spring from his presentation of major figures like John the Baptist, Jesus and even Paul as prophets whose lives fulfilled that of Israel's prophets in distinctive ways. These factors are consistent with Luke's prophetic theology but are not constitutive of it.

To establish Luke-Acts as a prophetic history, no passage is more fundamental than Lk 3:1-2. Coming immediately after the prologue, these verses provide the gospel narrative with a new introduction. Luke 1:1-4 had presented Luke-Acts in the tradition of hellenistic historiography. Luke 3:1-2 takes that tradition, with its careful attention to situating the beginning of a new and significant historical moment chronologically, and associates it with the established literary conventions used to introduce the work and message of Israelite prophets. To verify this, one need only compare Lk 3:1-2 with the statements which stand at the head of each prophetic book and introduce the work of Israel's prophets by indicating when the word came to them. In Haggai 1:1 and Zechariah 1:1, to whom the word came during the reign of Darius the Persian emperor, we even have a precedent for Luke's reference to the Roman emperor, Tiberius Caesar in Lk 3:1.

Luke-Acts is consequently far more than an application of hellenistic historiography to the origins of Christianity. Had it been no more than this, we might have grounds to accuse Luke of historicizing the gospel and robbing it of its kerygmatic impact. In Luke-Acts, prophesy dominates history and transforms it from within, making it an apt vehicle of the traditional gospel word. This can be seen not only from John's story in Lk 3:1-19 but also from the account of all that Jesus did and taught in Lk 4:14-24:53 and from the narrative of the Church's growth and development in Acts. The history Luke tells is not so much that of John the Baptist, Jesus and others as that of the word which came to John (Lk 3:1-2), was fulfilled in Jesus' word (Lk 4:31,36; 5:5), and spread through the efforts of the christian community and its mission (Acts 6:7; 12:24; 19:20).

Luke thus infused history with prophetic dynamism. As a result, the events of which he wrote, and which involved many who had not received the word and even tried to impede its progress, reveal the power of the gospel, confound Christianity's enemies and inspire Luke's readers with new hope. Historical deeds are prophetic acts, wonders and signs which communicate the gospel at deeply symbolic levels. The kerymatic word articulates the meaning of prophetic acts for new historical circumstances and invite the readers once again to speak and act with the power they had long known.

The prophetic nature of Luke-Acts' history served its pastoral intention admirably well. Like the ancient prophets, Luke's vision penetrated the troubled surface of the times, clothed them with understanding, led his readers to insight and called them to an appropriate response. We have already indicated that Luke-Acts must be approached as pastoral theology. We can now be more specific. Among pastoral theologies, Luke-Acts is a work of prophetic theology.

Luke's narrative theology is equally prophetic. In telling the christian story, Luke unveiled the meaning of various life contexts which had become problematic for his readers. He showed them how to see, understand and respond like so many in his account, beginning with Bethlehem's shepherds (Lk 2:20), who had come to see, understand and respond.

One of the major life contexts addressed by Luke's prophetic narrative is table fellowship. Meals with Jesus are important in all four gospel accounts. No other gospel, however, equals Luke's emphasis on meals. From a banquet in Levi's house (Lk 5:27-39) to the risen Lord's final appearance (Lk 24:36-53), meal accounts were introduced in nearly every major section of the gospel. Taken together, these accounts present a mosaic of problematic and conflict situations along with Jesus' response to these.

Some, notably the Pharisees but others as well, objected to the way Jesus' disciples ate and drank with tax collectors and sinners (Lk 5:27-32; 15:1-2; see also 7:36-50; 19:1-10) as well as to the fact that unlike the disciples of John and the Pharisees those of Jesus did not fast (Lk 5:33). There were also those who objected to Jesus' not performing the customary jewish ablutions before eating (Lk 11:38) and to his curing the sick during a sabbath meal (Lk 14:1-6). In such cases, Jesus responds by spelling out the nature of his prophetic and reconciling mission and by confronting those who objected with fundamental religious values. Such meal accounts enabled Luke's readers to appreciate the basis of practices which had become traditional among them and to persevere in them.

Some meal accounts deal more directly with the behavior of those who came together for meals with Jesus the Lord and with the implications of these meals for life in the christian mission. There were those who fretted about secondary things (Lk 10:38-42), who sought after places of honor at table (Lk 14:7-11), or who tended to invite the rich for eventual personal gain (Lk 14:12-14). In response Jesus appeals for attention to the Lord and his word, for humility, and for attitudes and behavior befitting the kingdom of God (Lk 14:15). The disciples also had to be told not to dismiss the crowd but to nourish it (Lk 9:10-17), not to lord it over the people but to serve them as Jesus himself had done (Lk 22:14-38). With accounts such as these, Luke meant not only to recall events long past but to sensitize his readers to their own situation and provide directions for a proper christian response.

Finally, there are meal accounts which deal directly with the problem of faith experience. Confused and without hope, two disciples welcome a stranger to their table. In the breaking of bread, they recognize the risen Lord, understand all that the Lord had taught them and return enthusiastically to their missionary community (Lk 24:13-35). The assembled community thinks that the Lord present in their midst is but a spirit. Requesting food, he shows them that he is present to them in the flesh and blood of the hungry calling them to their mission (Lk 24:36-49). These accounts serve Luke's most basic intention to bring his readers to genuine knowledge concerning things of which they had been informed (Lk 1:4).

The meal accounts also enabled Luke to address three additional areas of major concern, namely, the wealthy's lack of care for the poor, resistance to reconciliation and inappropriate attitudes among those who led the communities. All three of these extended beyond the meals, of course, but the meal context in which the entire community was gathered made them especially obvious.

To be poor was to be without food and hungry. Since the christian meal called for generous sharing among all the participants, hunger should have been abolished from the christian community. At one time this may have been the case (Acts 2:42-47; 4:32-35), at least as an ideal which guided behavior. No longer. Among the wealthy, public status, prestige and personal recognition had submerged the christian ideal of sharing (Acts 5:1-11). Other problems in the same area stemmed from the Church's growth and the diversification of its social base. As we see in Acts 6:1-6, the development of ministries did not always keep pace with the growth needs of the Church. The gospel's many passages on wealth and poverty and the need to share with everyone addressed problems such as these, which continued to emerge in analogous forms. At stake was no less than Christianity's messianic mission (Lk 14:12-14; 7:22; 4:18-19) to herald the kingdom of God (Lk 14:15).

Resistance to reconciliation revealed similar tendencies toward exclusiveness. Like the issue of wealth and poverty, it too surfaced at meals, which of their very nature were reconciling events. Jesus makes this very plain in the stories of Levi and Zacchaeus (Lk 5:27-32; 19:1-10). The parable of the prodigal son, in which the older brother refuses to join in the younger brother's reconciliation banquet, shows great sensitivity to the older brother's plight (Lk 15:11-32). The father's plea that the older brother once again accept the younger as his brother (Lk 15:31-32) could not have been lost on Luke's readers.

Finally, there was the matter of leadership in the communities. In a sense, all of Luke-Acts is addressed to the leaders of missionary communities and deals with their problems and concerns. Some of these problems emerged above all when the assembly was gathered for meals. Accordingly, Jesus frequently speaks to the attitudes and behavior of his hosts (see again Lk 7:36-50; 12:37-52; 14:12-14), those who presided at table. Or again, when the apostles felt overwhelmed by the needs of the crowd, he tells them not to send the crowd away but to share the little they had with them (Lk 9:10-17). At the Last Supper, he addresses the leaders' tendency to want to be served rather than to serve, and he teaches the apostolic community how to eat and drink at his table in the kingdom (Lk 22:24-30). As prophetic narratives to Theophilus, all of these meals and Jesus' teaching within them were ordained in various ways to the needs of Luke's readers and the leaders of their communities.

To meet the gospel's multifaceted challenge, Christians had to pray like the disciples had been taught to pray (Lk 11:1-13). Their Father would surely answer their prayer with the gift of the Holy Spirit (Lk 11:13) so long as they persevered in prayer (Lk 18:1-8) and prayed humbly (Lk 18:9-14). The Holy Spirit would give them the genuine understanding which motivated Luke pastorally, would enable them to appropriate Luke's narrative, would strengthen them in their christian identity as they faced persecutions in a time of historical transition, and would assure prophetic fidelity in contexts which were critical for the christian life and mission. Such, in sum, was Luke's message to urban gentile communities living in the ninth decade who were shaken in their missionary approach to the gospel by problems from within as well as from without.

## Objectives and Methods

I began by describing the life setting of the Lukan communities. This brief presentation was based on what Luke-Acts presupposes when it is approached as a pastorally motivated narrative with a historical design inspired by a prophetic theology. Accordingly, the second part of the introduction presented a summary of Luke's message from each of these points of view. In turn, this summary needs to be verified by the commentary and its exposition of Luke's message in relation to the gospel itself. At the same time, my hope is that it provides a good orientation for reading the commentary and suggests directions for developing it further. In this third section, I shall outline the objectives and methods underlying the commentary which constitutes the body of this volume.

First of all this commentary is a pastoral and theological interpretation of Luke's historical narrative. Its aim is to show how the gospel addressed the Lukan communities and helped them to form a new sense of christian identity and mission at a critical turning point in their history. Second, it suggests how Luke's gospel continues to address the Church, which recognizes this gospel as a formative message for itself today no less than it was for Christians during the closing decades of the first century.

This effort to discern Luke's message requires a sharp focus on the Lukan communities and on what the narrative assumes concerning the values, problems and struggles of these communities. It also calls for considerable experience and understanding of the Church in our time. This focus on the addressees obviates any tendency to reduce the gospel to an object for dissection and analysis and facilitates its interpretation within a process of literary and prophetic communication.

Accordingly, the commentary approaches the gospel from the standpoint of Luke's own retelling of the christian story. In such an effort, the gospel's relationship to the history of tradition, oral and written, and to the historical life of Jesus becomes secondary. The primary concern is to draw attention to Luke's insights concerning the meaning and implications of the tradition for a new time. Other considerations are pertinent only in the measure that they help to clarify the Lukan message. Not that Luke's relationship to earlier christian tradition and history are unimportant. It merely falls outside the scope of this study of Luke's message, which consequently needs to be complemented by other commentaries which pursue Luke's work with the goals and methods developed in the historical critical tradition of interpretation.

Luke's stories concerning the Pharisees illustrate the commentary's nature and perspective. The Pharisees represent a significant religious body in the story of Jesus, and it is possible through a close study of Luke and the other gospels to disengage the original context and development of their confrontation with Jesus. A study of Mark can also show how the Pharisees and Jesus' relationship to them were treated in one of Luke's sources. Such concerns, however, all pertain to the pre-history of Luke's own gospel. The search for Luke's message requires that we move beyond them and ask what significance the Pharisees might have for Luke's readers. As we shall see, his telling of their story shows that these historical figures evoke a number of negative tendencies in the christian community itself. Thus it is that the Pharisees of Jesus' story are frequently introduced as symbols for neo-Pharisees in the gentile communities addressed by Luke. To appreciate Luke's message, we must consequently be prepared to read this account on two levels, that of Jesus' setting in life and of pre-Lukan Christianity, and that of the Lukan era. Many elements in Luke's narrative are incomprehensible unless we view the Pharisees as Christians.

Commenting on Luke's retelling of the Christian story, we shall often refer to Luke's intention and to the situation of his addressees. However, it should be clear that aside from Lk 1:1-4 and Acts 1:1-2 we do not have direct access to the mind of the author who stands behind the text. What we do have is the way the author revealed himself in the narrative, especially through the narrator. Consequently, whenever we refer to Luke's intention, we speak of the gospel's intention, which is related to that of the author but which also transcends what the author may have consciously intended and which outlives him as the gospel moves into new and unforeseen historical and social contexts. Correlatively, whenever we refer to the Lukan communities, we speak of what the gospel narrative presupposes concerning its readership. We thus view the communities through the lens of the narrative which focuses on some aspects of these communities and presents them according to a hierarchy of importance based on its values and its appraisal of the situation.

Since Luke articulated his insights in narrative form, the search for his message also requires close attention to the story's unfolding. This calls for a grasp of how the various sections complement one another in a developmental movement towards the gospel's climax. At times, it also calls for paraphrase. To interpret a song, one may explain it, but ultimately one must sing it. To interpret a story one must tell it. Interpretation lies in the manner it is retold and in the various connections established with other parts of the story.

The commentary tries to present each unit with as much clarity as possible. Major units are both distinguished from one another and related to one another in such a way as to reveal their contribution to the whole as well as to the story's general progression. Such units and other broad divisions have been provided with an introduction, which also situates the various sub-units included in each. A reading of these is indispensable before reading the commentary on a particular sub-unit, since some of the general considerations are not repeated for each sub-unit.

The gospel includes four major units, and they have been given titles which express their literary form and general theme. These titles are:

I. The Preface

   An Orderly Account for You

II. The Prologue

   Jesus in His Origins and in His Destiny

III. Background and Preparation

   Jesus in History

IV. The Story of Jesus

   The Human Life and Message of the Son of God

From these titles, readers should note Luke's versatility in the use of literary forms as well as the appropriateness of each of these general forms for the distinctive purpose of each unit.

The titles for the various levels of sub-units are also important. At times, they refer to the unit's literary form, but usually they summarize the particular unit's content as it relates to the larger unit to which it belongs as well as to the other units in the same section. When these titles are directly related to a literary segment rather than to a general introduction, they are immediately followed by a brief quotation from the gospel text. The purpose of these is to highlight a key element in the text and to focus the reader's point of view in approaching it. As such, they are an integral part of the commentary.

To facilitate reading of the commentary, title pages were included with a summary outline of the units found in the gospel's more comprehensive units. The gospel's general outline is also given in the table of contents. By referring to these outlines, readers should find it easier to acquire a sense of Luke's message as a whole.

Luke wrote his gospel narrative from within the faith, not as an outside observer. This commentary was also written from within the faith. Hopefully, it will contribute to the fulfillment of Luke's intention, that as Christians of a new era "you will know the truth concerning the things of which you have been informed" (1:4) with regard to "all that Jesus began to do and teach, until the day when he was taken up, after he had given commandment through the Holy Spirit to the apostles whom he had chosen (Acts 1:1-2).

*I. The Preface.*

*An Orderly Account for You.*

*1:1-4.*

# I. THE PREFACE.
## *AN ORDERLY ACCOUNT FOR YOU.*
## 1:1-4.

**1** Inasmuch as many have undertaken to compile a narrative of the things which have been accomplished among us, [2]just as they were delivered to us by those who from the beginning were eyewitnesses and ministers of the word, [3]it seemed good to me also, having followed all things closely for some time past, to write an orderly account for you, most excellent Theophilus, [4]that you may know the truth concerning the things of which you have been informed.

LUKE'S GOSPEL opens with a short, one-sentence preface, whose clauses situate the work historically (1:1-2), define its scope and nature (1:3) and announce the author's intention (1:4). In both form and content, this preface evokes the world of hellenistic historiography and defines the author's intent to place historical writing at the service of the gospel. In Luke-Acts, the gospel tradition thus moves to a new phase of literary awareness and maturity.

In keeping with the genre of historical prefaces, and much like a christian letter-writer, the author addresses the reader in the person of Theophilus. Speaking in the first person to one who is summoned in the second person (1:3), he prepares him for a message which will be told in the third person narrative which is characteristic of the story-teller's art. Elegant in its Greek style, simple and straightforward in its movement, modest and engaging in its personal tone, the preface reveals a sensitive, cultured, respectful and concerned minister of the word, inviting the reader to take up the story and follow its unfolding.

Luke was not the first to introduce a gospel account by a preface to the reader. Mark, one of Luke's main sources, and a gospel synthesis of great influence in the Lukan communities, also included a preface (1:1). Because of its wording, however, which seems to refer to the gospel's second verse, the Markan preface is frequently read as part of that gospel's prologue (1:2-13). This is most unfortunate, for Mark's prefatory title is truly a distinctive literary element with its own mode of communication. Together with hellenistic historical models, the Markan preface provided Luke with a prototype for introducing the gospel, or more precisely for introducing the reader to the gospel narrative.

As a creative marriage of hellenistic historiography and christian literary tradition, the Lukan preface stands unique in the New Testament. This uniqueness reflects the distinctive nature of the work it presents.

Mark had seen his entire work as a narrative statement of the beginning of the gospel (1:1). His readers were consequently asked to see themselves as living in the gospel's continuation, in a new and critical moment whose meaning could be grasped by recalling the beginning. In a sense, that moment was viewed as a new beginning, and Mark's gospel constituted an urgent call for Christians once again to take up the gospel challenge of their origins. As such, the work rings throughout with the radical demands of gospel proclamation.

Luke's concern, however, was not so much with the gospel's beginning as with the continuity which could be discerned in the story of its early years, a continuity which transcended periodic disruptions and moments of seeming meaninglessness. His account is thus a historical narrative of events which were part of the story of the communities for which he wrote. Its purpose is to help them to grasp their own moment in history and to commit themselves to the future. As such, the work reflects the vision and mission of the christian prophet.

Mark's gospel had served the Christians well and its authority had been great, as is obvious from its use as a point of reference for the gospels according to Luke and Matthew. However, times had changed. The need was less for an immediate and uncompromising response than for an ability to assume a long-term role in history. With this realization, Luke undertook to review and retell the entire story of Jesus and his disciples in a manner which addressed the new juncture at which gentile Christianity in particular had arrived.

*An Orderly Account*

In Luke's own terms, his purpose was "to write an orderly account" (1:3). He does not indicate which principles govern the order in that account. No doubt he expected his readers, who were immersed in the situation for which he wrote, to discern that order and recognize its governing principles. Fortunately for us, however, who stand far removed from the gospel's original setting, he does compare his effort to earlier works which he describes as narrative in form (1:1). His own work consequently reflects the flow of narrative, in which personages and contexts are introduced and various events are presented in succession.

The order among events in a narrative, however, is not necessarily chronological. As Luke notes, his concern, like that of his predecessors, is with "the things which have been accomplished or fulfilled." The order is thus that of promise and fulfillment, and as the narrative itself will reveal two principles govern this process.

First, there is a certain divine necessity, which is reflected in Luke's frequent use of the term *dei* (it is necessary), and which is revealed in the scriptures. To perceive this necessity, the reader must be able to interpret the scriptures properly.

The second principle is thus one of interpretation, and it lies in the life of Jesus. Events are not only necessary according to the scriptures but according to the word and work of Jesus, or better according to the scriptures as interpreted by Jesus and the events in his life.

Even the teaching and life activities of Jesus, however, and their interpretation of the biblical tradition, do not provide a fully adequate or ultimate principle for ordering the Lukan narrative. For this we must turn to the author's perception of the christian life context of the Lukan communities. Writing of "the things which have been accomplished" not only in a past moment of history, but "among us," Luke turns to the problems and issues confronted by the communities. Their hierarchy or relative importance, as perceived by Luke, determines in large measure the ordering of the events in Jesus' story. The biographical development of Jesus' actual life provides the narrative with its most general over-all order, but it has little influence on the succession of particular events.

## Having Followed All Things Closely
## for Some Time Past

Luke's work is the result of an extensive period of close observation and reflection (1:3). In this, he stands in a tradition. Many others had undertaken to do the same. Of these, only Mark is known to us, and we have no indication that other efforts had proven so successful or helpful to the emerging Church. Together with Mark, however, they did provide a precedent which in a sense legitimated Luke's own effort.

For Luke's predecessors and for Luke himself, the direct source for writing an ordered narrative was not actual participation in the original events, but the transmission of those events "by those who from the beginning were eyewitnesses and ministers of the word." On the other hand, it was most important that Luke have participated in the communities whose life was shaped by those events. Luke does not write as an outsider but as one deeply involved in the unfolding of christian history.

The eyewitnesses of which Luke speaks did not represent a category distinct from the ministers of the word, but the earliest Christians who have undertaken this ministry which continued as a vital element in the life of the communities. Luke himself could be considered a literary minister of the word. Within this ministry, however, he relied on those who first assumed it, and who had been commissioned by the risen Lord (Lk 24:48; Acts 1:8) while eating and drinking with him after he rose from the dead (Acts 10:39-41).

Luke's concern was consequently not with historical events in themselves, as they might have been perceived by those whose eyes were not opened in faith. Rather, his raw materials consisted of events which had been seen in faith from the beginning and taken up as a gospel message for others. Luke's work is thus a hermeneutic or interpretation of the apostolic message for Christians living in a new and vastly different historical context.

*That You Might Know the Truth*

Already Luke has situated himself and his work in relation to a history which he expected his reader to recognize and appreciate. In the process, he has presented the scope and nature of his work and shown how it was consistent with christian tradition as reflected in the earliest ministry of the word. His purpose is that his readers "might know the truth" (1:4).

Developments in the christian communities and in their relationship to the greater environment in which they lived and to which they brought the gospel had obscured the solid truth of Christianity's heritage. The truth had to be reaffirmed. Its communication, however, could not be a matter of mere information or statement, since it bore on "the things of which" the readers "have been informed." Luke's concern was thus to bring his readers to new insight into matters which they already knew. Such insight depended on an ability to see how the gospel story remained a valid articulation of christian life in the eighties of the first century. It would be brought about by means of a new narrative, a retelling and reordering of the story with the Lukan readers in view. Such was Luke's intention.

The work is addressed to a particular person, Theophilus, a Christian of distinction who was expected to disseminate it. This person, however, is equally symbolic of all readers. Following Luke's story, Christians should come to recognize that the gospel word continues to speak and live in their communities, that any fears to the contrary are groundless, and that the basis of their missionary commitment is secure.

*II. The Prologue.*
   *Jesus in His Origins*
   *and in His Destiny.*
   *1:5-2:52.*

# OUTLINE

# II. THE PROLOGUE.
# JESUS IN HIS ORIGINS
# AND IN HIS DESTINY.
# 1:5-2:52.

AFTER THE SHORT, compact preface to Theophilus (1:1-4), which introduced the readers to the world of elegant Greek writing, Luke sets out the gospel's prologue (1:5-2:52), and the readers find themselves in a world of biblical language and imagery. The passage from one to the other is sudden and the contrast unmistakable, as though one had moved from Thucydides to the Septuagint. From its vantage point at the gentile ends of the earth, the gospel thus looks back to its jewish origins in the Davidic city of Jerusalem.

Clearly comfortable in the stylistic parameters of Greek historiography, Luke is no less skillful at jewish hellenistic writing in the biblical tradition. He thus demonstrates how Christianity and the articulation of the christian message are related to the Greco-Roman and jewish cultures. Transcending both of these, the gospel draws on their combined literary heritage to become historically incarnate in the complex Mediterranean world of the late first century.

As with the other gospel prologues (Mk 1:2-13; Mt 1:1-2:23; Jn 1:1-18), Lk 1:5-2:52 constitutes a synthesis of the entire work which follows. Like the instrumental overture which anticipates an opera's principal musical themes and prepares the audience for the dramatic, vocal and visual presentation, the prologue sets forth the author's basic themes, concerns and emphases in the form of an infancy narrative. While presenting the story of Jesus' conception, birth and early development, the author never loses sight of the events which would reveal that birth's significance for all who would one day recognize the risen Lord and join in the Christian mission.

The prologue's understanding thus depends on the readers' knowledge of the gospel as a whole. Once we have savored and penetrated Luke's narrative of the events which have been accomplished among us (1:1), a second reading of the prologue should consequently bring us to a greater depth of appreciation concerning the things of which we have already been informed (1:4).

As an infancy narrative, Luke's prologue stands closest to that of Matthew. Indeed, both prologues appear to have drawn on common traditions current in their respective gentile and jewish communities. These basic similarities, however, must not obscure their differences. While Matthew draws attention to Jesus' legal origins as a Jew and focuses on Jesus' relationship to Joseph, Luke is concerned with Jesus' origins as a human being and approaches his conception and birth from the point of view of Mary. We note also that while John the Baptist has no role in the Matthean prologue, in Luke he constitutes an indispensable point of reference for establishing Jesus' unique significance. In this the Lukan prologue stands closer to those of Mark and John. Finally, Luke's concern includes Jesus' destiny as well as his origins, a dual perspective which is absent in the prologues of Matthew, Mark and John. As a summary of the entire gospel, the Lukan prologue is thus uniquely comprehensive.

The central concern of Luke's prologue is to set forth Jesus' personal identity as a gospel statement which clarifies the identity of his readers and challenges them to missionary discipleship.

From the point of view of his origins, Jesus was indeed human, born of woman, historically related to the biblical past, and enjoying human relationships. In no way, however, do these characteristics of one born in the jewish world reveal the Savior's true identity. Jesus was also divine. Born of God, he transcended all earlier divine manifestations and every human relationship and he communicated God's life to all and through all who accepted the gospel, irrespective of their human origins (1:5-2:40).

From the point of view of his destiny, it was necessary that Jesus return to his Father, the creative source of his divine life. Born of God, he would return to God, and Christians must accept the end of his life and his consequent absence from history as an individual figure (2:41-52). Even as it narrates the story of Jesus' origins, the prologue thus points to his exodus from history (9:31) and his post-ascension life with God. Jesus' identity is thus presented in terms of his historical life and of his actual risen life in the time of the Church which Luke addressed.

The prologue's basic structure is that of two diptychs, in which the conception (1:5-25) and birth (1:57-80) of John prepare us to grasp the significance of Jesus' own conception (1:26-38) and birth (2:1-21). The first of these diptychs (1:5-38) is supplemented by an additional unit in which Jesus' relationship to John is carefully developed (1:39-56). The second (1:57-2:21) is followed by a unit on Jesus' relationship to Jerusalem, contemporary prophecy and the fulfillment of the law of the Lord (2:22-40). To these two diptychs and their supplements (1:5-56; 1:57-2:40), Luke appended a final unit which situates Jesus' infancy account in relation to the climactic events of his life (2:41-52).

# A. Annunciation

## A. 1. THE CONCEPTION OF JOHN THE BAPTIST. *HE WILL BE GREAT BEFORE THE LORD.* 1:5-25.

⁵In the days of Herod, king of Judea, there was a priest named Zechariah, of the division of Abijah; and he had a wife of the daughters of Aaron, and her name was Elizabeth. ⁶And they were both righteous before God, walking in all the commandments and ordinances of the Lord blameless. ⁷But they had no child, because Elizabeth was barren, and both were advanced in years.

⁸Now while he was serving as priest before God when his division was on duty, ⁹according to the custom of the priesthood, it fell to him by lot to enter the temple of the Lord and burn incense. ¹⁰And the whole multitude of the people were praying outside at the hour of incense. ¹¹And there appeared to him an angel of the Lord standing on the right side of the altar of incense. ¹²And Zechariah was troubled when he saw him, and fear fell upon him. ¹³But the angel said to him, "Do not be afraid, Zechariah, for your prayer is heard, and your wife Elizabeth will bear you a son, and you shall call his name John.

¹⁴And you will have joy and gladness,
and many will rejoice at his birth;
¹⁵for he will be great before the Lord,
and he shall drink no wine nor
strong drink,
and he will be filled with the Holy
Spirit,
even from his mother's womb.
¹⁶And he will turn many of the sons
of Israel to the Lord their God,
¹⁷and he will go before him in the
spirit and power of Elijah,
to turn the hearts of the fathers to
the children,

and the disobedient to the wisdom
  of the just,
to make ready for the Lord a people
  prepared."
[18]And Zechariah said to the angel, "How shall I know this? For I am an old man, and my wife is advanced in years." [19]And the angel answered him, "I am Gabriel, who stand in the presence of God; and I was sent to speak to you, and to bring you this good news. [20]And behold, you will be silent and unable to speak until the day that these things come to pass, because you did not believe my words, which will be fulfilled in their time." [21]And the people were waiting for Zechariah, and they wondered at his delay in the temple. [22]And when he came out, he could not speak to them, and they perceived that he had seen a vision in the temple; and he made signs to them and remained dumb. [23]And when his time of service was ended, he went to his home.

[24]After these days his wife Elizabeth conceived, and for five months she hid herself, saying, [25]"Thus the Lord has done to me in the days when he looked on me, to take away my reproach among men."

The prologue's first diptych opens with a panel on the conception of John the Baptist. First the author introduces John's parents, Zechariah and Elizabeth, and situates them historically in relation to the reign of Herod the Great and to their biblical lineage (1:5). Righteous before God, they were nevertheless childless, for Elizabeth was barren and both were now elderly (1:6-7). Luke thus evokes the patriarchal figures of Abraham and Sarah (Gen 17:15-21; 18:9-15) and other great biblical personages who remained childless in their old age and for whom only a divine intervention would overcome this human limitation.

Second, Luke positions Zechariah in the temple where he was fulfilling his priestly duties while the multitude remained outside at prayer (1:8-10). It is there in the temple that an angel appeared to him with the announcement that

Elizabeth would bear a son who was to be named John (1:11-13). Here, as later in Luke's gospel and Acts, prayer is the context for God's creative self-manifestation and revelation.

The angel then continues with a canticle announcing John's greatness and outlining his way of life and the scope of his mission (1:14-17). With the spirit and power of Elijah, John would make ready a people for the Lord (see 7:27). Like Elijah he would thus be a messenger announcing the Lord's advent (Mal 3:1; 4:5-6). Looking to the future, the canticle focuses on the happy results of John's mission. It also notes that John would be filled with the Holy Spirit from his mother's womb (1:15b). The significance of this last indication will become clear in the narrative of Mary's visit to Elizabeth, where John the prophet is quickened by the presence of the unborn Jesus who had been conceived by the creative power of the Holy Spirit.

While exuberant in its praise of John, the canticle is very careful to describe his origins and his mission as continuous with God's great interventions in the course of Israelite history. Each term and phrase was consequently selected to present John as the climax of biblical prophetic history. The annunciation of Jesus' conception, on the other hand, would show how he transcended that history and gave it a new significance (see 16:16).

The narrative then focuses on Zechariah's failure to believe the good news which had been brought to him by one who stands in the presence of the Lord. Without faith, Zechariah is struck dumb, unable to utter the good news (1:18-23). His wife Elizabeth, however, recognizes that God has acted on her behalf and taken away the barrenness which had been a sign of God's disfavor and a reproach among men (1:24-25).

The annunciation of John the Baptist's conception and birth is thus an important statement concerning salvation history and the way in which the biblical past was oriented towards the Lord's advent. However, the passage does far more than make a theological comment or establish a number of points. If we accept that the prologue is a brief synthesis of the entire gospel, we must also view its personages as human symbols typifying the disciples and the life situations developed in the remainder of the gospel. As such, Zechariah and Elizabeth express some aspect of every disciple's challenge. Further, from the point of view of narrative communication, the unit invites the disciples, including the modern readers, to identify with the person of Zechariah in confronting the gospel promise of their pre-christian history as well as their prior failure to believe the word of the Lord (1:18,20).

In spite of their inability to rise to the challenge of biblical faith, God had overcome the barrenness and old age of Elizabeth, Zechariah and all whom they represent. Through God's intervention, the promise of biblical history would be fulfilled in spite of unbelief (1:20). The one who would prepare the Lord's coming was conceived and the reproach taken away (1:24-25). By divine grace, biblical history and the readers' pre-christian past became fruitful and gave life to John, God's preparatory agent for a new and definitive moment of history. To the extent that the Lord Jesus is not fully present in and through the life of the Church, Zechariah, Elizabeth and their son continue to challenge Luke's readers to prepare the way of the Lord.

## A. 2. THE CONCEPTION OF JESUS.
### *HE WILL BE CALLED THE SON OF THE MOST HIGH.*
1:26-38.

> [26]In the sixth month the angel Gabriel was sent from God to a city of Galilee named Nazareth, [27]to a virgin betrothed to a man whose name was Joseph, of the house of David; and the virgin's name was Mary. [28]And he came to her and said, "Hail, O favored one, the Lord is with

you!" ²⁹But she was greatly troubled at the saying, and considered in her mind what sort of greeting this might be. ³⁰And the angel said to her, "Do not be afraid, Mary, for you have found favor with God. ³¹And behold, you will conceive in your womb and bear a son, and you shall call his name Jesus.

³²He will be great, and will be called
    the Son of the Most High;
  and the Lord God will give to him
    the throne of his father David,
³³and he will reign over the house of
    Jacob for ever;
  and of his kingdom there will be no
    end."

³⁴And Mary said to the angel, "How shall this be, since I have no husband?" ³⁵And the angel said to her,
  "The Holy Spirit will come upon
    you,
  and the power of the Most High
    will overshadow you;
  therefore the child to be born
    will be called holy,
  the Son of God.

³⁶And behold, your kinswoman Elizabeth in her old age has also conceived a son; and this is the sixth month with her who was called barren. ³⁷For with God nothing will be impossible." ³⁸And Mary said, "Behold, I am the handmaid of the Lord; let it be to me according to your word." And the angel departed from her.

In the second panel of this first diptych, the scene shifts from Jerusalem to Nazareth, where the angel Gabriel, the same who had appeared to Zechariah (1:19), now comes to Mary (1:26-27). From the very start, Luke's effort is to show how Jesus' origins transcended those of John, however extraordinary the latter may have been.

First, the narrative focuses on Jesus' mother rather than on his father. In the case of John, it is Zechariah who received the angelic messenger and Elizabeth is introduced as a secondary personage. The son whom Elizabeth would conceive is presented as that of Zechariah and it is he would give him the name John (1:13). In Jesus' case, the angel came to Mary, and Joseph is simply introduced as the man to whom she was betrothed. While Joseph remains a secondary figure, he is nevertheless significant since he belongs to the royal house of David and it is through Joseph that Jesus would have David as his father (1:32). The son whom Mary would conceive, however, is presented as her son and not as Joseph's son, and it is she who would give him the name Jesus (1:31).

All of these contrasting elements are related to a second and far more fundamental difference between the origins of Jesus and John. Whereas John was conceived by a barren woman and by parents who were both advanced in years (1:7), Jesus would be conceived by a virgin, who was betrothed to Joseph (1:27) but who as yet did not have him as a husband (1:34). The divine intervention which would result in his conception was consequently of an altogether different order. In the case of John, God intervened to overcome ordinary human inability to conceive, and as in the Old Testament this intervention manifested his wonderful provident care for those who were righteous. The divine manifestation, however, took place through the human agency of Zechariah and Elizabeth. In the case of Jesus, God intervened as creator. Mary's son would not be born through the human agency of Mary and Joseph but by the power of the Most High and the Holy Spirit which would come upon Mary (1:35), that same Spirit who moved over the waters at the moment of creation (Gen 1:2) and which God breathed into Adam's inert clay when he became a living being (Gen 2:7).

Consequently, whereas John would be filled with the Holy Spirit from his mother's womb but after his conception, Jesus would actually be conceived by the Holy Spirit.

Since the Spirit was the true source of Jesus' entire life, and no moment in his life was other than Spirit-filled, he would not only be great as John was great before the Lord (1:15), but he would be called the Son of the Most High (1:32). Conceived by the power of the Most High, he would be the Son of God (1:35).

The annunciation is thus an extremely fundamental christological statement, spelling out Jesus' divine identity in terms of his conception. As a narrative addressed to Christians living several decades after Jesus' death-resurrection, however, it is also an important ecclesiological statement, challenging all to accept the Lord's on-going invitation to give historical life to the Son of God, whose kingdom would thus be without end (1:33).

As the readers identify with Mary, her story becomes their story. With her, they are greeted, learn of God's abiding presence with them, become aware of their dignity and are called to bear a son through the power of the Spirit of the Most High, a son who is truly the Son of God. Be they married or physically virginal, there is no way that they could conceive and bring forth divine life through their own human creativity or agency. Their conception of God's Son springs from God's own creative act, and they recognize that in relation to divine life they are indeed virginal. In her womanhood, Mary is a symbol for all Christians, whether men or women, and all are challenged to be servants of the Lord, accepting that he be conceived in them according to the heavenly word (1:38). The annunciation of Jesus' birth is thus a statement concerning the relationship between the human life of the Church and the divine life which she is called to bear.

## A. 3. JESUS COMES TO JOHN.
### *THE BABE IN MY WOMB LEAPED FOR JOY.*
1:39-56.

> <sup>39</sup>In those days Mary arose and went with haste into the hill country, to a city of Judah, <sup>40</sup>and she entered

the house of Zechariah and greeted Elizabeth. ⁴¹And when Elizabeth heard the greeting of Mary, the babe leaped in her womb; and Elizabeth was filled with the Holy Spirit ⁴²and she exclaimed with a loud cry, "Blessed are you among women, and blessed is the fruit of your womb! ⁴³And why is this granted me, that the mother of my Lord should come to me? ⁴⁴For behold, when the voice of your greeting came to my ears, the babe in my womb leaped for joy. ⁴⁵And blessed is she who believed that there would be a fulfilment of what was spoken to her from the Lord." ⁴⁶And Mary said,

"My soul magnifies the Lord,
⁴⁷and my spirit rejoices in God my
    Savior,
⁴⁸for he has regarded the low estate
    of his handmaiden.
  For behold, henceforth all
    generations will call me blessed;
⁴⁹for he who is mighty has done great
    things for me,
  and holy is his name.
⁵⁰And his mercy is on those who fear him
  from generation to generation.
⁵¹He has shown strength with his arm,
  he has scattered the proud in the
    imagination of their hearts,
⁵²he has put down the mighty from
    their thrones,
  and exalted those of low degree;
⁵³he has filled the hungry with good
    things,
  and the rich he has sent empty away.
⁵⁴He has helped his servant Israel,
  in remembrance of his mercy,
⁵⁵as he spoke to our fathers,
  to Abraham and to his posterity for ever."
⁵⁶And Mary remained with her about three months, and returned to her home.

The annunciation of the conception of John (1:5-25) and Jesus (1:26-38) is followed by a supplementary unit in which Mary leaves Galilee for a city of Judah to visit her pregnant kinswoman Elizabeth (1:39-56). The visit begins in Elizabeth's sixth month (1:36,39), continues for about three months (1:56), and ends, paradoxically, just prior to the birth of John. The paradox, however, is merely historical and not theological. In terms of salvation history, Luke is careful to separate the person of Jesus from that of John, just as he would later separate Jesus' adult mission from that of John (3:21-22; 16:16). The coming of Jesus marks the beginning of a radically new historical era.

Ostensibly, the principal personages in this account are Mary and Elizabeth, and we note that Zechariah has been displaced by his wife during the nine months of his silence. Only after John's birth would he re-emerge as a key figure in the account of John's origins (1:62-79). In reality, however, the main personages in the visitation are the unborn infants, Jesus and John, and their mothers' primary function is to articulate the significance of their pre-natal encounter. Filling important but secondary roles, Elizabeth and Mary also symbolize the dynamic link between the readers' pre-christian past and their present christian challenge.

Bearing the life of Jesus, who was conceived by the Holy Spirit (1:35), Mary assumes the initiative in going to Elizabeth (1:39-40). As a result of her greeting, John leaped in his mother's womb (1:41). The one who would "make ready for the Lord a people prepared" (1:17) is thus quickened and "filled with the Holy Spirit, even from his mother's womb" by the one for whom he would exercise his mission. Jesus is thus the source of John's prophetic value and greatness. For Luke, Jesus and the New Testament did come in fulfillment of John and the Old. Transcending the promise, however, the fulfillment does not draw its meaning from the biblical past but from the Spirit's life-giving creativity. Hence Mary's initiative. It is Mary who visits Elizabeth in a city of Judah and not Elizabeth who travels to Nazareth of Galilee. In Mary, the New Testament reaches out to the Old, transforms it, and gives it its ultimate significance.

As a result of Mary's greeting and of John's new life in the Spirit, Elizabeth herself is filled with the Holy Spirit (1:41) and she proclaims the significance of what has just taken place (1:42-45). Extolling the blessedness of Mary and her child (1:42), she marvels that she should have received this visit from the mother of her Lord (1:43), through whom her own son had sprung to life (1:44). The Old Testament thus proclaims its debt and witnesses to the New, a debt historically grounded in Mary's faith that the Lord's word to her would be fulfilled (1:45). The author thus contrasts Mary's faith with Zechariah's failure to believe the Lord's words (1:20) and her greeting with his inability to utter the Lord's word (1:22). In Mary and in the Church which she represents, faith is thus a condition for speaking God's life-giving word.

Mary's response is cast in the form of a canticle, the *Magnificat*, whose form and content was inspired by Hannah's prayer in 1 Sam 2:1-10. Declaring the greatness of the Lord and rejoicing in God her Savior (1:46-47), Mary contrasts her humble condition with the greatness of what God has done (1:48-49). Her attention then turns to the extraordinary reversals of divine history, in which God's strength and greatness reduces human pride, might and wealth to no account, exalts those who humbly recognize their position before God and fills the hungry with good things (1:50-53). Mindful of his merciful love, God thus fulfills his promise to Abraham and his posterity for ever (1:54-55).

The canticle announces and summarizes some of the major themes of Luke-Acts, in particular the work's concern for the poor and politically weak, for christian leadership which must not assume the ways of human power, for the quality of christian nourishment at the Lord's table, and for the fulfillment of God's promise of blessing to Abraham and his true posterity.

## B. Manifestation.

## B. 1. THE BIRTH OF JOHN THE BAPTIST.
### *THE PROPHET OF THE MOST HIGH.*
### 1:57-80.

⁵⁷Now the time came for Elizabeth to be delivered, and she gave birth to a son. ⁵⁸And her neighbors and kinsfolk heard that the Lord had shown great mercy to her, and they rejoiced with her. ⁵⁹And on the eighth day they came to circumcise the child; and they would have named him Zechariah after his father, ⁶⁰but his mother said, "Not so; he shall be called John." ⁶¹And they said to her, "None of your kindred is called by this name." ⁶²And they made signs to his father, inquiring what he would have him called. ⁶³And he asked for a writing tablet, and wrote, "His name is John." And they all marveled. ⁶⁴And immediately his mouth was opened and his tongue loosed, and he spoke, blessing God, ⁶⁵And fear came on all their neighbors. And all these things were talked about through all the hill country of Judea; ⁶⁶and all who heard them laid them up in their hearts, saying, "What then will this child be?" For the hand of the Lord was with him.

⁶⁷And his father Zechariah was filled with the Holy Spirit, and prophesied, saying,
⁶⁸"Blessed be the Lord God of Israel,
   for he has visited and redeemed his
       people,
⁶⁹and has raised up a horn of salvation
       for us
   in the house of his servant David,
⁷⁰as he spoke by the mouth of his
       holy prophets from of old,
⁷¹that we should be saved from our
       enemies,
   and from the hand of all who hate us;

[72]to perform the mercy promised to
    our fathers,
  and to remember his holy covenant,
[73]the oath which he swore to our
    father Abraham, [74]to grant us
  that we, being delivered from the
    hand of our enemies,
  might serve him without fear,
[75]in holiness and righteousness before
    him all the days of our life.
[76]And you, child, will be called the
    prophet of the Most High;
  for you will go before the Lord to
    prepare his ways,
[77]to give knowledge of salvation to
    his people
  in the forgiveness of their sins,
[78]through the tender mercy of our
    God,
  when the day shall dawn upon us
    from on high
[79]to give light to those who sit in
    darkness and in the shadow of
    death,
  to guide our feet into the way of
    peace."
[80]And the child grew and became strong in spirit, and he
was in the wilderness till the day of his manifestation
to Israel.


The prologue's second diptych opens with the birth of
John the Baptist, an event which is heralded by all as a sign
that the Lord had shown great mercy to Elizabeth (1:57-58)
and through her to God's entire people, as Zechariah
would later proclaim (1:68-72). The narrative focuses not
so much on the actual birth, which is merely stated by way

of introduction (1:57), as on the naming of John (1:59-66), a name which expressed John's special identity and role in history. In his canticle, Zechariah spells out the significance of that role (1:67-79). John's birth story ends with a brief summary which gazes across the years to the day John would embark on his public mission (1:80).

The naming of John took place on the occasion of his circumcision. The neighbors and kinsfolk, who gathered for this important family event, expected the child to be named after his father, that is Zechariah (1:59). Elizabeth intervened however, and affirmed that he would be named John (1:60), the name which had been announced by Gabriel (1:13). Objecting to this departure from family tradition (1:61), the gathering appealed to Zechariah (1:62). Still unable to speak, the latter communicated by writing, "His name is John," a firm declaration which evoked wonderment on the part of the neighbors (1:63).

Luke's emphasis on the naming of John draws the reader's attention away from the actual birth, which was of little consequence apart from John's special role. The name expresses the person as no description can. Transcending all classifications, it is a person's proper word, speaking his unique identity and singular contribution to history. As such the meaning of the name can be drawn only from the person's life and its experiential perception and appreciation by others. In the present context, we must consequently turn to Luke's story of John, as told here in the prologue and in other parts of the gospel, if we wish to know the significance of John's name. The name's etymology, "The Lord has been gracious," is consequently of little interest. It may indeed say something about John, something which could also be attributed to others, but it does not say who John is.

By emphasizing the naming of John, Luke leads us to reflect on John's personal significance rather than on the mere fact of his birth. By disassociating John's name from his family history, he draws attention to the divine and transcendent source of his significance. The extraordinary circumstances of John's conception called for an extraordinary name. Conceived by divine intervention, John was named by divine mandate, and both Elizabeth and Zechariah were instrumental in its fulfillment.

With the naming of John, Zechariah regained his speech. The one who had not believed (1:20) turns to God with a blessing (1:64). The event inspired fear in all who were present or who later came to hear of it (1:65). It was seen that somehow renewed ability to speak was a sign connected with the naming of John. Attention thus focuses not on the wonder observed but on the person of John. For the moment, however, John's identity remains a mystery and an open-ended question (1:66). Luke himself articulates the mystery by noting that "the hand of the Lord was upon him" (1:66).

The story of John's birth and naming continues with Zechariah's prophetic canticle. Like Mary's *Magnificat* (1:46-55), Zechariah's *Benedictus* may have been introduced in a Lukan revision of the prologue. Like the former, it presupposes many of the major themes which would be developed in Luke-Acts. Be that as it may, the canticle greatly enriches the account of John's origin by its poetic anticipation of John's actual story.

The *Benedictus* contains two distinct units. First we have a blessing or *berakah* (1:68-75). Spoken in divine praise, it spells out the narrator's earlier statement that Zechariah opened his mouth in divine blessing (1:64). Its theme is God's redemption of his people by a mighty Savior. As the prophets had spoken, God had remembered his covenant promise to Abraham, that his people might serve him without fear. Zechariah's blessing, which in context echoes Mary's *Magnificat*, thus refers to Jesus, the object of John's prophetic mission.

The second part of the *Benedictus* is quite different in form and style. Begun as a blessing (1:68-75), Zechariah's canticle is transformed into a hymn celebrating the birth of his son (1:76-79). John will be the prophet of the Most High, one who prepares the way of the Lord by giving his people the knowledge of a salvation which would come from the experience of forgiveness. The canticle thus incorporates the basic theme of Is 40:3, a classical locus for interpreting John's mission, and one which Luke himself cites in 3:4 and 7:27. The hymnic celebration of John's birth thus focuses entirely on his relationship to Jesus and his salvific mission.

The unit's concluding summary indicates John's growth and spiritual strengthening and brings the prophet to the wilderness where the reader will once again join him in the account of Jesus background and preparation (3:2). The story of Jesus' birth and the prologue itself end with similar summary statements (2:40,52).

## B. 2. THE BIRTH OF JESUS.
### *A SAVIOR, WHO IS CHRIST THE LORD.*
2:1-21.

**2**  In those days a decree went out from Caesar Augustus that all the world should be enrolled. [2]This was the first enrollment, when Quirinius was governor of Syria. [3]And all went to be enrolled, each to his own city. [4]And Joseph, also went up from Galilee, from the city of Nazareth, to Judea, to the city of David, which is called Bethlehem, because he was of the house and lineage of David, [5]to be enrolled with Mary, his betrothed, who was with child. [6]And while they were there, the time came for her to be delivered. [7]And she gave birth to her first-born son and wrapped him in swaddling cloths, and laid him in a manger, because there was no place for them in the inn.

[8]And in that region there were shepherds out in the field, keeping watch over their flock by night. [9]And an angel of the Lord appeared to them, and the glory of the Lord shone around them, and they were filled with fear. [10]And the angel said to them, "Be not afraid; for behold, I

bring you good news of a great joy which will come to all the people; [11]for to you is born this day in the city of David a Savior, who is Christ the Lord. [12]And this will be a sign for you: you will find a babe wrapped in swaddling cloths and lying in a manger." [13]And suddenly there was with the angel a multitude of the heavenly host praising God and saying,

[14]"Glory to God in the highest,
    and on earth peace among men with
        whom he is pleased!"

[15]When the angels went away from them into heaven, the shepherds said to one another, "Let us go over to Bethlehem and see this thing that has happened, which the Lord has made known to us." [16]And they went with haste, and found Mary and Joseph, and the babe lying in a manger. [17]And when they saw it they made known the saying which had been told them concerning this child; [18]and all who heard it wondered at what the shepherds told them. [19]But Mary kept all these things, pondering them in her heart. [20]And the shepherds returned, glorifying and praising God for all they had heard and seen, as it had been told them.

[21]And at the end of eight days, when he was circumcised, he was called Jesus, the name given by the angel before he was conceived in the womb.

The story of Jesus' birth is considerably different from that of John. Divided into three units, it begins by narrating the circumstances which prepared and accompanied Jesus' actual birth (2:1-7), continues with the story of the shepherds (2:8-20), and ends with a brief statement concerning the naming of Jesus (2:21). In John's case, the birth was simply noted (1:57), the circumstances of the naming were greatly developed (1:59-66), and there is nothing to parallel the heavenly manifestation to the shepherds. These differences are altogether consonant with Luke's effort to show how Jesus was historically related to John but in no way reducible to the religious history which climaxed in him.

## *The Birth of Mary's First-Born Son.*
*2:1-7.*

Joseph and Mary lived in Nazareth of Galilee, a fact clearly attested in early christian tradition. However, according to another tradition, which is at least theological if not historical, Jesus was born in Bethlehem of Judah, the city of David (2:1-7; Mt 2:1-6). This relationship to Bethlehem was an important element in christological and scriptural reflection on Jesus, who was acclaimed as Son of David (18:38-39). At the same time, it posed a problem, at least for the narrative telling of Jesus' origins. How could Jesus be presented both as a Nazarene and as a Bethlehemite? Matthew solved this problem by beginning Jesus' story at Bethlehem. Only later would he show how Jesus came to be associated with Nazareth (Mt 2:19-23). Luke, on the other hand, began his story with the annunciation at Nazareth. Consequently, his problem was to show how Jesus came to be born at Bethlehem.

From a historical point of view, Luke's account is extremely difficult. Since the author is generally well-informed in political matters, every effort has been made to uncover the imperial decree which allegedly was issued while Quirinius was governor of Syria (2:1-2). None of these have been truly successful. Apart from this difficulty and several others, however, Luke's intention is quite clear.

The birth of Jesus is situated in the greater world of the Roman empire, in relation to the imperial province of Syria and in the client-kingdom of Judea. He is thus mindful of Christianity's movement from Judea to Syria, the area from which he very likely wrote Luke-Acts, and on to the ends of the earth (Acts 1:8), symbolized by Rome (Acts 19:21; 28:14-31). The circumstances which led to Jesus' birth thus announce the historical development and universal scope of the Church as set forth in Luke-Acts. In view of this general intention, Luke could very well have prescinded from the precise historical and chronological factors which surrounded Jesus' birth.

It is not enough to note that Luke 2:1-5 situates the Church in the political world of the first century. The passage also presents Joseph and his betrothed as loyal subjects of Rome and Augustus. In light of Luke's general effort to show how Jesus and the Church were just and legitimate in terms of Roman law, the indication is significant. It contributes to the author's apologetic for Roman recognition, an apologetic urgently required to counter the persecutions which were arising in various quarters. In a sense, Luke 2:1-5 is Luke's own appeal to Caesar (see Acts 25:10-12).

The description of Jesus' actual birth (2:6-7) must be read in light of 2:1-5. Set in the vastness of imperial Rome and in the biblical context of the royal house of David, Jesus' birth is that of a poor man, a simple and humble event which contrasts with the political world about him. Consequently, Jesus' messianic royalty has nothing to do with worldly aspirations and ways of ruling (see 22:24-27).

What is true of Jesus is also true of his disciples and the Church. Clearly affirmed in 22:24-27, this relationship is also inscribed in 2:7, which refers to Mary's "first-born son" (*prototokos*). The designation "first-born son," prepares the reader for Jesus' presentation to the Lord as the first-born in 2:22-24. However, unlike the term "only son" (*monogenes*, 7:12), it also leaves open the possibility and may actually imply that Mary had further children. This possibility may be excluded as a biological fact, but not as a theological statement. Mary would have further children, namely all who would come to be associated with her son after the passion-resurrection. In Lukan terms this is most clearly stated in the narrative of Paul's conversion: "Saul, Saul, why do you persecute me?" (Acts 9:4; 22:7; 26:14). In Acts 1:14, Mary herself is expressly singled out in the community of those who continued to give historical expression to the life of her son. The designation 'first-born son" is thus a statement about Jesus' relationship to his future followers.

## *The Gospel Proclaimed to Shepherds.*
### *2:8-20.*

After noting John's birth (1:57), his story had immediately focused on the giving of the name, an event which
caused considerable wonderment and which raised the
question of John's identity (1:58-66). With regard to Jesus,
the naming is briefly stated in 2:21 as a fulfillment of
Gabriel's command (1:31). The wonderment which surrounds Jesus, however, has nothing to do with his naming.
Nor does it raise the question of his identity. Rather it
springs from the report of shepherds who had heard the
good news concerning Jesus' birth.

Jesus had been announced to the shepherds as a Savior,
Christ the Lord (2:10-11). They had been given a sign,
namely that they would find the Lord "wrapped in swaddling clothes and lying in a manger" (2:12; see 2:7). This
they had verified (2:16) and the wonderment sprang precisely from the contrast between the Savior's lordship and
the humble circumstances of his birth. For the shepherds,
the announcement and the event were truly good news, and
they responded by glorifying and praising God (2:20).
Christ the Lord was part of their world. Humbly born, he
was a Savior for the humble (see 1:46-55), those with whom
God was pleased (2:14).

Luke's main point, which links God's glory in the highest
with peace on earth for the humble (2:14) would have been
lost had the passage merely raised the matter of Jesus'
identity. The narrative called for a manifestation of Jesus'
life and mission, a statement which would anticipate the
actual unfolding of the implications of his name. This need
was met by the angelophany. The message of the angel and
the song of the heavenly host thus fills the function which
Zechariah's canticle had filled in the story of John's birth.
In the context of the prologue, this first proclamation of
the gospel thus continues the series of christological statements begun in the annunciation of Jesus' conception
(1:31-33,35) and pursued in the visitation (1:39-55) and

Zechariah's song of blessing (1:68-75). Like these earlier passages, the unit is also ecclesiological, affirming the true nature of the Church as the humble recipient and proclaimer of the gospel.

## B. 3. JESUS COMES TO JERUSALEM.
*MINE EYES HAVE SEEN THY SALVATION.*
   2:22-40.

22And when the time came for their purification according to the law of Moses, they brought him up to Jerusalem to present him to the Lord 23(as it is written in the law of the Lord, "Every male that opens the womb shall be called holy to the Lord") 24and to offer a sacrifice according to what is said in the law of the Lord, "a pair of turtledoves, or two young pigeons." 25Now there was a man in Jerusalem, whose name was Simeon, and this man was righteous and devout, looking for the consolation of Israel, and the Holy Spirit was upon him. 26And it had been revealed to him by the Holy Spirit that he should not see death before he had seen the Lord's Christ. 27And inspired by the Spirit he came into the temple; and when the parents brought in the child Jesus, to do for him according to the custom of the law, 28he took him up in his arms and blessed God and said,

29"Lord, now lettest thou thy servant
   depart in peace,
   according to thy word;
30for mine eyes have seen thy
   salvation
31which thou hast prepared in the
   presence of all peoples,
32a light for revelation to the Gentiles,
   and for glory to thy people Israel."

33And his father and his mother marveled at what was said about him; 34and Simeon blessed them and said to Mary his mother,

"Behold, this child is set for the fall
and rising of many in Israel,
and for a sign that is spoken against
[35](and a sword will pierce through
your own soul also),
that thoughts out of many hearts may
be revealed."
[36]And there was a prophetess, Anna, the daughter of Phanuel, of the tribe of Asher; she was of a great age, having lived with her husband seven years from her virginity, [37]and as a widow till she was eighty-four. She did not depart from the temple, worshiping with fasting and prayer night and day. [38]And coming up at that very hour she gave thanks to God, and spoke of him to all who were looking for the redemption of Jerusalem.

[39]And when they had performed everything according to the law of the Lord, they returned into Galilee, to their own city, Nazareth. [40]And the child grew and became strong, filled with wisdom; and the favor of God was upon him.

In 2:1-21, Luke showed how Jesus' birth was related to Judaism, the Greco-Roman world, the life of the Church and the gospel mission. In 2:22-40, he develops Jesus' relationship to Israel's hope for salvation, a hope based on a historical and prophetic promise which reached out even to the gentiles. He also shows how salvation would entail suffering for those who were associated with Jesus' origins, for the disciples and for the world they would address. Jesus' advent is thus seen both as the fulfillment of biblical promise and as the promise of his salvific passion and future persecutions and struggles.

Within the prologue, the passage parallels Jesus' encounter with John (1:39-56) and complements the literary diptych concerning the birth of John (1:57-80) and Jesus (2:1-21). Structurally, it includes an introduction, part of whose function is to bring Jesus to Jerusalem (2:22-24), a body, whose context is the Jerusalem temple and which presents the witness of Simeon (2:25-35) and Anna (2:36-38), and a conclusion, in which Jesus returns to Nazareth (2:39-40). The events in Jerusalem (2:25-38) are thus framed by the journey to and from that city (2:22-24, 39-40).

In addition to the journey motif, which provides the passage with a sense of movement, purposefulness and unity (compare with 1:39-40,56), the introduction and conclusion also develop Jesus' fulfillment of the law, which called for the mother's purification (Lv 12:2-8) and the consecration of the first-born to the Lord (Ex 13:2,12). The fulfillment of the law brought God's favor on the child and this was reflected in his maturation. As the concluding summary indicates, Jesus grew, became strong and was filled with wisdom (2:40; see 1:80).

Through Mary and Joseph, Jesus fulfilled the jewish law just as he had fulfilled the law of Rome (2:1-5). What was true of Jesus' origins would be equally true of the entire course of his life as well as of the life of the Church. Luke has thus introduced an important literary thread which would make its way through the whole Lukan tapestry of christian origins.

## The Witness of Simeon and Anna.
### 2:25-38.

Jesus' fulfillment of the law's various prescriptions (2:22-24, 39-40; see also 2:27) pointed to a deeper theological fulfillment. The Lord's Christ or Messiah (2:26) responded to Israel's deepest hope for salvation. In Jesus' advent, Israel's life and mission found its ultimate fulfillment.

Through the witness of Simeon and Anna, which is presented in two complementary sub-units (2:25-35, 36-38), Israel itself acknowledges the end of a long period of history and the beginning of a new era. Transformed into a new and universal Israel, the old Israel could depart in peace. In terms of Israel's own life, the fulfillment, which included both Israel and the gentiles (2:32) far transcended the promise.

Simeon was a righteous and devout man. His "looking for the consolation of Israel" (2:25) evokes Is 40:1-5, a passage which sums up the messianic expectations of the time and which the early Christians frequently cited to articulate the relationship between the missions of John the Baptist and Jesus (3:4-6). Simeon's witness, however, does not spring from ordinary reflection on the jewish tradition, but from the Holy Spirit, which had provided him with a special revelation (2:26), which moved him to go to the temple at the moment Jesus' parents brought in the child (2:27), which led him to recognize Jesus as the consolation and salvation of Israel (2:28-30) and to proclaim him as such (2:25). The same Holy Spirit had moved Elizabeth and Zechariah to recognize and proclaim the significance of Jesus (1:41-45, 67-79).

Salvation had not been prepared in the secret of Israel's own life but in the presence of all. In Jesus it now shone as a light which would extend revelation to the gentiles and glorify God's people Israel (2:31-32). Simeon's little canticle, a prayer of blessing like the first part of Zechariah's canticle (1:68-75), explicitly refers to what Simeon had been promised by the Holy Spirit (2:29,26). It is Luke's simplest and most eloquent expression of Christianity's relationship to Israel.

After blessing God (2:28) and before departing from history (2:29), Simeon bestows God's blessing on Jesus' father and mother (2:33-34). The promise made to Abraham was thus being fulfilled in the new Israel. Jesus would also bless his disciples before ascending to God (24:50-51). Simeon then announces the sufferings which would accompany the unfolding of the fulfillment, sufferings manifested in the passion of Jesus but also in the life of the post-ascension community (2:34-35). Luke's readers should thus be able to situate their own sufferings with regard to their origins, which entailed the fall and the rising of many in Israel (see 20:17-18). The sword which pierced the soul of the mother of the first-born was piercing that of the Church, the mother of all who shared his life.

Simeon's witness is supplemented by that of Anna, an aged prophetess, a jewish woman of heroic life who never left the temple and worshipped through unceasing fasting and prayer (2:36-37). Like Simeon, she came forward while Jesus and his parents were there. Her response, which presupposed that of Simeon, is briefly summarized as giving thanks to god. Simeon's word had been limited to the small circle of Jesus and his parents. Anna's word, which also expressed the voice of Israel, is directed to all who came to the temple "looking for the redemption of Jerusalem" (2:38). All who now came to the temple are greeted with the gospel of God's redemption through Jesus.

## II. C. Jesus' Ultimate Destiny.
## I Must be in my Father's House.
## 2:41-52.

[41]Now his parents went to Jerusalem every year at the feast of the Passover. [42]And when he was twelve years old, they went up according to custom; [43]and when the feast was ended, as they were returning, the boy Jesus stayed behind in Jerusalem. His parents did not know it, [44]but supposing him to be in the company they went a day's journey, and they sought him among their kinsfolk and acquaintances; [45]and when they did not find him, they returned to Jerusalem, seeking him. [46]After three days they found him in the temple, sitting among the teachers, listening to them and asking them questions; [47]and all who heard him were amazed at his understanding and his answers. [48]And when they saw him they were astonished; and his mother said to him, "Son, why have you treated us so? Behold, your father and I have been looking for you anxiously." [49]And he said to them, "How is it that you sought me? Did you not know that I must be in my Father's house?" [50]And they did not understand the saying which he spoke to them. [51]And he went

> down with them and came to Nazareth, and was obedient
> to them; and his mother kept all these things in her
> heart.
>
> [52]And Jesus increased in wisdom and in stature, and
> in favor with God and man.

From many points of view, the prologue could already
be considered as complete. Jesus conception (1:26-38) and
be considered as complete. Jesus' conception (1:26-38) and
those of John the Baptist (1:5-25, 57-80). The prophetic
voice of the Old Testament has been quickened by the
advent of one who fulfills it (1:39-56), and its living voice
has witnessed to Jesus' salvific death and the universality
of the christian mission (2:22-40). In the process, Jesus
and his mission have been situated with regard to the
Roman Empire, Judaism, the law, prophecy and the
temple.

There remained, however, one major theme to develop,
that of Jesus' departure from history and his ultimate
destiny. This is presented in the prologue's present conclusion, which also situates Jesus with regard to Israel's
interpretation of the law and the living voice of Israelite
wisdom (2:41-52). Since the unit stands outside the prologue's basic structure, it may have been added once Luke-
Acts had already been written. Be that as it may, the passage
does correspond to two of Luke-Acts' major themes, that of
the exodus or ascension of Jesus (9:31,51; 24:50-53; Acts
1:9-12), and that of Jesus' interpretation of the law and
the prophets (24:25-27, 44-47). Both of these themes had
become essential in a gospel message for Christians who
deeply felt the absence of Jesus, for whom the gospel had
become opaque, and who consequently were losing touch
with their sense of mission.

As in 2:22-40, the narrative framework consists in a
journey to and from Jerusalem (2:41,51). In the previous
unit, however, Jerusalem and the temple witnessed to the
meaning of Jesus' mission. In the present unit, that witness
is related to Jesus' passage to the Father.

Again as in 2:22-40, Jesus goes to Jerusalem with his parents. In the first visit, however, the course of Jesus' life and its implications for his parents were clarified by Simeon and Anna. In this second visit, Jesus himself interprets the event and disassociates the ultimate meaning of his life from his parental origins. Jesus' destiny transcends created humanity and the boundaries of human history.

The story evokes another journey to Jerusalem, that which begins in 9:51 and which also brings Jesus to Jerusalem as the feast of Passover was approaching (2:41; 22:1). In that larger story, Jesus would also celebrate the Passover (2:43; 22:7-38) and be lost (2:43-45; 22:47-23:56), only to be found after three days (2:46; 24:1-49). In both cases, the loss of Jesus creates confusion and consternation (2:48; 24:19-24) and Jesus explains the divine necessity which called for his absence (2:49; 24:25-27). Again as in the great journey narrative, Jesus absence is situated in the context of his ultimate destiny which requires his being with the Father (2:49; 24:50-53).

In light of the relationship between 2:41-52 and 9:51-24:53, Jesus' visit to Jerusalem at the age of twelve (2:42), that is at his entry into adulthood, must be seen as a narrative statement concerning the journey of his entire adult life. In 2:41-52, Jesus journeys with his parents. In 9:51-24:53, his journey is in the company of his disciples, that is with those who "hear the word of God and do it" (8:21; 11:28). It is they who are Jesus' true parents and relatives (8:19-20; 11:27). In both cases, Jesus' absence is a matter of divine necessity.

The concluding summary (2:52) is similar to the previous summary, which concluded Jesus' first visit to Jerusalem (2:41). Both emphasize Jesus' wisdom. In the present case, however, the implications of Jesus' wisdom are much clearer. The wisdom which springs from the fulfillment of the law (2:40) transcends the law as well as the interpretations of its teachers (2:46-47). In his wisdom, Jesus points to life's ultimate fulfillment beyond the sphere of history in which the law operates.

*III. Background and Preparation.*
   *Jesus in History.*
   *3:1 - 4:13.*

## OUTLINE

# III. BACKGROUND AND PREPARATION. JESUS IN HISTORY. 3:1 - 4:13.

AFTER THE PREFACE (1:1-4) and the prologue (1:5-2:52), Luke lays out the background and preparation for Jesus' mission (3:1-4:13) as it will be presented in the remainder of his gospel. It may well be that this unit had originally been intended as the gospel's introduction. Beginning with a solemn historical declaration, which would have been most appropriate as the work's opening statement, the section corresponds to Mark's prologue (Lk 3:1-18, 21-22; 4:1-13; Mk 1:2-8, 9-11, 12-13) and includes a genealogy of Jesus akin to that which stands at the head of Matthew's gospel (Lk 3:23-38; Mt 1:1-17). Be that as it may, 3:1-4:13 now forms the gospel's second major unit and includes many of the pastoral preoccupations and literary themes which are characteristic of Luke's message to Christians living in the ninth decade.

In its present context, the section positions Jesus' divine mission in relation to recent prophetic history (3:1-22), universal biblical history (3:23-38) and Israel's classic struggle with evil (4:1-13). The prologue, on the other hand, had situated Jesus' divine identity in relation to his human origins and relationships (1:5-2:52). Luke 3:1-4:13 thus complements the prologue by focusing on the roots and significance of Jesus' historical mission. Both in his personal identity and in his adult mission, Jesus is God's Son (1:35; 3:22) and his life must be seen as an expression of God's Spirit. Conceived by the power of the Holy Spirit (1:35), he exercises his mission by the power of that same Spirit (3:22) as he victoriously confronts the forces of evil (4:1).

## A. Jesus and Recent Prophetic History. The word of God came to John. 3:1-22.

**3** In the fifteenth year of the reign of Tiberius Caesar, Pontius Pilate being governor of Judea, and Herod being tetrarch of Galilee, and his brother Philip tetrarch of the region of Ituraea and Trachonitis, and Lysanias tetrarch of Abilene, [2]in the high priesthood of Annas and Caiaphas, the word of God came to John the son of Zechariah in the wilderness; [3]and he went into all the region about the Jordan, preaching a baptism of repentance for the forgiveness of sins. [4]As it is written in the book of the words of Isaiah the prophet,

"The voice of one crying in the
wilderness:
Prepare the way of the Lord,
make his paths straight.
[5]Every valley shall be filled,
and every mountain and hill shall
be brought low,
and the crooked shall be made
straight,

and the rough ways shall be made
 smooth;
[6]and all flesh shall see the salvation
 of God."

[7]He said therefore to the multitudes that came out to be baptized by him, "You brood of vipers! Who warned you to flee from the wrath to come? [8]Bear fruits that befit repentance, and do not begin to say to yourselves, 'We have Abraham as our father'; for I tell you, God is able from these stones to raise up children to Abraham. [9]Even now the axe is laid to the root of the trees; every tree therefore that does not bear good fruit is cut down and thrown into the fire."

[10]And the multitudes asked him, "What then shall we do?" [11]And he answered them, "He who has two coats, let him share with him who has none; and he who has food, let him do likewise." [12]Tax collectors also came to be baptized, and said to him, "Teacher, what shall we do?" [13]And he said to them, "Collect no more than is appointed you." [14]Soldiers also asked him, "And we, what shall we do?" And he said to them, "Rob no one by violence or by false accusation, and be content with your wages."

[15]As the people were in expectation, and all men questioned in their hearts concerning John, whether perhaps he were the Christ, [16]John answered them all, "I baptize you with water; but he who is mightier than I is coming, the thong of whose sandals I am not worthy to untie; he will baptize you with the Holy Spirit and with fire. [17]His winnowing fork is in his hand, to clear his threshing floor, and to gather the wheat into his granary, but the chaff he will burn with unquenchable fire."

[18]So, with many other exhortations, he preached good news to the people. [19]But Herod the tetrarch, who had been reproved by him for Herodias, his brother's wife, and for all the evil things that Herod had done, [20]added this to them all, that he shut up John in prison.

> ²¹Now when all the people were baptized, and when
> Jesus also had been baptized and was praying, the heaven
> was opened, ²²and the Holy Spirit descended upon him in
> bodily form, as a dove, and a voice came from heaven,
> "Thou art my beloved Son; with thee I am well pleased."

In a sense, Jesus' divine mission was grounded in the
work of John the Baptist, a major personage who also
figures prominently in the infancy narrative. Accordingly,
Luke begins this preparatory section by situating and
presenting John and his message (3:1-20). To be more
precise, however, the unit does not concern John himself
so much as the word of God which came to John and which
he uttered to the various categories of people who followed
him out to the wilderness. Consequently, the author's
interest does not lie in John's mission as a baptizer but in
his prophetic appeal for repentance and reform in preparation for one who would be mightier than he. For Luke then,
John must be seen primarily as a prophet, and Jesus'
mission is grounded in the divine word which John
mediated.

Having related Jesus' mission to the word which came to
John, Luke then disassociates it from John's baptism and
shows how the true source of Jesus' mission is the Holy
Spirit (3:21-22). Consequently, while Jesus was indeed
baptized by John, his mission was not merely a religious
response to the reformer's baptism. Rather, sprung from
God's creative and empowering Spirit, it far surpasses the
work of John the prophet and the many centuries of salvation history which had led to it.

As the fulfillment of John's prophetic word, Jesus'
mission thus stood in continuity with that of John. As a new
expression of the Holy Spirit, however, it was also dis-
continuous, transcending all earlier manifestations of God's
saving presence. With this distinction in mind, we can well
appreciate why the proper subject of Luke's history is not
John but the word of God (3:2), why John's essential role

is prophetic, and why, as opposed to Mk 6:14-29, his mission terminates before that of Jesus begins (3:18-20,21). We also understand why the Holy Spirit descends upon Jesus after the baptism and while Jesus is at prayer (3:21-22).

## John the Prophet.
### 3:1-20.

Luke begins by situating the word's coming to John chronologically, politically, religiously and geographically (3:1-2). With an elaborate synchronism which is characteristic of historical writing in hellenistic times, he positions the advent of God's word in the year 26 or 27 and within the political world of the Roman Empire, of which the ancient land of Israel now formed a part, and in the religious priestly world of Jerusalem's temple. In a work which would see God's word open outwards to the ends of the earth and where Jesus and his disciples would come in conflict with both political and religious leaders at all levels, this introduction appears most appropriate.

Geographically, however, the event took place far from the political and religious centers of power, in the very wilderness region (see 1:80) where Jesus would be led to confront the powers of evil (4:1-13). Although the christian mission would be immersed in the religious world of Jerusalem and the political world of Rome, its true source is thus quite distinct from both of these spheres of life and influence.

Luke's effort would be no ordinary hellenistic history, whether Greek or jewish, but a prophetic history of the word. Accordingly, the opening verses also evoke the characteristic biblical manner of introducing a prophetic work. Like the latter, Lk 3:1-2 notes the coming of God's word and identifies its recipient by giving the prophet's name and his immediate filiation. Prophetic introductions also situated the word's advent in terms of Israel's political history, and in the case of Haggai (1:1) and Zechariah (1:1), the scope of that history included even Darius, the ruler of

Persia, in whose empire Judah constituted a satrapy. In prophetic writing, however, such synchronisms were shorter and far more modest than in hellenistic historiography.

The above observations indicate that Luke has wedded the world of hellenistic historical writing to that of biblical prophecy. Cultured christian readers, steeped in the Septuagint and educated in Greek historical literature, would thus find themselves at home in the emerging christian literature which integrated and transcended both. In Luke's work, the biblical world confronts the Greco-Roman world, as the fulfillment of God's word to John spreads from its origins in the mission of Jesus (4:21,43; 5:5) and the life of the Jerusalem community (Acts 6:7) to the various centers of the Roman empire (Acts 8:4,25; 12:24) and all the way to the Roman capital itself (Acts 28:30-31). Born as a word to the Jews, the christian word would reach out to all peoples (Acts 1:8; 11:1), thereby fulfilling Israel's universal mission.

Following this introduction, the narrator interprets John's prophetic word, which called for a baptism of repentance for the forgiveness of sins (3:3), in terms of Isaiah 40:3-5. John's role is thus comparable to that of Deutero-Isaiah who was asked to comfort the Israelites in exile (40:1-2) and to prepare the way for the Lord's coming. We note that Luke omitted Mark's reference to "my messenger" (Mk 1:2), a citation from Malachi 3:1 which evoked the figure of Elijah (Mal 4:5-6) whose return would announce the Lord's definitive coming. Similarly, he also excluded Mark's physical description of John as a new Elijah (Mk 1:6). We should recall, however, that Luke had already presented John as an Elijan figure in the prologue (1:17) and that he would once again do so in 7:27. There was consequently no need to repeat the statement at this point.

We then have a general summary of John's preaching (3:7-9) in which appeals to a physical relationship to Abraham our father (3.8) are counted as ineffectual efforts to escape God's punishing wrath (3:7,9). Every tree which does not bear good fruit, that is fruits that befit repentance (3:3), is cut down and thrown into the fire (3:8,9). A true son of Abraham is thus one who bears fruit and apart from this whether or not one has Abraham for a father is absolutely insignificant (see 13:28-30; 19:9). As in the case of Jesus' conception (1:26-38), of John's word (3:1-2) and of the universal mission to the gentiles (Acts 2:1-13; 10:1-11:18), human origins are of no consequence. What does matter is that one respond to the life which God himself creatively brings forth through the Holy Spirit.

In turn, the multitudes, the tax collectors and the soldiers then ask what they must do, and John responds with a message adapted to the concrete social situation of each. The multitudes must share with the needy (3:10-11), tax collectors must require no more than is appointed them (3:12-13) and soldiers must refrain from violent robbery and false accusations as means to supplement inadequate wages (3:14).

John's prophetic activity was bound to raise the question of his personal identity. He consequently assures the people that he himself is not the Messiah (3:15) and asks that they direct their expectations to another who would be far mightier and whose baptism would be in the Holy Spirit and in fire (3:16). The author thus draws attention to the Spirit-life of the Church in history and to history's definitive consummation in a fiery judgment for the unrepentant (3:17). Such was the preaching of the gospel which led to John's incarceration by Herod the tetrarch (3:18-20; see 3:1).

*God's Beloved Son.*
*3:21-22.*

Along with all the people, Jesus was baptized by John (3:21a). However, while this event was significant, it did not constitute the springboard for Jesus' mission. Accordingly, Luke merely notes that it has occurred and focuses the reader's attention on a post-baptismal moment when Jesus was at prayer. There is consequently no baptismal narrative. Instead we have a divine manifestation which is completely distinct from the baptism itself. The manifestation includes the opening of the heavens, a descent of the Holy Spirit and a heavenly proclamation (3:21b-22).

The uniqueness of Luke's presentation emerges most clearly from a comparison with Mark 1:9-11. In the latter we also have a divine manifestation with the opening of the heavens, a descent of the Spirit and a heavenly word. Unlike Luke 3:20-21, however, these have been carefully integrated in a baptismal narrative and occur at the very moment when Jesus emerges from the water.

Luke's account thus transforms a baptismal event into a descent of God's Spirit. The Spirit is the creative source of Jesus' mission just as it had been the source of his very life (1:35). This reinterpretation of Jesus' baptism is closely related to Luke's presentation of the Church's origins.

In Acts 1:5, the risen Jesus promises that the apostolic community would "be baptized with the Holy Spirit" (see 2:1-4). The descent of the Spirit is thus interpreted as a baptism. At first reading, this appears to be a reversal of the order established for Jesus in Luke 3:20-21. Luke's statement in Acts, however, actually constitutes a redefinition of baptism as a descent of the Spirit. The Christians, who had developed a baptism akin to that of John were consequently not to reduce it to the latter. As a gift of the Spirit, christian baptism was unique. In 3:20-21, the descent of the Spirit is thus Jesus' true baptism. This presentation is consistent with the story of Jesus' conception, where all human considerations give way to the Spirit's intervention. As we shall see, a similar theology governs the Lukan genealogy of Jesus (3:23-38).

The human context of the event, namely while Jesus is praying, is closely related to the event itself, whose elements constitute an important synthesis of biblical theology. The opening of the heavens recalls Is 63:19, where Isaiah prays that God open the heavens for a definitive act of redemption in a final exodus. Jesus' prayer is answered, and the Holy

Spirit descends in bodily form, like a dove, a comparison which associates the Spirit with the people of Israel (Hos 11:11; Ps 68:14). Symbolically, Jesus is thus presented as the fulfillment of Israel's expectations, and Israel itself, through whom the Spirit is manifested, witnesses to that redemptive fulfillment. As in liturgical texts (see 22:17-20), a word announces and interprets the significance of the event taking place. The quotation in 3:21, a composite reference to Ps 2:7 and Is 42:1, articulates the meaning of the Spirit's descent upon Jesus: Jesus' mission is that of God's beloved Son with whom he is well-pleased.

### B. Jesus and Universal History.
### Jesus, the son of Adam, the son of God.
### 3:23-38.

23Jesus, when he began his ministry, was about thirty years of age, being the son (as was supposed) of Joseph, the son of Heli, 24the son of Matthat, the son of Levi, the son of Melchi, the son of Jannai, the son of Joseph, 25the son of Mattathias, the son of Amos, the son of Nahum, the son of Esli, the son of Naggai, 26the son of Maath, the son of Mattathias, the son of Semein, the son of Josech, the son of Joda, 27the son of Joanan, the son of Rhesa, the son of Zerubbabel, the son of Shealtiel, the son of Neri, 28the son of Melchi, the son of Addi, the son of Cosam, the son of Elmadam, the son of Er, 29the son of Joshua, the son of Eliezer, the son of Jorim, the son of Matthat, the son of Levi, 30the son of Simeon, the son of Judah, the son of Joseph, the son of Jonam, the son of Eliakim, 31 the son of Melea, the son of Menna, the son of Mattatha, the son of Nathan, the son of David, 32the son of Jesse, the son of Obed, the son of Boaz, the son of Sala, the son of Nahshon, 33the son of Amminadab, the son of Admin, the son of Arni, the son of Hezron, the son of Perez, the son of Judah, 34the son of Jacob, the son of Isaac, the son of Abraham, the son of

Terah, the son of Nahor, [35]the son of Serug, the son of Reu, the son of Peleg, the son of Eber, the son of Shelah, [36]the son of Cainan, the son of Arphaxad, the son of Shem, the son of Noah, the son of Lamech, [37]the son of Methuselah, the son of Enoch, the son of Jared, the son of Mahalaleel, the son of Cainan, [38]the son of Enos, the son of Seth, the son of Adam, the son of God.

Unlike Mt 1:1-17, Jesus' genealogy is not related to his birth but to the origins of his ministry, which began when he was about thirty years of age (3:23a). It is thus intended to situate Jesus' active role in life within the broad sweep of history. From Luke's point of view, that role, which began after Jesus' baptism (3:21-22), could not be understood in terms of John the Baptist alone. This important relationship could only situate Jesus in immediate religious history. It was also necessary to view Jesus' ministry in the context of universal history. Nor could a truly universal history begin with Abraham, as it did in Mt 1:1-17. Since the christian mission reached out to all human beings, including Jews and gentiles, its historical horizon had to include the entire history of the race, beginning with Adam.

Genealogies are closely related to the biblical manner of naming someone. Usually, this included only a person's given name and that of his immediate progenitor. In the case of Jesus, the name was Jesus son of Joseph, and this provided adequate identification in his immediate social context. To identify Jesus in terms of biblical history, however, Luke presented his entire genealogy, indicating his lineage all the way back to his remotest human origins. Luke 3:23-38 is thus a summary recapitulation of history as it led to the mission of Jesus. Carefully selected, each name evokes a story which illumines the significance of his mission.

In the prologue (1:5-2:52) and in the unit on Jesus' relationship to John the Baptist (3:1-22), Luke showed how Jesus' identity transcended his human origins and immediate historical preparation. Jesus was of God as well as of

man, and his full identity sprang from the creative intervention of the Holy Spirit. Accordingly, the genealogy
which **situated** his ministry could not be limited to the
tracing of a merely human lineage, even a biblical one.
At best, this would have situated Jesus in the line of religious
history as defined by the parameters of God's guiding
presence in the Old Testament. Jesus' ministry, however,
fulfilled the promise through an altogether unexpected
divine intervention which transcended the continuum of
previous history. The genealogy thus complements the
limited perspective of an ordinary genealogy by relating
Jesus to God.

From the beginning, Luke both affirms and denies
Joseph's parentage of Jesus. By means of a parenthesis,
"being the son (as was supposed) of Joseph" (3:23), he
evokes the annunciation of Jesus' birth (1:26-38) and asks
his readers to see Jesus as more than the heir to a long
biblical history. The genealogy is thus relativized and
subordinated to Jesus' divine sonship.

Jesus' genealogy is clearly consistent with 1:5-3:22.
However, it also goes further in its reflection and situates
Jesus with regard to the moment of creation. Ultimately,
Jesus is son of Adam, who is son of God (3:38). The creation
motif had been implied in the role of the Holy Spirit who
came upon Mary (1:35). It is now explicitly introduced in
Adam's divine sonship. As with the origins of the human
race, Jesus' divine sonship cannot be accounted for in
historical terms alone, but only as an expression of God's
personal creativity.

### C. Jesus and the Struggles of Humanity.
### Full of the Holy Spirit . . tempted by the devil.
### 4:1-13.

**4** And Jesus, full of the Holy Spirit, returned from the
Jordan, and was led by the Spirit ²for forty days in the
wilderness, tempted by the devil. And he ate nothing in

those days; and when they were ended, he was hungry.
³The devil said to him, "If you are the Son of God, command this stone to become bread." ⁴And Jesus answered him, "It is written, 'Man shall not live by bread alone.'"
⁵And the devil took him up, and showed him all the kingdoms of the world in a moment of time, ⁶and said to him, "To you I will give all this authority and their glory; for it has been delivered to me, and I give it to whom I will. ⁷If you, then, will worship me, it shall all be yours."
⁸And Jesus answered him, "It is written,

'You shall worship the Lord your
    God,
and him only shall you serve.'"

⁹And he took him to Jerusalem, and set him on the pinnacle of the temple, and said to him, "If you are the Son of God, throw yourself down from here; ¹⁰for it is written,

'He will give his angels charge of
    you, to guard you,'

¹¹and

'On their hands they will bear you
    up,
lest you strike your foot against a
    stone.'"

¹²And Jesus answered him, "It is said, 'You shall not tempt the Lord your God.'" ¹³And when the devil had ended every temptation, he departed from him until an opportune time.

After showing Jesus' relationship to recent prophetic history (3:1-22) and to universal history (3:23-38), the gospel turns to his victorious struggle with evil (4:1-13). Like the two previous units, this new development presents essential background and prepares the readers "to know the truth concerning the things of which" they had "been informed" (1:4).

Each gospel episode has a message of its own and contributes to the unfolding of the total gospel message. Jesus' response to the devil's threefold temptation sensitizes readers to an important aspect of that total message and enables them to view each episode as an expression of Jesus' victory over evil. With Luke's intended readers, we thus never lose sight of what ultimately is at stake.

To appreciate the passage, we must reflect on its internal development, its immediate literary context and its contribution to the gospel as a whole.

Although Lk 4:1-13 echoes the conclusion of the Markan prologue (Mk 1:12-13), its closest literary parallel is with Mt 4:1-11. Indeed, the content and actual wording of Lk 4:1-13 and Mt 4:1-11 leave little doubt that the two are based on the same richly elaborated tradition. As we examine Lk 4:1-13, we shall consequently pay close attention to Mt 4:1-11.

Both Luke and Matthew include three temptations (compare with Mk 1:12-13), and both present Jesus' response to these through identical passages from scripture. In the underlying tradition as well as in these two gospels, the passage evokes the classic temptations of Israel's desert experience during the exodus. Jesus' life is thus seen as a recapitulation of Israelite history. His response to Israel's key temptations, however, contrasts with that of Israel and finally fulfills the latter's vocation (4:4,8,12; Dt 8:3; 6:13,16).

Several important differences between Lk and Mt help us to situate the passage in the gospel as a whole. First, we note Luke's emphasis on the role of the Holy Spirit. Not only is Jesus led by the Spirit (Lk 4:1b, Mt 4:1), he returns from the Jordan full of the Holy Spirit (Lk 4:1a). The temptation episode is thus closely related to Jesus' true baptism (3:21-22) as well as to the inauguration of his mission (4:14,18). Second, the third and climactic temptation occurs at the temple in Jerusalem, and not, unlike Matthew, on the mountain (Lk 4:9-12; Mt 4:8-10). Indeed, Luke does not situate any of the temptations on a mountain. The order of the temptations thus reflects Luke's orientation of the christian journey toward Jerusalem (9:51-24:53), and Jesus' victory over temptation is an important statement concerning the christian way to God. Finally, unlike Matthew, Luke notes that "when the devil had ended every temptation, he departed from" Jesus "until an opportune time" (4:13). This complete account of the temptations of Jesus is thus presented as a theological reflection on the end of Jesus' life. In Luke's gospel, the devil re-emerges in the figure of Satan, who enters Judas at the beginning of the passion narrative (22:3). Jesus' historical response to temptation in the passion is necessary for his entry into glory (24:26).

In the first temptation, Jesus rejects the view that his divine sonship cancels out his humanity (4:3-4). Jesus is indeed Son of God, but he is also fully human and his messianic mission will in no way escape the limitations of the human condition.

In the second temptation, Jesus rejects the view that his mission is political (4:5-8). As messiah, he fulfills a divine mission and that mission is an act of worship. Had he sought political power, he would have played out his role in the worldly arena and rejected the total gift of himself to God, a gift consummated in his passion and death. In so doing, he would have been subject to the devil's illusory power.

In the third temptation, Jesus rejects the view that his divine sonship entails a special protection in the human sphere (4:9-12). Even for the messiah, any effort to circumvent human limits would be a divine affront and a betrayal of God's intention concerning human life. In accepting the passion, Jesus does not expect God to save him from death.

Jesus' response to the three temptations shows the christian community how it should respond to its own basic temptations. In the Lukan historical context, these temptations have arisen in the areas of table fellowship, political relationships and persecution, all three of which are fundamental preoccupations in Luke-Acts.

Christians must not expect to be nourished automatically and for the simple reason that they are Christians. They must learn to situate the need for food among other life needs which are more basic. Christians should understand that their persecutions and political difficulties are normal for men and women bent on divine values. To greet political power with mere political power would be bowing to the enemy. Finally, Christians must not expect God to free them from the human condition. Trust in God should not be confused with the kind of foolhardy behavior which tries to control God and limit his freedom.

Luke's message in 4:1-13 is not limited to the passage's internal literary development and its thematic relationship to the remainder of Luke-Acts. The specific context in which the temptation account is presented is also significant.

Unlike Matthew, Luke situated the temptations immediately after the genealogy of Jesus. The two are not unrelated. We have already noted how 4:1-13 insists on Jesus' humanity. Jesus is indeed Son of God, but his messianic mission unfolds within the human sphere. Such considerations move us beyond Israelite history and require that we view Jesus' temptations in terms of humanity's most basic struggle with evil. The conclusion of the genealogy, which associated Jesus with both Adam and God (3:38) had prepared us for this development. The problem in the genealogy, however, was to show how the son of Adam was also son of God. In the temptation story, the problem is the reverse, and Luke means to show how the son of God is fully son of Adam.

Jesus' mission marks humanity's complete victory over evil. Adam had fallen short of that victory. No ordinary son of Adam, Jesus rose to its challenge. Unlike Adam, he accepted the limitations of created humanity, and it is thus that he manifested the ideal of divine sonship. Jesus' divine sonship was revealed in his humanity, and his victory over evil was effected in his acceptance of creaturely limitations.

*IV. The Story of Jesus.*
   *The Human Life and Message*
   *of the Son of God.*
   *4:14 - 24:53.*

## OUTLINE

# IV. THE STORY OF JESUS. THE HUMAN LIFE AND MESSAGE OF THE SON OF GOD. 4:14 - 24:53.

THE PREFACE (1:1-4), the prologue (1:5-2:52) and the background units (3:1-4:13) have brought us to the story of Jesus (4:14-24:53) and the beginning of the mission (4:14-44). In these three sections, Luke addressed us concerning his intention, presented the mystery of Jesus in his ultimate origins and destiny, and situated him in history.

Jesus' story begins with an introductory unit in which events at Nazareth and Capernaum (4:14-44) reflect the story of his mission (5:1-9:50) and his journey (9:51-24:53) in terms of their historical point of departure. The introduction is thus a programmatic statement of the entire gospel, and in many ways it also includes the story of the post-ascension communities in Acts.

The story of Jesus then takes up his mission (5:1-9:50), which is inextricably bound up with the origins of the Church. This account of the Church's remotest beginnings corresponds to Luke's preoccupation with Jesus' own origins in the prologue and background sections. As in the latter, the disciples and apostles are thus presented in light of their human and historical origins. In no way, however, do these account for their specifically christian role in history. Through its relationship to Jesus, the Church springs from God's own transcendent word.

After the account of Jesus' mission, the story continues with Jesus' journey narrative (9:51-24:53). Together with the disciples and apostles, Jesus journeys to Jerusalem, the place of his ascension (9:51; 24:50-53). The life of the Church is thus presented from the point of view of its ultimate destiny. The latter, it will be recalled, constituted an important aspect of Luke's message in the prologue. Although the Church continues its mission in history, Jesus' ascension to God points to its eventual movement beyond history. The Church's mission cannot be grasped in purely historical terms. Through its relationship to Jesus, it assumes the challenge of the passion in its exodus from history (9:31) into God's promised dwelling.

Luke's narrative of the story of Jesus can be summarized as the human life and message of the Son of God. In view of the disciples' association with Jesus, it can also be seen as the human life and message of those who share in his divine sonship.

## A. Introduction.
### Jesus, His Mission and His Journey.
### 4:14-44.

Luke's account of Jesus' historic mission opens with a marvelous programmatic statement, in which a series of episodes from the beginning of Jesus' ministry evoke the entire course and meaning of his life (4:14-44).

The unit begins with an introductory summary which situates Jesus in the Galilee of his human and religious origins (4:14-15). It then focuses on his initial self-presentation in Nazareth, the city where he had been brought up, and more specifically in the synagogue which he had regularly frequented (4:16-30). After a transitional summary, which brings Jesus to Capernaum, the city which knew him as a young adult (4:31-32), the unit presents a number of incidents in the Capernaum synagogue and in the home of Simon (4:33-43). It ends with a brief concluding summary concerning Jesus' preaching in the synagogues of Judea (4:44).

As in the prologue (1:5-2:52) and in the section on the historical background and the ultimate meaning of Jesus' mission (3:1-4:13), Luke's main concern is with Jesus' identity and its implications for his mission. In this new unit, however, the question of Jesus' identity (4:21,34,36,41) arises directly from his mission and its impact on those he reached (4:16-20,33,35,40). Conversely, Jesus' identity sheds light on the nature of his mission.

Those who had gathered in the Nazareth synagogue assumed that Jesus' mission should be confined to the Jews and that they would benefit from it no less than the Jews of Capernaum (4:23). In his challenging response, Jesus affirms that his prophetic mission is to move from the Jews to the entire Gentile world (4:24-27). The people of Capernaum likewise felt that Jesus' mission should unfold for their benefit (4:42). Jesus responds that as the Son of God and the Messiah (4:41), he must leave them, for he was sent to preach the good news to the other cities also (4:43).

The universal mission is thus intrinsically and indissolubly linked to Jesus' identity. Contact with Jesus' word and deed introduces his addressees to the mystery of his person and the latter reveals the universal scope of his mission. Consequently, an important element in Luke's message is to show how Jesus' mission, which began with the Jews of Galilee (4:14) already contained the seeds of Christianity's movement to the ends of the earth (Acts 1:8).

Since in fact Jesus' historical mission was confined almost exclusively to the Jewish world, Luke's concern in 4:14-44 is obviously with the meaning of Jesus' entire life and its implications for the life of the Church which would receive and fulfill the universal commission (Acts 1:8). Accordingly, what is ostensibly presented as a number of episodes at the beginning of Jesus' public career is actually a narrative summary of "all that Jesus began to do and teach, until the day when he was taken up" (Acts 1:1-2).

## A. 1. INTRODUCTORY SUMMARY.
### JESUS IN GALILEE.
#### 4:14-15.

> [14]And Jesus returned in the power of the Spirit into Galilee, and a report concerning him went out through all the surrounding country. [15]And he taught in their synagogues, being glorified by all.

Jesus began his mission in his own native Galilee. The introductory summary in which those beginnings are presented (4:14-15) includes several important elements which enable us to understand the episodes and the summarizing statements which immediately follow (4:16-30, 31-32, 33-43,44), as well as the subsequent account of the mission to Galilee (5:1-9:50).

We note, first of all, that the summary contains two distinct statements (4:14,15) each of which presents Jesus' activity (4:14a,15a) as well as the popular reaction to it (4:14b,15b). This twofold concern will be characteristic of Luke's entire presentation of the gospel. In 4:16-30, for example, he carefully distinguishes Jesus' message and self-communication (4:16-20a,21,23-27) from the assembly's response and reaction (4:20b,22,28-30). The same is true of the transitional summary (4:31,32) and of the events in Capernaum (4:33-35, 38-42a and 4:36-37,42b).

The first statement (4:14) is very generic, noting only that Jesus returned to Galilee and that his reputation spread. Nothing is said of the nature of his activity or of the quality of his reputation. However, the author does note that Jesus came "in the power of the Spirit." It is this power which would give rise to the question of his identity (4:22), endow his teaching with authority (4:32), make him victorious over unclean spirits (4:33-36) and demons (4:41) and enable him to cure a severe fever (4:38-39) and diseases (4:40). It is with this same Spirit that he was sent to preach the good news (4:18,43). In the prologue and in the background unit, Luke had already indicated how the Spirit distinguished Jesus from all other human beings (1:35), disassociated him from the movement of John the Baptist (3:21-22) and made him victorious over evil (4:1).

With regard to the report and reputation of Jesus, Luke notes that it spread throughout the surrounding country, a theme which is explicitly recalled in 4:37 and 5:15. He thus prepares us for future developments in which the gospel word would continue to spread in ever-widening circles (Acts 6:7; 12:24; 13:49; 19:20).

The second statement (4:15) is more specific than the first (4:14). Returning to Galilee, Jesus devoted himself to teaching, and this he did in the synagogues, places which were set aside for prayer and study and which nourished Jewish life away from Jerusalem's temple. We also learn that the reports concerning Jesus (4:14) were favorable. All those who heard Jesus in the sabbath assembly glorified him. As in 4:14b, Luke emphasizes the universality of the people's response. This second statement thus provides an immediate introduction for the episodes in the Nazareth and Capernaum synagogues (4:16-30, 31-43). The first furnished a more general introduction for the entire Galilean mission (4:16-9:50). This same pattern from the generic and implicit to the specific and explicit is repeated in the Nazareth and Capernaum episodes.

## A. 2. JESUS AT NAZARETH.
### *IS NOT THIS JOSEPH'S SON?*
### 4:16-30.

> [16]And he came to Nazareth, where he had been brought up; and he went to the synagogue, as his custom was, on the sabbath day. And he stood up to read; [17]and there was given to him the book of the prophet Isaiah. He opened the book and found the place where it was written,

18"The Spirit of the Lord is upon me,
    because he has anointed me to
        preach good news to the poor.
    He has sent me to proclaim release
        to the captives
    and recovering of sight to the blind,
        to set at liberty those who are
        oppressed,
19to proclaim the acceptable year of
        the Lord."

20And he closed the book, and gave it back to the at-
tendant, and sat down; and the eyes of all in the synagogue were fixed on him. 21And he began to say to them,
"Today this scripture has been fulfilled in your hearing."
22And all spoke well of him, and wondered at the gracious
words which proceeded out of his mouth; and they said,
"Is not this Joseph's son" 23And he said to them, "Doubtless you will quote to me this proverb, 'Physician, heal
yourself; what we have heard you did at Capernaum, do
here also in your own country.'" 24And he said, "Truly
I say to you, no prophet is acceptable in his own country.
25But in truth, I tell you, there were many widows in
Israel in the days of Elijah, when the heaven was shut up
three years and six months, when there came a great
famine over all the land; 26and Elijah was sent to none
of them but only to Zarephath, in the land of Sidon, to a
woman who was a widow. 27And there were many lepers
in Israel in the time of the prophet Elisha; and none of
them was cleansed, but only Naaman the Syrian."
28When they heard this, all in the synagogue were filled
with wrath. 29And they rose up and put him out of the
city, and led him to the brow of the hill on which their
city was built, that they might throw him down headlong.
30But passing through the midst of them he went away.

The episode at Nazareth (4:16-30) is divided into two
sections. In the first, Luke situates Jesus with regard to
the city of his origins and its synagogue (4:16-22). Since

Jesus and his mission constitute the fulfillment of messianic expectations (4:18-19,21), he cannot be understood merely in terms of his human and religious upbringing as a Galilean from Nazareth. The Spirit which fills Jesus' word with power (4:14,18) evokes wonderment and praise, and it becomes obvious that his identity transcends his human and Jewish origins (4:22).

Jesus reading from Isaiah (4:18-19; Is 61:1-2a) and his interpretation of the passage (4:21) form the heart of this first section. Observe that the citation ends immediately before Isaiah's announcement of the divine day of vengeance (61:2b). The latter does not fall within Jesus' historical mission of reconciliation (see 9:52-55). Note also how Luke has used otherwise meaningless details to frame the reading from Isaiah (4:16b-17,20). These details create a feeling of expectation, heighten the importance and intensity of the actual reading, and graphically focus the assembly's attention on Jesus. Once Jesus has interpreted the passage (4:21), the intensity is slowly released through the articulation of the popular reaction (4:22).

From the point of view of Jesus' entire life, this first section corresponded to the emergence of Jesus' mission and the initial favorable but questioning reaction which greeted it. The second section focuses on Jesus' challenge, on his rejection of a purely Jewish mission and on the unfavorable reaction which these received (4:23-30). It corresponds to the end of Jesus' life and the frustrated effort to destroy him. The passion, resurrection and ascension were thus occasioned by Jesus' assumption of a mission to all human beings.

Paradoxically, the effort to destroy Jesus (4:28-30a) led to his glorification (4:30b; see 4:15). This, of course, was not the intention of the Jews of Nazareth. However, since it was necessary for the Christ to suffer in order to enter into his glory (24:26), they unwittingly did glorify him. In the episode at Nazareth, Luke thus shows himself a master of irony. Jesus' true glorification (4:15) is not realized in shallow and selfish admiration (4:22-23).

Jesus begins by interpreting the expectations of the synagogue assembly, and he does so by means of a popular proverb, "Physician, heal yourself." His interpretation of the proverb illustrates the sense of solidarity which pervaded Jewish attitudes and which saw the healing of Jesus' fellow Nazarenes as inextricably bound up with his own personal well-being (4:23). Jesus, however, is not bent on his own well-being, and he responds with a second popular proverb to the effect that "no prophet is acceptable in his own country" (4:24). Jesus's mission is not to himself but to others, and so must it be with all who claim a relationship to him.

After this general challenging statement (4:23-24), Jesus adduces two instances from biblical history, in which Israelite prophets had been sent to nourish and to cure Gentiles in spite of pressing needs in Israel (4:25-27; see 1 Kgs 17:1, 8-16 and 2 Kgs 5:1-14). As a result, the initial favorable response to Jesus (4:22) is transformed into violent wrath, and an effort is made to destroy him (4:28-30a). In Luke's account, the hill on which Nazareth was built becomes symbolic of the hill of Calvary, and the Jews of Nazareth prefigure the leaders of the Jewish nation who would do all in their power to destroy Jesus on its gibbet. However, Jesus is filled with the power of the Spirit (4:14, 18), and the effort proves unsuccessful. Foiling their intentions, Jesus passes through their midst and walks away (4:30b). For the moment this brief and undeveloped statement, which evokes the resurrection and ascension, remains clothed in the same mystery which concealed Jesus' identity (4:22) from those who tried to limit his mission to their own human and religious sphere (4:23).

## A. 3. TRANSITIONAL SUMMARY.
## JESUS GOES TO CAPERNAUM.
### 4:31-32.

> [31]And he went down to Capernaum, a city of Galilee. And he was teaching them on the sabbath; [32]and they

were astonished at his teaching, for his word was with
authority.

In the introductory summary (4:14-15), we read that
Jesus was teaching in the synagogues of Galilee and that all
who heard him were moved to glorify him. This was followed by an episode at Nazareth which ended in a violent
but unsuccessful attack on Jesus' life (4:16-30). A transitional summary now brings Jesus from Nazareth to Capernaum, another city in Galilee (4:31-32). Although mention
had already been made of Jesus' activities in that city (4:23),
they are about to be narrated for the first time.

The summary notes that Jesus went to Capernaum, refers
to his teaching on the sabbath (4:31) and describes the
assembly's reaction along with its basis in reality (4:32).
From verse 33 we learn that Jesus' sabbath teaching took
place in the synagogue as it had at Nazareth.

The second part of the summary describes the assembly's
astonishment at Jesus' teaching (4:32). This preoccupation
with the response of those who heard Jesus pursues the
theme introduced in the summary of 4:14-15 and developed
in 4:22. Astonishment, however, goes beyond the spreading
reputation (4:14b) and the wonderment over Jesus' gracious
words (4:22a). Correspondingly, the grounds for this
astonishment, that is the authority with which Jesus spoke
(4:32b), brings Jesus' identity into far sharper focus than
the question concerning his parental origins (4:22). The
source of Jesus' authority is the power of the Spirit (4:14,18).
The authority of Jesus is one of the main concerns in the
passage which follows (4:33-43).

## A. 4. JESUS AT CAPERNAUM.
### *I KNOW WHO YOU ARE.*
### 4:33-43.

<sup></sup>33And in the synagogue there was a man who had the
spirit of an unclean demon; and he cried out with a loud
voice, 34"Ah! What have you to do with us, Jesus of

Nazareth? Have you come to destroy us? I know who you are, the Holy One of God." [35]But Jesus rebuked him, saying, "Be silent, and come out of him!" And when the demon had thrown him down in the midst, he came out of him, having done him no harm. [36]And they were all amazed and said to one another, "What is this word? For with authority and power he commands the unclean spirits, and they come out." [37]And reports of him went out into every place in the surrounding region.

[38]And he arose and left the synagogue, and entered Simon's house. Now Simon's mother-in-law was ill with a high fever, and they besought him for her. [39]And he stood over her and rebuked the fever, and it left her; and immediately she rose and served them.

[40]Now when the sun was setting, all those who had any that were sick with various diseases brought them to him; and he laid his hands on every one of them and healed them. [41]And demons also came out of many, crying, "You are the Son of God!" But he rebuked them, and would not allow them to speak, because they knew that he was the Christ.

[42]And when it was day he departed and went into a lonely place. And the people sought him and came to him, and would have kept him from leaving them; [43]but he said to them, "I must preach the good news of the kingdom of God to the other cities also; for I was sent for this purpose."

Jesus' work at Capernaum includes two narrative units, which present him first in the prologue (4:33-37) and then in the house of Simon (4:38-41). Like 4:16-30, the passage climaxes in Jesus' departure from the town (4:42-43).

As in the Nazareth episode, the author is concerned with Jesus' identity (4:34,36,41) and the continuing spread of his reputation (4:37,40). Reports that he was the Messiah, however, had to be silenced (4:41b), since they would only intensify the efforts of those who did not grasp what it meant for Jesus to be Messiah and who consequently tried to prevent him from continuing on his mission (4:42).

The vital link between Jesus' mission and his identity is thus an important element in Luke's message, as it had been in 4:16-30. In 4:33-43, however, Jesus' mission does not lead to a destructive assault on his person but to attempts to restrain him from going away (4:42). At Nazareth, Jesus' going away was the result of an effort to end his life. At Capernaum, his departure is presented as a divine necessity which Jesus consciously accepted and equated with his own intention (4:43).

While in the synagogue, Jesus encounters a man with an unclean spirit. This spirit of evil recognizes the Spirit of good in Jesus. Radically incompatible, the Spirit of good overcomes the unclean spirit, and the latter is banished at Jesus' command (4:33-35). Luke thus recalls Jesus' triple encounter with the devil in the desert, when, filled with the Holy Spirit and led by it, Jesus successfully confronted the seductive power of evil (4:1-13). In 4:33-35, the confrontation is situated in the course of Jesus' mission. As all recognize, it demonstrates the authoritative power of his word (4:36-37). For the people, however, the event merely intensifies the mystery of Jesus' identity; only the unclean spirit knows that Jesus of Nazareth is actually the Holy One of God (4:34).

After a brief summary concerning Jesus' growing renown (4:37), the account moves away from the synagogue to the home of Simon (4:38-41). It is in such homes that Jesus would focus much of his work and in which the Christian community would continue to develop after Jesus' death-resurrection. The passage thus reflects the general movement away from the Jewish synagogue and into the home environment which characterized the early Church. Simon's introduction into the narrative prepares us for his call and mission (5:1-11) and follows a general Lukan pattern of mentioning an important personage at some point before his story actually begins.

With his word Jesus heals Simon's mother-in-law of a high fever, and she becomes the first woman to serve Jesus (4:39; see 8:2-3). The women mentioned in 8:2-3 also had been healed of evil spirits and infirmities. As we note from 4:40-41, where Jesus heals the many who came to Simon's door, the curing of diseases and the expulsion of demons are extremely closely related and at times one and the same.

As in 4:34, the demons recognize that Jesus is the Son of God (4:41). The titles Holy One of God and Son of God recall the angel's word to Mary that due to the Spirit and the power of the Most High, "the child to be born," that is Jesus, "will be called holy, the Son of God" (1:35). At this point in the Gospel, however, Jesus' identity has been announced (1:32,35) or proclaimed (4:34,41) only by angels and demons, not by the human beings for whom Jesus' mission is destined. When the latter finally recognize Jesus for what he is, it will be in conjunction with an acknowledgement of human sinfulness and with the origins of a christian mission (5:8-10).

The Capernaum episodes end with Jesus' departure from the city, the effort to keep him from going, and the explicit announcement of the purpose of his mission (4:42-43). Pressure to limit Jesus' work to the people of Capernaum does not prevent him from going away. He was sent to "preach the good news of the kingdom of God to the other cities also" (4:43). As in the passion, Jesus' departure is consequently by choice and not by reason of an effort to destroy him (4:28-30).

## A. 5. CONCLUDING SUMMARY.
### JESUS IN JUDEA.
#### 4:44.

[44]And he was preaching in the synagogues of Judea."

The brief concluding summary focuses on the preaching that Jesus had announced in 4:43. However, that preaching is said to be in the synagogues of Judea and not in those of Galilee as we might have expected from 4:14-15, 31-32, from the events in 4:16-30, 33-43, and from the subsequent narrative which maintains Jesus' sphere of activity in Galilee and not in Judea. Is Judea then a slip of the pen or a literary contradiction? Not so.

In context, Judea refers to the very territory which Luke called Galilee in 4:14 and 31. Galilee was the name ordinarily used by the Jews, while Judea was the Greco-Roman designation for the entire Jewish nation, including Galilee. In a section which emphasizes Christianity's movement from the Jews to the Gentiles, the concluding summary's substitution of Judea for Galilee highlights one of the author's main concerns. It was from Jerusalem and Judea that the gospel witness was to reach out to the ends of the earth (24:47; Acts 1:8). By situating Jesus' preaching "in the synagogues of Judea," Luke implies that the universal gospel mission was grounded in the vocation of Judaism itself. The synagogue also had received a universal mission. It was now being fulfilled by Christianity (see 4:23-27).

## B. The Mission.
## Jesus and the Origins of the Church.
## 5:1 - 9:50.

The story of Jesus began with an introductory unit (4:14-44), a programmatic anticipation of the entire narrative of Jesus' mission (5:1-9:50) and journey to God (9:51-24:53). It now takes up Jesus' mission and presents the story of the Church's origins in the life and work of Jesus (5:1-9:50).

The mission unfolds in four major sections, each of which opens with a narrative statement concerning the disciples (5:1-11; 6:12-16; 8:1-3; 9:1-17). The same pattern would be used to distinguish the structural units of Acts, whose first part develops the life and mission of the post-ascension community (1:15-26; 6:1-7; 13:1-3; 15:36-41).

The first major section deals with the call of the disciples and the implications of that call with regard to their origins in Judaism and the synagogue (5:1-6:11). As the section ends, we find the disciples in solidarity with Jesus, the definitive fulfillment of the law. As such they are disassociated from the Pharisees and their interpretations of the law, which have been superseded by the authoritative word and deed of the Son of Man.

The second section focuses on the Church as a new Israel. Jesus selects twelve of his disciples and appoints them to be his apostles. As the new sons of Jacob, they would lead the new Israel in its life and mission, both of which would include Jews and gentiles. For the gentiles, Christianity implied radical healing through the word of Jesus. For the Jews, it required nothing short of resurrection.

After calling the first disciples (5:1-6:11) and appointing twelve of their number as the apostles (6:12-7:50), Jesus forms the new Israel for its mission (8:1-56). The third section in the story of Jesus thus focuses on the apostolic community's responsibilities as those who will continue Jesus' work in history. Its formation takes place in the company of Jesus. Following Jesus in his mission, the Church learns by observing Jesus as he reaches out to both Jew and gentile.

The first part of Jesus' story concludes with the mission of the new Israel. Called to discipleship, appointed as the Twelve, and formed in the ministerial and apostolic school of Jesus, the disciples are sent on mission (9:1-50). The section emphasizes the implications of the mission, the need to pursue it after Jesus' departure from history, and the special problems which the disciples will encounter in its fulfillment.


## B. 1. JESUS AND HIS FIRST DISCIPLES.
### 5:1-6:11

Jesus would not remain alone in the gospel mission. Nor would it cease with his death-resurrection. After presenting the identity, message and mission of Jesus

(4:14-44), Luke focuses on the disciples and shows how their own life, work and mission is rooted in a special call (5:1-6:11). Stemming from Jesus, this call establishes the disciples in a new way of life patterned on that of Jesus himself.

The section, which includes five units, opens by the lake of Gennesaret where Jesus calls Simon Peter and his companions to missionary discipleship (5:1-11). The scene then shifts from the lake to one of the cities, where Jesus demonstrates his healing power, a power exercised with due respect for the law and religious legal authority (5:12-16). This simple conflict-free event provides the ultimate basis and justification for the attitudes and behavior of Jesus and his disciples as they then confront the scribes and the Pharisees in a triple challenge concerning their religious integrity and relationship to the law. The first confrontation takes place in a home: the healing of a paralytic reveals Jesus' power to forgive sins (5:17-26). The second takes place at a banquet hosted by Levi the tax-collector: the forgiveness of sins is related to the call of disciples, a call which results in the repentant disciples' radically new way of life (5:27-39). The third takes place on two sabbath days, in the grainfields and in the synagogue: the new way, with its genuinely biblical grasp of life-values, transcends the Pharisees' interpretation of sabbath observance (6:1-11).

As in the prologue (1:5-2:52), the preparation and background unit (3:1-4:13) and the programmatic narrative of Jesus' life and mission (4:14-44), Luke's main concern is with christian identity. In this section, however, his focus is on that of the disciples. Jesus' own identity remains a preoccupation, but only in so far as it provides the basis for that of his disciples.

Attention rests on the disciples' relationship to Jesus and his mission. Called by one who forgives sins, their own religious integrity is grounded in repentant faith. Called to his mission, they also join him in the work of reconciliation. On both counts, they stand accused by the Pharisees and the scribes. Jesus himself responds in word and deed to the accusations. Associated with Jesus, the disciples stand unassailable, secure in the authoritive power of the one who called them.

Like Jesus in 4:22 and 5:26, the disciples can expect a positive response to their life and work. However, they can also expect a negative reaction, such as Jesus received at Nazareth (4:28-30). The entire section ends with just such a reaction and its strong intimations of the passion (6:11). As the section comes to a close, we find the disciples clearly associated with Jesus' fulfillment of the law and disassociated from the Pharisees and their self-righteous, exclusivistic interpretation of it.

## 1. a. The Call of Simon,
### *Henceforth you will be catching men.*
### 5:1-11

**5** While the people pressed upon him to hear the word of God, he was standing by the lake of Gennesaret. ²And he saw two boats by the lake; but the fishermen had gone out of them and were washing their nets. ³Getting into one of the boats, which was Simon's, he asked him to put out a little from the land. And he sat down and taught the people from the boat. ⁴And when he had ceased speaking, he said to Simon, "Put out into the deep and let down your nets for a catch." ⁵And Simon answered, "Master we toiled all night and took nothing! But at your word I will let down the nets." ⁶And when they had done this, they enclosed a great shoal of fish; and as their nets were breaking, ⁷they beckoned to their partners in the other boat to come and help them. And they came and filled both the boats, so that they began to sink. ⁸But when Simon Peter saw it, he fell down at Jesus' knees, saying, "Depart from me, for I am a sinful man, O Lord." ⁹For he was astonished, and all that were with him, at the catch of fish which they had taken; ¹⁰and so also were James and John, sons of Zebedee, who were partners with Simon. And Jesus said to Simon, "Do not be afraid; henceforth you will be catching men." [11]And when they had brought their boats to land, they left everything and followed him.

In keeping with a traditional pattern already set in Mark 1:14-20, the call of the first disciples (5:1-11) follows a general statement concerning Jesus' mission (Lk 4:14-44). Luke's presentation, however, is extremely different from that of Mark. Drawing on diverse traditions, he created a new literary synthesis, in which Simon's future preeminence is inscribed in the very moment of his call, and in which the challenges and successes of the passion and of the post-Easter mission are boldly announced.

There can be no mistaking Luke's effort to single out the position of Simon among those who were first called. As in Mark 1:16-20, we note the presence of Simon, James and John, as well as Jesus' promise that the fishermen would henceforth be catching men, together with their leaving all to follow Jesus. However, we also note that Simon stands alone in the entire first part of the narrative (5:1-9), that his brother Andrew is altogether absent, that Simon is the owner of the fishing boat (5:3), that James and John remain unmentioned until 5:10, where they are introduced as Simon's partners, and that the latter do not receive a distinct call. Luke has thus transformed Mark's paralleling of two call incidents (1:16-18, 19-20) into a single well-integrated event with Simon as the key personage. Simon's fishing partners would retain their relative role in the fishing of men.

Luke's setting and the whole development of the incident is also dramatically different from that of Mark 1:16-20. Whereas in Mark Jesus was simply passing by the sea, in Luke he was teaching a large multitude by the sea, a dynamic context drawn from Mark's introduction to Jesus' parable teaching (4:1). The call of Simon is thus related to Jesus' teaching of the crowds, to his need for a boat and to the fact that Simon facilitated Jesus' fulfillment of his teaching mission (5:1-3). According to Luke's account we must also conclude that Simon knew Jesus and moved in his company (see 4:38-39) well before the moment which came to symbolize his call.

Since Jesus' teaching of the crowd is perceived as the word of God (5:1), his command to Simon (5:4) and the subsequent call (5:10-11) must also be viewed as expressions of God's word. As a response to Jesus' word, Simon's call and mission are thus grounded in the very word of God.

In addition to Mark 1:16-20 and 4:1, we also note the influence of an early christian tradition which received a distinct literary development in the Johannine epilogue (Jn 21:1-14). After teaching the crowds (Lk 5:1-3), Jesus ordered Simon out into the deep to net some fish. Overcoming his objections of futility, Simon did so and was astounded by an extraordinary catch (5:4-7).

Different from Mark 1:16, where Simon already was casting a net when Jesus came upon him, and from John 21:3-5, which narrates Simon's lack of success prior to Jesus' command, Luke's account introduces Jesus at the outset. Earlier failures belonged to a previous venture and are simply recalled (5:5a). The call of Simon thus parallels the Spirit's descent on Jesus, which had been carefully separated from John's baptism (3:21-22). Like Peter's previous unsuccessful fishing, the latter is merely recalled as a distinct event.

The marvelous catch is an extraordinary sign which evokes a faith response from Simon (see Jn 21:6-7). Henceforth the narrator no longer refers to him as Simon but as Simon Peter (5:8), a name which announced the apostle's future foundational role as the rock, and which Mark, and Luke himself, associated with his position among the Twelve (Mk 3:16; Lk 6:14).

Formally, Simon's response is a confessional statement in which he acknowledges both Jesus' lordship and his personal unworthiness to be in Jesus' company (5:8-9).

Peter's future confessional statement (Mk 8:29; Lk 9:20) is thus anticipated and directly related to the nature and dynamics of his call. At the same time, Jesus' rebuke of Peter (Mk 8:33), which Luke omits in 9:20-22, has been transformed into the apostle's own humble plea that Jesus depart from him, a sinner (Lk 5:8).

The author's emphasis on Peter's unworthiness prepares us for Jesus' word to him in the farewell discourse (22:31-34) as well as for Peter's actual denial during the passion (22:54-62). His use of the title "Lord" announces Peter's primary post-resurrection experience (24:12,34) as well as the basis for the mission to the Gentiles (Acts 10:36), when Peter would provide the link between Christianity's origins in Judaism and Paul's mission to the Gentile world (Acts 10:1-11:18). It also moves the reader beyond the question raised in the Nazareth synagogue (4:22) and prepares the way for Herod's perplexity (Lk 9:7-9), Jesus' question to the disciples (Lk 9:18-20a), Peter's confession (Lk 9:20b) and the disclosure of Jesus' divine sonship at the transfiguration (Lk 9:35), where once again we encounter Peter, John and James (9:28).

1. b. Fidelity to the Law.
> *Go . . . as Moses commanded.*
> 5:12-16.

> [12]While he was in one of the cities, there came a man full of leprosy; and when he saw Jesus, he fell on his face and besought him, "Lord, if you will, you can make me clean." [13]And he stretched out his hand, and touched him, saying, "I will; be clean." And immediately the leprosy left him. [14]And he charged him to tell no one; but "go and show yourself to the priest, and make an offering for your cleansing, as Moses commanded, for a proof to the people." [15]But so much the more the report went abroad concerning him; and great multitudes gathered to hear and to be healed of their infirmities. [16]But he withdrew to the wilderness and prayed.

No doubt this brief story about Jesus' cure of a leper had its own independent origin and development in early christian tradition. Luke drew the story from Mark 1:40-45, where it falls between two sets of episodes situated in or around Capernaum (1:21-39; 2:1-3:6). However, ignoring the Markan context, he placed the account immediately after the call of Simon and his companions. In relation to Luke's message, this new context is just as significant as the narrative's own internal development.

Simon Peter had recognized his personal sinfulness and the way it separated him from Jesus. However, since he was open to Jesus and acknowledged his lordship (5:8), this sinfulness did not militate against his call to christian discipleship (5:10). In 5:12-16, Luke dwells on Jesus' power to cleanse any outcast, even the most unclean. Lepers, be it noted, were cut off from human society. In relation to 5:1-11, the passage constitutes a powerful statement about the source and non-exclusiveness of discipleship. Jesus' call and the human response to it does not depend on someone's worthiness but on Jesus' powerful cleansing act.

Through its emphasis on compliance with the law and respect for religious authority, the unit also anticipates the pharisaic accusation that Jesus and his disciples live and act with disregard for the law. Since he is Lord (5:8,12), the Son of man has authority on earth to forgive sins (5:24) to call sinners to repentance (5:32) and to interpret sabbath observance (6:5). Since the law is meant for salvation and life, its fulfillment can never stand in the way of life or destroy it (6:9). In the narrow view of the Pharisees, Jesus and his disciples may appear to be transgressing the law. In reality, however, they are fulfilling it, and the legitimacy of Jesus' interpretation and application of the law is amply demonstrated by his healing and life-giving power. Jesus' command that the former leper show himself to the priest and make an offering for his cleansing should provide the people with a proof of Jesus' messianic fulfillment of the law (5:14).

Jesus' charge that the man tell no one (5:14) has a dual intention. In one sense it is not an absolute charge, but a temporary one, since Jesus intends that the people have a proof once the law has been observed. In another sense, however, it is related to Jesus' spreading reputation and the danger that large numbers come to Jesus seeking a purely physical cure. Thus it is that Jesus withdraws to the wilderness for prayer (5:15-16). It is there in the wilderness and in communion with God that every temptation to false messianism is overcome (see 4:1-13).

## 1. c. Healing and the Forgiveness of Sins.
*Why do you question in your hearts?*
5:17-26.

[17]On one of those days, as he was teaching, there were Pharisees and teachers of the law sitting by, who had come from every village of Galilee and Judea and from Jerusalem; and the power of the Lord was with him to heal. [18]And behold, men were bringing on a bed a man who was paralyzed, and they sought to bring him in and lay him before Jesus; [19]but finding no way to bring him in, because of the crowd, they went up on the roof and let him down with his bed through the tiles into the midst before Jesus. [20]And when he saw their faith he said, "Man, your sins are forgiven you." [21]And the scribes and the Pharisees began to question, saying, "Who is this that speaks blasphemies? Who can forgive sins but God only?" [22]When Jesus perceived their questionings, he answered them, "Why do you question in your hearts? [23]Which is easier, to say, 'Your sins are forgiven you,' or to say, 'Rise and walk'? [24]But that you may know that the Son of man has authority on earth to forgive sins"—he said to the man who was paralyzed—"I say to you, rise, take up your bed and go home." [25]And immediately he rose before them, and took up that on which he lay, and

> went home, glorifying God. [26]And amazement seized them all, and they glorified God and were filled with awe, saying, "We have seen strange things today."

The first of three conflict episodes deals precisely with the relationship between Jesus' authority to forgive sins and his power to heal (5:17-26). These two aspects of Jesus' power had been treated separately in 5:1-11 and 5:12-16. We now have an explicit indication that they are one and the same. The episode thus reinforces Luke's contextual association of the cure of a leper with the call of a sinner.

The passage also continues to raise the question of Jesus' identity (4:22) and authority (4:36). Focus, however, is not so much on the fact of his authority as on its nature. Jesus' authority is divine and it is expressed in the forgiveness of sins. The mystery in this is that Jesus holds this authority as Son of man, that is in his very humanity.

A paralytic is lowered into Jesus' presence through an opening in the roof (5:18-19). Seeing this demonstration of faith, Jesus tells the man that his sins are forgiven (5:20). The event takes place in the company of Pharisees and teachers of the law or scribes who have come from all over Galilee, Judea and Jerusalem (5:17). Consequently, their objection that Jesus blasphemes by appropriating divine power to forgive sins (5:21) speaks the attitude not merely of one or other Pharisee but of the Pharisees and scribes in general.

Addressing the objectors, Jesus asks why they question in their hearts (5:22). He thus turns their attention inward and asks that they examine not him but themselves in the issue. Continuing, Jesus then articulates the question which should arise from the self-scrutiny and reflection to which he has invited them. Actually, which is easier to say, "Your sins are forgiven you" or "Rise and walk" (5:23)? Clearly the two are equally difficult, and anyone who can say the second can also say the first. Concluding his response, Jesus orders the paralytic to rise, take up his bed and go home (5:24). The effectiveness of Jesus' word in the physically observable order (5:25) demonstrates Jesus' power to forgive sins. Jesus does not merely claim to be able to forgive sins; he actually does so. By emphasizing the forgiveness of sins in a healing account, Luke also points to the deeper, spiritual need which should motivate those who approach him for physical healing (see 5:14-16). The unit ends by indicating the reaction of the gathering (5:26).

1. d. Forgiveness and a New Way of Life.
*New wine must be put into fresh wineskins.*
5:27-39.

> [27]After this he went out, and saw a tax collector, named Levi, sitting at the tax office; and he said to him, "Follow me." [28]And he left everything, and rose and followed him.
>
> [29]And Levi made him a great feast in his house; and there was a large company of tax collectors and others sitting at table with them. [30]And the Pharisees and their scribes murmured against his disciples, saying, "Why do you eat and drink with tax collectors and sinners?" [31]And Jesus answered them, "Those who are well have no need of a physician, but those who are sick; [32]I have not come to call the righteous, but sinners to repentance."
>
> [33]And they said to him, "The disciples of John fast often and offer prayers, and so do the disciples of the Pharisees, but yours eat and drink." [34]And Jesus said to them, "Can you make wedding guests fast while the bridegroom is with them? [35]The days will come, when the bridegroom is taken away from them, and then they will fast in those days." [36]He told them a parable also: "No one tears a piece from a new garment and puts it upon an old garment; if he does, he will tear the new, and the piece from the new will not match the old. [37]And

no one puts new wine into old wineskins; if he does, the new wine will burst the skins and it will be spilled, and the skins will be destroyed. [38]But new wine must be put into fresh wineskins. [39]And no one after drinking old wine desires new; for he says, 'The old is good.'"

The second conflict episode deals with the purpose of Jesus' mission, which is to call sinners to conversion (5:27-32) and with the new way of life which this conversion implies (5:33-39). The way of life of Jesus' disciples transcends that of the disciples of both John the Baptist and the Pharisees.

The account begins with the call of Levi (5:27-28), a brief unit which was patterned on the call of Jesus' first disciples (Mk 1:16-20) and which literary tradition had associated with a meal in Levi's house (Mk 2:13-14, 15-17). Luke retained this association (5:27-28, 29-32). The story thus begins in the tax office, where Levi is called to follow Jesus, but it soon transfers to a banquet setting in Levi's house. Participating in an unjust system of taxation, Levi and his fellow tax collectors were classed with sinners. Indeed, in the religious mentality of the time, the terms tax collectors and sinners were practically interchangeable. The basic issue is consequently that Jesus calls sinners, an issue which held important implications for christian table fellowship.

Levi's call in 5:27-28 might lead us to assume that he is the principal personage in the story. However, although 5:29 presents him as the host and the one who provides the banquet, he in no way figures in the dialogue. The principal personages are actually the Pharisees and the scribes, and it is their objection which called for Jesus' response. Note also that the Pharisees do not focus specifically on Levi but on tax collectors and sinners. The story thus deals with a general problem. Levi merely presents the occasion in which the problem surfaces.

Since joining in a meal was in itself an eloquent gesture of solidarity, we can understand the Pharisees' objection to the disciples' association with tax collectors and sinners. What the Pharisees failed to appreciate, however, is that solidarity is mutual. Jesus did indeed affirm solidarity with sinners. However, by joining Jesus at table, sinners also expressed solidarity with him. The central issue is thus the quality of Jesus' person and the nature of his mission. In Lk 5:29-32, Jesus is one who calls sinners to repentance, and a meal is the social and experiential locus in which his call is both uttered and heard. The meal is thus a healing and reconciling event in which Jesus breaks through the divisions maintained by the Pharisees and their scribes.

By transferring the object of reproach from Jesus (Mk 3:16) to the disciples (5:30), Luke reveals his concern with problems in the life of the early christian community. He thus resituates the primitive locus of Jesus' outreach to sinners in the ongoing context of christian table fellowship. What Jesus had done in his historical life, the disciples must now do in theirs.

In terms of Luke's broader effort, this meal is the first of many stages in the historical origins of "the breaking of bread" (Lk 24:35). Within this larger context, the call of Levi emphasizes one of the most important aspects of the specifically christian meal, namely that it is a reconciling call to repentant discipleship.

In Mark, Levi's call and the ensuing meal constitute a complete conflict story (2:13-17), independent of the conflict story which follows it (2:18-22). Luke's account, on the other hand, joins the two stories into one unit (5:27-39). The objection that Jesus' disciples do not act like those of John and those of the Pharisees is part of the table conversation in Levi's house. To grasp Luke's message, this context must be taken into consideration.

As in 5:29-32, the Pharisees' concern is not with Jesus' behavior but with that of his disciples (5:33). The unit thus continues to address a post-ascension problem within the christian community. This context influences the wording of the problem. The Pharisees only appear to be the objectors. Their reference to "the disciples of the Pharisees"

points to a future when the Pharisees themselves had dis-
appeared from history and a new group had taken up
their ancient objection. As a reference to Jesus' day, the
text would normally have read "our disciples" rather than
"the disciples of the Pharisees."

The objection is more general than that of 5:29-32. Once
Jesus affirmed the need to call sinners to repentance and to
join with them at table, the neo-Pharisees object to the
disciples' eating and drinking as such. Jesus had referred
to the Pharisees and others as righteous (5:32). The latter
now bring up an odious comparison between Jesus' disciples
and the righteous, namely the disciples of John and the
Pharisees.

Jesus responds to the objection with a question (5:34),
which he himself answers (5:35), with two short parables
(5:36, 37-38) and a concluding statement (5:39).

The question and the answer introduce the image of a
wedding feast and focus on the difference between the
bridegroom's presence at the feast and his future departure.
In so doing, they distinguish between the behavior which
was appropriate during Jesus' historical life and that which
would be required after the ascension. The same preoccupation recurs in Jesus' farewell discourse (22:35-36). It had
been good to feast in Jesus' company. Now, however, the
christian community must be prepared to fast (5:34-35),
at least on certain days (18:12).

The parables comment on Christianity's incompatibility
with the way of life from which it had sprung. Whether
feasting or fasting, the Christians represent a new reality,
irreducible to John's movement or to the pharisaic synagogue. Efforts to combine the new and the old do not
respect the reality of the new and eventually destroy both
the old and the new (5:36-38).

Jesus' concluding statement explains why the objectors
find it so difficult to accept Jesus and his way of life. They
are like people who have found that the old wine is good
and who have no desire to try the new (5:39). Satisfied with

their way of life, the neo-Pharisees are unable to risk the full challenge of christian discipleship.

## 1. e. The New Way of Life and Sabbath Observance.
### *The Son of Man is lord of the sabbath.*
### 6:1-11.

**6** On a sabbath, while he was going through the grain-fields, his disciples plucked and ate some heads of grain, rubbing them in their hands. ²But some of the Pharisees said, "Why are you doing what is not lawful to do on the sabbath?" ³And Jesus answered, "Have you not read what David did when he was hungry, he and those who were with him: ⁴how he entered the house of God, and took and ate the bread of the Presence, which it is not lawful for any but the priests to eat, and also gave it to those with him?" ⁵And he said to them, "The Son of man is lord of the sabbath."

⁶On another sabbath, when he entered the synagogue and taught, a man was there whose right hand was withered. ⁷And the scribes and the Pharisees watched him, to see whether he would heal on the sabbath, so that they might find an accusation against him. ⁸But he knew their thoughts, and he said to the man who had the withered hand, "Come and stand here." And he rose and stood there. ⁹And Jesus said to them, "I ask you, is it lawful on the sabbath to do good or to do harm, to save life or to destroy it?" ¹⁰And he looked around on them all, and said to him, "Stretch out your hand." And he did so, and his hand was restored. ¹¹But they were filled with fury and discussed with one another what they might do to Jesus.

The third and final conflict deals with freedom from the pharisaic interpretation of sabbath observance. Called to discipleship (5:1-11) in a gesture which fulfills the law (5:12-16), the disciples are healed and their sins forgiven

(5:17-26). So reconciled, their way of life transcends that of the disciples of John and of the Pharisees (5:27-39). In their new life, traditional sabbath observance is relativized by the fundamental purpose of the law as interpreted by the authoritative word of Jesus (6:1-11).

The issue is developed in two closely related stages, which are temporarily situated on distinct sabbaths (6:1-5, 6-11). The first introduces the particular problem of working on the sabbath to obtain food (6:1-5). The second takes up the general question of doing good and saving life on the sabbath (6:6-11). Proceeding from a particular case to a universal question, these two stages are comparable to 5:27-32 and 33-39.

As in 5:27-39, the problem is raised by the Pharisees and it resides in the behavior of Jesus' disciples rather than in his own. However, once the narrative has affirmed that the disciples' freedom is grounded in their relationship to the Son of man who is lord of the sabbath (6:5), it focuses on Jesus himself and the broader implications of that lordship.

Geographically, the passage moves from the grainfields (6:1-5) to the synagogue (6:6-11). The Pharisees' furious reaction to Jesus' saving and life-giving action on the sabbath (6:11) announces the passion, Jesus' ultimate act of salvation. Situated in the synagogue, it also provides the grounds for Christianity's disassociation from this important jewish institution and prepares us for the following section on the institution, formation and commissioning of the new Israel (6:12-9:50). After 6:11, the story of Jesus' mission and the origins of the Church unfolds away from the synagogue and in the various contexts which would characterize the life of the Church.

In 6:1-5, Jesus responds to the Pharisees' objection by recalling an incident in the life of David (6:3-4, 1 Sam 21:1-6). An incident which normally would have violated the house of God is thus associated with one which would normally have transgressed the sabbath law. Since the Davidic precedent is included in the scriptures and their prophetic interpretation of the law, it wielded great authority with the Pharisees. Jesus thus responds to the Pharisees on their own terms, as indeed he had done in the Nazareth synagogue when he challenged the entire congregation (4:24-27). Human life takes precedence over sabbath observance.

The first stage ends by comparing Jesus to David. Jesus is not merely a new David but the Son of man, and it is as such that he is lord of the sabbath (6:5). Jesus' superiority over David will be developed in 20:41-44, where Jesus argues with the Sadducees that David himself acknowledged the lordship of his son.

*A fortiori*, what is true of David must be true of the Son of man. What Jesus has affirmed must now be demonstrated. Foiled by Jesus' argument and infuriated by his claim, the Pharisees seek a way to accuse him. The occasion presents itself on a sabbath while Jesus is in the synagogue together with the scribes and the Pharisees and a man whose right hand was withered (6:6-7). Knowing their thoughts, Jesus asks the man to stand in the midst of the congregation (6:8). He then confronts the scribes and the Pharisees directly: the real issue is whether one can do good and save life on the sabbath. Jesus then proceeds to cure the man (6:9-10).

Jesus' question is also a clear indictment of the scribes and Pharisees. How can they object to Jesus' doing good, when in their own attitude and in their search to accuse him, they are doing harm and destroying life on the sabbath? Furious at being completely undone and unwilling to change, the scribes and the Pharisees have no alternative: they must find a way to rid themselves of Jesus (6:11).


## B. 2. JESUS AND THE NEW ISRAEL.
### 6:12-7:50.

In 5:1-6:11, Luke presented the call to discipleship along with its relationship to Jesus' identity and mission and to

the life situation of those who were called. In so doing, he
disassociated the disciples from the pharisaic interpretation
of the law and developed some of the basic characteristics
of the new way of salvation. He also emphasized the role of
Simon, who would be the foundation stone of the christian
community, and laid the groundwork for the apostolic
mission. In 6:12-7:50, Luke now narrates Jesus' establishment of the new Israel, whose leaders would later be formed
(8:1-56) and actually sent on that mission (9:1-50).

From several points of view, 6:12-7:50 is thematically
parallel to 5:1-6:11, and this is reflected in the section's
literary structure. The section, which includes six units,
opens with a passage on the disciples (see 5:1-11) in which
Jesus selects twelve disciples whom he names apostles
(6:12-16). It continues with a unit which provides the
foundation for all that follows (see 5:12-16); in this unit,
Luke presents an ethical synthesis for life in the new Israel
(6:17-49). We then have an important cure (see 5:17-26)
which highlights the faith of the gentiles (7:1-10). In an
additional event (see 5:27-32), Jesus raises a young Jew
from the dead (7:11-17). This is followed by a discussion
on Jesus' relationship to John the Baptist (see 5:33-39),
a discussion in which Jesus responds to two disciples whom
John sent to him (7:18-35). Finally, the section concludes
with a unit on salvation (see 6:1-11); dining with a Pharisee,
Jesus shows how salvation is related to faith and love
(7:36-50).

Thematic and structural similarities, however, should not
obscure this section's unique contribution to the development of the gospel. In 5:1-6:11, Luke had set forth the newness of the christian way and the antagonism which it
aroused among the leaders of the synagogue. In 6:12-7:50,
he spells out the ultimate implications of that way, which
amounts to nothing less than a new Israel (6:12-16) with a
new and demanding ethic (6:17-49). Open to the Gentiles
(7:1-10), the new Israel called the Jews to resurrection and
new life (7:11-17). It not only fulfilled but far surpassed

the promise of the old Israel (7:18-35). In the new Israel, the measure of forgiveness is the quality of love, and those who respond to Jesus in faith are gifted with peace (7:36-50).

In 4:14-44 and 5:1-6:11, the synagogue provided an important context for Jesus' teaching and activity. In summary statements (4:15,44) and in narrative episodes (4:16, 33; 6:6), this relationship to the synagogue had been carefully noted. However, beginning with 6:12-7:50 and throughout the remainder of Jesus' Galilean ministry (8:1-56; 9:1-50), Jesus and his disciples never again set foot in the synagogue. The new Israel transcends the synagogue. In 6:12-7:50, its life context is the mountainside (6:12-16), a level place (6:17-49), the open streets (7:1-10) and the gate of the city (7:11-17), an undisclosed place (7:18-35), and a house (7:36-50). The new Israel has moved out of the synagogue into the arena of daily life.

2. a. The Foundations of the New Israel.
   *Twelve whom he named apostles.*
   6:12-16.

> [12]In these days he went out to the mountain to pray; and all night he continued in prayer to God. [13]And when it was day, he called his disciples, and chose from them twelve, whom he named apostles; [14]Simon, whom he named Peter, and Andrew his brother, and James and John, and Philip, and Bartholomew, [15]and Matthew, and Thomas, and James the son of Alphaeus, and Simon who was called the Zealot, [16]and Judas the son of James, and Judas Iscariot, who became a traitor.

In 5:1-6:11, Luke's great concern with the disciples became evident from the section's introductory unit, in which Jesus called Simon and his companions to missionary discipleship (5:1-11), as well as from two further units (5:27-39; 6:1-11), where attention focused explicitly on the disciples (see 5:30, 33-35; 6:1-5). Indeed, the entire section deals with the disciples' distinctive identity vis-a-vis the law, the Pharisees, the scribes and the synagogue. This same concern appears in 6:12-16, a unit which introduces 6:12-7:50 and in which Jesus selects twelve from among his disciples to be his apostles.

The event takes place on the mountain after Jesus spent a night in prayer (6:12), as he frequently did in the course of his mission (5:16). The selection of the Twelve thus springs from Jesus' communing with God, a fact which highlights the significance of this new moment in the emergence of the christian community.

The twelve apostles represent an extremely important group in Luke's theology of christian history. In direct continuity with Jesus and his mission, they constituted the first stage in the development of church leadership. Further stages, namely that of the prophetic teachers (Acts 13:1-3) and that of the elders, whose function was to oversee the life of local communities (Acts 14:23), would build on their foundations.

For Luke, however, as for the long history of tradition which preceded him (see 1 Cor 15:5), the Twelve (6:13) represented far more than the list of individual apostles included in their number (6:14-16). Evoking the twelve sons of Jacob (Gen 35:22-26), from whom sprang the twelve tribes of Israel (Gen 49:28), Jesus' selection of twelve apostles announced the beginning of a new Israel. The blessings which God had promised to Abraham (Gen 12:1-3; 15:1-21) were transmitted through the twelve sons of Jacob (Gen 49). Their fulfillment in Jesus (1:55) would be transmitted through the twelve apostles (24:51; Acts 3:25-26).

At the head of the list stands Simon, who alone received a new name from Jesus (5:14). The name Peter, which was anticipated in the passage on Simon's call (5:8), indicates Simon's identity and role among the Twelve. In the course of Luke-Acts, Simon is the rock in whom all the others find their strength (22:32). Through his leadership the

Twelve were restored to their full complement (Acts 1:15-26). His experience of the risen Lord (24:34), his preaching (Acts 2:14-41) and his apostolic and pastoral practice (Acts 8:14-15; 11:1-18) set the norms against which all the others were measured. Respecting ancient tradition (1 Cor 15:5), Luke presents Peter both as one of the Twelve and as distinct from them. In Acts 2:14, he actually distinguishes Peter from the Twelve by referring to the others as the Eleven. Like Joseph (Gen 49:22-26), Peter remains ultimately unmoved by the enemy (22:31-32), deriving his strength from the Rock of Israel (Gen 49:24).

The list of the Twelve ends with "Judas Iscariot, who became a traitor" (6:16). Even as he posits the foundations of the new Israel, Luke looks to the passion and Jesus' betrayal from within the select apostolic circle.

## 2. b. The Ethic of the New Israel.
*To you that hear.*
6:17-49.

[17]And he came down with them and stood on a level place, with a great crowd of his disciples and a great multitude of people from all Judea and Jerusalem and the seacoast of Tyre and Sidon, who came to hear him and to be healed of their diseases; [18]and those who were troubled with unclean spirits were cured. [19]And all the crowd sought to touch him, for power came forth from him and healed them all.

[20]And he lifted up his eyes on his disciples, and said:

"Blessed are you poor, for yours is the kingdom of God.

[21]"Blessed are you that hunger now, for you shall be satisfied.

"Blessed are you that weep now, for you shall laugh,

[22]"Blessed are you when men hate you, and when they exclude you and revile you, and cast out your name as evil, on account of the Son of man! [23]Rejoice in that day,

and leap for joy, for behold, your reward is great in heaven; for so their fathers did to the prophets.

24"But woe to you that are rich, for you have received your consolation.

25"Woe to you that are full now, for you shall hunger.

"Woe to you that laugh now, for you shall mourn and weep.

26"Woe to you, when all men speak well of you, for so their fathers did to the false prophets.

27"But I say to you that hear, Love your enemies, do good to those who hate you, 28bless those who curse you, pray for those who abuse you. 29To him who strikes you on the cheek, offer the other also; and from him who takes away your coat do not withhold even your shirt. 30Give to every one who begs from you; and of him who takes away your goods do not ask them again. 31And as you wish that men would do to you, do so to them.

32"If you love those who love you, what credit is that to you? For even sinners love those who love them. 33And if you do good to those who do good to you, what credit is that to you? For even sinners do the same. 34And if you lend to those from whom you hope to receive, what credit is that to you? Even sinners lend to sinners, to receive as much again. 35But love your enemies, and do good, and lend, expecting nothing in return; and your reward will be great, and you will be sons of the Most High; for he is kind to the ungrateful and the selfish. 36Be merciful, even as your Father is merciful.

37"Judge not, and you will not be judged; condemn not, and you will not be condemned; forgive, and you will be forgiven; 38give, and it will be given to you; good measure, pressed down, shaken together, running over, will be put into your lap. For the measure you give will be the measure you get back."

39He also told them a parable: "Can a blind man lead a blind man? Will they not both fall into a pit? 40A disciple is not above his teacher, but every one when he is fully taught will be like his teacher. 41Why do you see the speck that is in your brother's eye, but do not notice the log that is in your own eye? [42]Or how can you say to your brother, 'Brother, let me take out the speck that is in your eye,' when you yourself do not see the log that is in your own eye? You hypocrite, first take the log out of your own eye, and then you will see clearly to take out the speck that is in your brother's eye.

[43]"For no good tree bears bad fruit, nor again does a bad tree bear good fruit; [44]for each tree is known by its own fruit. For figs are not gathered from thorns, nor are grapes picked from a bramble bush. [45]The good man out of the good treasure of his heart produces good, and the evil man out of his evil treasure produces evil; for out of the abundance of the heart his mouth speaks.

[46]"Why do you call me 'Lord, Lord,' and not do what I tell you? [47]Every one who comes to me and hears my words and does them, I will show you what he is like: [48]he is like a man building a house, who dug deep, and laid the foundation upon rock; and when a flood arose, the stream broke against that house, and could not shake it, because it had been well built. [49]But he who hears and does not do them is like a man who built a house on the ground without a foundation; against which the stream broke, and immediately it fell, and the ruin of that house was great."

Having defined the Church as a new Israel (6:12-16), Luke turns to its fundamental characteristics. In a discourse which includes many of the sayings found in Matthew's sermon on the mount (Mt 5-7), he begins by presenting an ethical synthesis of life in the new Israel (6:17-49). The unit includes a narrative introduction (6:17-20a) and the discourse proper (6:20b-49), which is divided into two parts (6:20b-26, 27-49).

The discourse differs from most of the other discourses in Luke, which are occasioned by specific sets of circumstances and deal with particular problems. Luke's concern in 6:20b-49 is rather with the general stance and attitudes which underlie all christian life and behavior. Accordingly, it is not presented as a response to a special problem but as a general statement to all the disciples (6:20-26), who are called to extend and continue Jesus' work of teaching and healing (6:18-20), and to the people (6:27-49), who will come to them as they had come to him and who will form the new Israel.

Accompanied by the Twelve (6:17a), Jesus first addresses his disciples (6:20-26) in the hearing of a great multitude of people (6:17; 7:1). The presence of the Twelve is significant. Standing in solidarity with Jesus as he spoke on the plain, they would be faithful transmitters and exponents of Jesus' ethical teaching. The teaching itself bears on the life of the disciples as related to those among whom they live and whom they are called to serve. The crowd, which included people from all Judea, Jerusalem and the seacoast of Tyre and Sidon (6:17b) indicates the disciples' universal mission (see 2:31-32; 4:24-27).

*Message to the Disciples.*
*6:20b-26.*

Jesus' word to the disciples confronts their concrete human condition, points to genuine values, and contrasts these with the response which can be expected from those who do not share the attitudes of the new Israel (6:20b-26). Its four beatitudes (6:20b-23) and four woes (6:24-26) parallel one another, and each woe is antithetical to its corresponding beatitude.

Unlike Matthew 5:3-10, Luke applies the beatitudes directly to the disciples, who are addressed in the second person. The same is true of the woes. Accordingly, the poor, the rich, those who hunger, those who are full, those who weep, and those who laugh are all members of the Lukan communities. Consequently, the author's intention was not to compare the Christians with non-Christians, but to lead his readers to recognize their social differences as well as the paradox of life in the new Israel. This paradox stands out very clearly in the mystery of christian suffering and persecution (6:22,26a), a mystery which is historically continuous with the way the fathers of the persecutors treated the prophets (6:23,26b) Like Jesus (4:24), the disciples are thus viewed as prophets (see Acts 13:1).

*Message to the People.*
*6:27-49.*

After addressing his disciples in the hearing of the people (6:20-26), Jesus speaks to the multitudes of people who have come to hear him (6:17, 27-49). This second part of the discourse includes a series of traditional sayings of Jesus (6:27b-38) and a number of parables (6:39-49), which distinguish the attitudes and behavior of those who accept Jesus' teaching from the life of sinners. This same message would be that of the disciples.

The sayings emphasize two points: love of one's enemies (6:27-28,32,35) and generosity in giving (6:29-30, 34-35,38). It is not enough to love those who love us or to give to those who can be expected to reciprocate. Such love and such giving are no greater than those of sinners (6:32,34). Nor can love remain merely a matter of attitude; it must be translated into action, and this is referred to as doing good (6:27,33,35). Concretely, the primary way of doing good is to give to others, especially to the needy who must beg (6:30a) or who are reduced to stealing (6:29b,30b). Sensitivity to the poor and the sharing of goods, both of which will emerge as christian ideals (Acts 2:42, 44-45; 4:32-5:11; 11:27-30; 12:25), are thus inscribed in the ethic of the new Israel.

In these matters, Jesus provides a rule of thumb: we must do to others as we would have them do to us (6:31). Ultimately, however, the norm is God's own goodness, which does not discriminate between those who love him and those who do not. Only in this way will we truly be God's sons (6:35), expressing the merciful love of our Father (6:36). Actually, the rule and measure which we apply in dealing with others will be applied to us (6:35,38).

The parables also emphasize two points: the need for personal faith and conversion in order to help our brother (6:39-45), and the need to put into practice what Christ teaches us (6:46-49).

One who fails to recognize his own blindness and whose eyes have not been opened in faith cannot lead, teach or heal his brother (6:39, 41-42). In this, the people are no better than the disciples, who are prophets and teachers (see 6:23,26; Acts 13:1). However, by learning from the disciples they can become like them (6:40). Once they have responded to Jesus and have accepted his teaching, their behavior and their actions will likewise be good (6:43-46), and they will be able to lead, teach and heal their brother (6:39-42).

It is not enough to proclaim Christ as Lord. One must also do what he tells us (6:46). In this way, Christians contribute to making Christ's lordship a historical and social reality. For those who do not act on Jesus' word, "Lord" remains an empty title. Without foundations, their christian life is swept away with the first storm (6:47-49).

## 2. c. The Faith of the Gentiles.
### *I am not worthy.*
### 7:1-10.

> **7** After he had ended all his sayings in the hearing of the people he entered Capernaum. ²Now a centurion had a slave who was dear to him, who was sick and at the point of death. ³When he heard of Jesus, he sent to him elders of the Jews, asking him to come and heal his slave. ⁴And when they came to Jesus, they besought him earnestly, saying, "He is worthy to have you do this for him, ⁵for he loves our nation, and he built us our synagogue." ⁶And Jesus went with them. When he was not far from the house, the centurion sent friends to him, saying to him, "Lord, do not trouble yourself, for I am not worthy to have you come under my roof; ⁷therefore I did

not presume to come to you. But say the word, and let my servant be healed. [8]For I am a man set under authority, with soldiers under me: and I say to one, 'Go,' and he goes; and to another, 'Come,' and he comes; and to my slave, 'Do this,' and he does it." [9]When Jesus heard this he marveled at him, and turned and said to the multitude that followed him, "I tell you, not even in Israel have I found such faith." [10]And when those who had been sent returned to the house, they found the slave well.

After the discourse on the plain (6:17-49), Jesus reenters Capernaum for the first time since his divinely ordained departure at the end of 4:31-44 (7:1). On this occasion, however, his ministry would not be to the Jews but to a Gentile, a centurion who had asked Jewish elders to intercede with Jesus on behalf of his servant who was seriously sick (7:2-3). The passage thus focuses on the mission to the Gentiles, which Jesus had announced in the Nazareth synagogue (4:25-27).

In the context of 6:12-7:49, the story presents one of the principal characteristics of the New Israel, which would include the Gentiles. The latter, it will be recalled, had been among the many who came to hear Jesus and be healed (6:17-18).

The role of the elders is significant. These Jewish leaders were the antecedents of the presbyters of elders who led the Gentile communities for which Luke is writing. In 7:1-10, it is they who mediate Jesus' mission to the Gentiles. Their request is presented from a Jewish point of view: the centurion is *worthy* of Jesus' attention since he loves the Jewish people and has even built the Capernaum synagogue (7:4-5). This very synagogue had witnessed Jesus' authoritative power when he freed a man from the spirit of an unclean demon (4:33-36).

The intercession of the elders sufficed to turn Jesus toward the centurion's house (7:6a). However, as Jesus approached, the centurion sent friends to protest his *unworthiness* that Jesus actually come under his roof. Jesus' authoritative word was all that was needed to heal the servant (7:6b-8). Luke thus reinforces the historical foundations of Gentile Christianity with an extraordinary manifestation of faith, which surpasses even that of Israel (7:9). In so doing, he also sets up a new milestone in the history of the word which first came to John (3:2) but which was now identified with the word of Jesus (4:22,36; 5:1,5).

2. d. The New Life of the Jews.
   *God has visited his people.*
   7:11-17.

> [11]Soon afterward he went to a city called Nain, and his disciples and a great crowd went with him. [12]As he drew near to the gate of the city, behold, a man who had died was being carried out, the only son of his mother, and she was a widow; and a large crowd from the city was with her. [13]And when the Lord saw her, he had compassion on her and said to her, "Do not weep." [14]And he came and touched the bier, and the bearers stood still. And he said, "Young man, I say to you, arise." [15]And the dead man sat up, and began to speak. And he gave him to his mother. [16]Fear seized them all; and they glorified God, saying, "A great prophet has arisen among us!" and "God has visited his people!" [17]And this report concerning him spread through the whole of Judea and all the surrounding country.

Leaving Capernaum, accompanied by his disciples and a great crowd, Jesus then went to a city called Nain (7:11). At the gate of the city, he was met by a woman, a widow, who accompanied her deceased son and who was followed by another large crowd (7:12). As opposed to 7:1-10, the story's human environment is entirely jewish. For the gentiles, participation in the new Israel had required faith and radical healing. For the Jews, it implied resurrection. At Jesus' word, the dead young man of the old Israel would rise to new life in the new Israel.

As in 7:6, Jesus is introduced as Lord (7:13). The Son of man, who held power to forgive sins (5:24) and who was lord of the sabbath (6:5) is also Lord of life. Through his power the old Israel will not be excluded from participating in the new. The actual use of that power springs from Jesus' compassionate attitude toward the dead (7:13). As we note in 15:24 and 32, Luke equates death with being lost and life with being found. Like the father in the parable of the prodigal son, Jesus greets the widow's dead or lost son with compassion.

The resurrection is effected through Jesus' word. When Jesus commands life, it is communicated, and the young man manifests his regained life by speaking (7:14-15). Seeing him speak, those who witnessed the event were filled with fear, much like those who were present at the birth and naming of John and who had seen Zechariah regain his speech (1:64-65). Jesus is recognized as a great prophet, and like Zechariah the assembly proclaims that God has visited his people (7:16; 1:68). As in the naming of John, the author also notes that a report of the event was spreading through the whole of Judea (7:17; 1:65). Unlike the former incident, however, that report also spread out of Judea through all the surrounding country. Luke thus relates Israel's new life to the greater gentile environment.


2. e. The Fulfillment of the Expectations of Israel.
  *Blessed is he who takes no offense at me.*
  7:18-35.

> [18]The disciples of John told him of all these things.
> [19]And John, calling to him two of his disciples, sent them

to the Lord, saying, "Are you he who is to come, or shall we look for another?" [20]And when the men had come to him, they said, "John the Baptist has sent us to you, saying, 'Are you he who is to come, or shall we look for another?'" [21]In that hour he cured many of diseases and plagues and evil spirits, and on many that were blind he bestowed sight. [22]And he answered them, "Go and tell John what you have seen and heard: the blind receive their sight, the lame walk, lepers are cleansed, and the deaf hear, the dead are raised up, the poor have good news preached to them. [23]And blessed is he who takes no offense at me."

[24]When the messengers of John had gone, he began to speak to the crowds concerning John: "What did you go out into the wilderness to behold? A reed shaken by the wind? [25]What then did you go out to see? A man clothed in soft clothing? Behold, those who are gorgeously appareled and live in luxury are in kings' courts. [26]What then did you go out to see? A prophet? Yes, I tell you, and more than a prophet. [27]This is he of whom it is written,

'Behold, I send my messenger
    before thy face,
who shall prepare thy way before
    thee.'

[28]I tell you, among those born of women none is greater than John; yet he who is least in the kingdom of God is greater than he." [29](When they heard this all the people and the tax collectors justified God, having been baptized with the baptism of John; [30]but the Pharisees and the lawyers rejected the purpose of God for themselves, not having been baptized by him.)

[31]"To what then shall I compare the men of this generation, and what are they like? [32]They are like children sitting in the market place and calling to one another,
'We piped to you, and you did not
    dance;

we wailed, and you did not weep.'
[33]For John the Baptist has come eating no bread and drinking no wine; and you say, 'He has a demon.' [34]The Son of man has come eating and drinking; and you say, 'Behold, a glutton and a drunkard, a friend of tax collectors and sinners!' [35]Wisdom is justified by all her children."

Luke's evocation of the events which surrounded the naming of John (7:15-17) has set the stage for this new unit in which the missions of John and Jesus are both related and distinguished. In an exchange between John and Jesus (7:18-24) and a brief discourse which Jesus presents to the crowds (7:25-35), the author takes up the issues already developed in the poetic lines of Zechariah's *Benedictus* (1:68-75, 76-79). Given the cure of the centurion's servant (7:1-10) and the raising of the widow's son (7:11-17), the passage also presents Jesus' fulfillment of John's preparatory mission in the universal perspectives of Simeon's canticle (2:29-32).

The exchange between John and Jesus is initiated by the former, who sent two of his disciples to Jesus the Lord (see 7:6,13). In the passage, Luke's concern is with John's disciples rather than with John himself. At the time of writing, John was long dead. His disciples, however, had continued the Baptist's work, and it is they who were immediately relevant to the christian community. Accordingly, the unit opens by introducing John's disciples (7:18). Just as Jesus' disciples turn to Jesus for an authoritative word, John's disciples turn to John. The latter, however, who had been quickened by Jesus for his life and mission (1:44), does not personally respond to his disciples, but sends them to Jesus with their question. The question, which concerns Jesus' identity and mission, is carefully articulated and attributed first to John and then to his disciples, who repeat it *verbatim* (7:19-20).

After the disciples' question, the narrator interrupts the dialogue with a summary of Jesus' extraordinary activities as a healer (7:21). The activities are situated "in that hour," that is while John's disciples are with Jesus. The summary thus sets the stage for Jesus' response to them.

Jesus' answer is indirect. Presupposing that John's disciples had observed how he cured many of diseases, plagues, and evil spirits and gave sight to the blind (7:21), Jesus tells the disciples to report to John concerning what they had seen and heard (7:22a). The response thus appeals to the disciples' experience of what Jesus actually did, and Jesus' word is authoritative in part because it articulates their experiential knowledge of those deeds. For Luke, Jesus' entire life can be summarized in terms of deeds and word (24:19; Acts 1:1). The present passage demonstrates the relationship between these two aspects of Jesus' mission.

After appealing to the disciples' experience, Jesus assumes the role of teacher and expresses what they had seen and heard in biblical terms (7:22b). In phrases inspired by Is 29:18-19; 35:5-6 and 61:1, he points out that his mission is indeed the fulfillment of God's promise. He is the one who was to come, and they need look for no other. Consequently, the meaning of Jesus' deeds and the authority of his word also stem from their relationship to the scriptures. Through its reference to Is 61:1, Jesus' response is related to his inaugural self-presentation in the Nazareth synagogue (4:18-19). From the point of view of theological methodology, it is also related to 24:25-27, 44-47, where Jesus interprets events in biblical terms and asks the apostolic community to recall how he had done so while he was still with them (24:44). In 4:18-19 and 7:22, Luke provides two such instances.

The dialogue between Jesus and John's disciples ends with a brief declaration which applies the response to Jesus' listeners: "And blessed is he who takes no offense at me" (7:23). The concluding statement is clearly intended as a challenge. To appreciate this challenge, the reader must have a sense of what called it forth. For this we need only recall the terms of John's preaching which had presented the one who was to come in the role of a definitive eschatological judge (3:16-17). Jesus, however, had come as a healer and reconciler, and in the scriptural interpretation of his mission he omitted reference to the day of divine vengeance (Is 61:2; see 4:18-19). Hence the question of John and his disciples; hence Jesus' challenge. At the beginning of the journey narrative, Jesus would rebuke his own disciples for wanting to bring down fire on those who did not receive him (9:53-55).

Once the messengers of John had left, Jesus began to address the crowds concerning John (7:24a). His brief discourse includes two sections, both of which take up and challenge attitudes toward John and Jesus. In the first, Jesus compares and contrasts John's mission with his own (7:24-28). In the second, he compares and contrasts their respective behavior with regard to eating and drinking (7:29-35).

Jesus begins his discourse by evoking descriptions of John which were patently inappropriate (7:24b-25). In so doing, he challenges those whose personal and social stance is nothing more than a reed shaken by the wind and whose soft clothing contrasts with John's way of life. He then presents John as a prophet whose life, and mission transcends that of ordinary prophets (7:26). Citing Mal 3:1, Jesus interprets John's mission in biblical terms (7:27) just as he had interpreted his own (7:22).

The first part of the discourse ends by comparing John with all who are born of woman and by contrasting him with the least in the kingdom of God (7:28). John is greater than all whose life is merely human. However, the least in the kingdom, that is among those whose life is more than human, is greater than he. Like Jesus, those who participate in the new Israel are born of the Spirit and their life cannot be appreciated in human terms alone. The passage thus draws out the implications of Jesus' virginal conception for the disciples.

As in 7:21, the narrator now intervenes with a background statement which is required by the discourse's second section. Its purpose is to distinguish the crowds and the tax collectors from the Pharisees and their lawyers. Since the former had accepted John's baptism, they justified God on hearing Jesus' word. The latter, however, had not been baptized by John and they rejected Jesus' teaching concerning God's purpose for them (7:29-30). In the discourse proper, the sons of this generation are thus disassociated from the crowds and the tax collectors and equated with the Pharisees and the lawyers who accepted neither John nor Jesus (7:33-34).

The discourse opens with a rhetorical question (7:31) which Jesus answers with a comparison (7:32). Invoking a popular saying, Jesus accuses the men of this generation of insincerity and lack of religious seriousness (7:32). Such men reject the penitential way of the one who was more than a prophet (7:26) as well as the joyful way of those who are entering the kingdom of God (7:28). Their accusation that Jesus' disciples compare unfavorably with those of John (see 5:33) is consequently unwarranted and lacking in authority (7:33-34).

Since the Pharisees and the lawyers had rejected John as well, they were in no position to accuse Jesus and his disciples. Further, had they accepted John, they would understand why Jesus was a friend of tax collectors and sinners (see 5:29-32). Accepting John's call to repentance (3:12-13), the latter had been baptized by him (7:29). Along with the crowds, they had become children of wisdom, and wisdom was justified (7:35) in their manifestation of God's justice (7:29). In his justice, God does not reject those who repent and enter into Jesus' reconciling friendship.

## 2. f. Salvation through Faith and Love.
### *Go in peace.*
### 7:36-50.

³⁶One of the Pharisees asked him to eat with him, and he went into the Pharisee's house, and took his place at table. ³⁷And behold, a woman of the city, who was a sinner, when she learned that he was at table in the Pharisee's house, brought an alabaster flask of ointment, ³⁸and standing behind him at his feet, weeping, she began to wet his feet with her tears, and wiped them with the hair of her head, and kissed his feet, and anointed them with the ointment. ³⁹Now when the Pharisee who had invited him saw it, he said to himself, "If this man were a prophet, he would have known who and what sort of woman this is who is touching him, for she is a sinner." ⁴⁰And Jesus answering said to him, "Simon, I have something to say to you." And he answered, "What is it, Teacher?" ⁴¹"A certain creditor had two debtors; one owed five hundred denarii, and the other fifty. ⁴²When they could not pay, he forgave them both. Now which of them will love him more?" ⁴³Simon answered, "The one, I suppose, to whom he forgave more." And he said to him, "You have judged rightly." ⁴⁴Then turning toward the woman he said to Simon, "Do you see this woman? I entered your house, you gave me no water for my feet, but she has wet my feet with her tears and wiped them with her hair. ⁴⁵You gave me no kiss, but from the time I came in she has not ceased to kiss my feet. ⁴⁶You did not anoint my head with oil, but she has anointed my feet with ointment. ⁴⁷Therefore I tell you, her sins, which are many, are forgiven, for she loved much; but he who is forgiven little, loves little." ⁴⁸And he said to her, "Your sins are forgiven." ⁴⁹Then those who were at table with him began to say among themselves, "Who is this, who even forgives sins?" ⁵⁰And he said to the woman, "Your faith has saved you; go in peace."

Throughout this section on the new Israel, Luke has referred to Jesus either as Lord (6:46; 7:6,13,19) or as the Son of man (7:34). In this concluding unit, a sinful woman treats him as Lord (7:37-39) but the narrator refers to him by his personal name (7:40), as the question of Jesus' identity surfaces once again (7:39,49). The use of the name Jesus is thus related to the unit's special concerns.

To accept Jesus' establishment of the new Israel, along with its ethic and the way it reaches out to both gentiles and Jews and in particular to sinners, one must recognize him as Lord and as the human being *par excellence*. Such recognition requires both love and faith, two keys to forgiveness and salvation, and the grounds for receiving the Lord's peace (7:47-48,50). Without these, Jesus' identity remains a question, and one does not enter into the *shalom* of the new Israel.

In the gospel's previous section, Jesus took part in a feast held in the house of a tax collector. While at table, the Pharisees objected to Jesus' dining with sinners (5:29-32). A similar objection now arises at a meal in the house of a Pharisee (7:36). Table fellowship with tax collectors does not preclude table fellowship with Pharisees. No one is excluded from dining with Jesus. The problem in the Pharisee's house revolves around a woman, a sinner who comes to him at table and touches him in an effusive gesture of repentance. For the Pharisee, however, her repentance is of no consequence. If Jesus were truly a prophet, he would not allow the woman to touch him (7:37-39). The question of Jesus' identity is thus raised in the story's opening episode (7:39; see 7:49).

The story about the woman who anoints Jesus is closely related to similar stories in Mk 14:3-9, Mt 26:6-13 and Jn 12:1-8. The account's narrative components are thus deeply rooted in christian tradition. Like the other three evangelists, Luke developed its basic potential in a unique manner and in the particular context which best suited his general purpose.

After an introductory statement which presents the physical context and the principal personage (7:36), the story unfolds in several phases. First, we have an episode which gives rise to the Pharisee's problem (7:37-39). Second, we have Jesus' response to the Pharisee (7:40-47), a dialogue in which a brief parable (7:41-42) is interpreted on its own terms (7:43) and in terms of the woman's response to Jesus which is contrasted with that of the Pharisee (7:44-47). Third, we have Jesus' response to the woman. At this point, the Pharisee's question concerning Jesus' identity becomes that of all who were at table (7:48-50).

The parable, which is about a creditor and two debtors, draws attention to varying degrees of love (7:41-42). In its present form, the parable does not concern the creditor or the love which might have inspired his cancellation of the debts. As is clear from Jesus' question, focus is on the two whose debt is forgiven and how the degree of their love corresponds to the amount of the debt forgiven them. The Pharisee carefully concedes that the one who had the greater debt must have responded with the greater love, and Jesus forcefully accepts his judgment (7:43).

The Pharisee's response then becomes the point of departure for a comparison between the woman's loving gesture toward Jesus and the Pharisee's own limited welcome (7:44-46). The woman is forgiven because she loved much (7:47a). This application of the parable is quite puzzling. The normal conclusion would have been that the woman loved much because she had been forgiven many sins. It thus appears that the parable had originally belonged to another context and that Luke's incorporation of the story was not altogether successful.

The second part of the application follows directly from the parable: he who is forgiven little, loves little (7:47b). Its wording, however, which avoids any mention of whether the love preceded forgiveness or resulted from it, is indicative of Luke's literary malaise. The saying could be read in the sense of 7:47a, where love preceded and invited forgiveness. We must conclude that the latter constitutes

Luke's message as he struggles to reinterpret a parable which had called for a related but different conclusion.

Jesus' response to the woman confirms the view that Luke's basic point is found in 7:47a. The woman had already demonstrated her love (7:37-38), and Jesus consequently forgives her sins (7:49). Her love had sprung from a faith response to Jesus, whom she recognized as Lord. The woman has thus been saved by loving faith, and her salvation called forth the Lord's peace (7:50).

## B. 3. JESUS AND THE FORMATION OF THE NEW ISRAEL.
### 8:1-56.

Luke now turns his attention to Jesus' formation of the new Israel (8:1-56). Those who had been called (5:1-11) and who were designated as the Twelve (6:12-16) needed to be prepared for their mission. This would not be accomplished in isolation but by joining Jesus in the continuation of his own mission.

The section opens with an introductory summary concerning Jesus' activities and those who accompanied him (8:1-3). It is then divided into three units. The first deals with the hearing of God's word (8:4-21). In this unit, Jesus teaches the crowds with a parable, interprets it for his disciples, and emphasizes their responsibility as his true kin. The second unit once again raises the question of Jesus' identity (8:22-39). This time the question is stimulated by the manifest power of Jesus' word in calming a windstorm at sea. The answer is given in a dramatic demonstration of that same power among the tombs in the Gentile territory of Gerasa. The third unit focuses on the new life which comes from Jesus' word and person (8:40-56). It includes the story of Jairus' daughter, whom Jesus raises from the dead, and that of a woman with a flow of blood, who was cured upon touching Jesus.

Throughout the section, Luke pursues his concern with the history of the word (3:2; 5:1), which was to be identified with Jesus' word (6:46-49). The disciples now learn the nature and scope of that word as it affects their own responsibility in the new Israel. The disciples themselves are defined as "those who hear the word of God and do it" (8:21).

3. a. Introductory Summary:
   Jesus, the Twelve and the Women.
   8:1-3.

> **8** Soon afterward he went on through cities and villages, preaching and bringing the good news of the kingdom of God. And the twelve were with him, ²and also some women who had been healed of evil spirits and infirmities: Mary, called Magdalene, from whom seven demons had gone out, ³and Joanna, the wife of Chuza, Herod's steward, and Susanna, and many others, who provided for them out of their means.

The introductory summary (8:1-3) is reminiscent of 4:14-15 and 4:44. Once again Jesus goes through the cities and villages preaching. In the present summary, however, the content of the preaching is explicitly noted: "the good news of the kingdom of God" (8:1). Further, since the new Israel has already been disassociated from the synagogue, no mention is made of the latter. Jesus' teaching in the synagogue (6:6-11) ended prior to the naming of the Twelve (6:12-16). Finally, the summary is more concerned with those who accompanied Jesus than with his own precise activities.

Luke's mention of the women provides a link with 7:36-50, in which Jesus' forgiveness of a sinful woman concludes 5:1-7:50. However, since the women play no further role in 8:1-56, we must assume that they are also introduced to prepare the reader for their function in the passion-resurrection narrative (23:49,55; 24:10, 22-23), where they are identified as the women who had followed Jesus from Galilee. In 8:1-3, Luke states that these women had been healed of evil spirits and infirmities. Like the men, the women consequently had needed to be healed in order to become Jesus' followers.

From a socio-economic and political point of view, at least some of the women enjoyed considerable status. One of them was the wife of Herod's steward, and as a group they provided for Jesus and the apostolic community out of their means. Luke's description of these women must have been inspired, at least in part, by the fact that prominent women played an important role in the development of the early Church (Acts 17:4).

### 3. b. Hearing the Word of God.
*Take heed then how you hear.*
8:4-21.

⁴And when a great crowd came together and people from town after town came to him, he said in a parable: ⁵"A sower went out to sow his seed; and as he sowed, some fell along the path, and was trodden under foot, and the birds of the air devoured it. ⁶And some fell on the rock; and as it grew up, it withered away, because it had no moisture. ⁷And some fell among thorns; and the thorns grew with it and choked it. ⁸And some fell into good soil and grew, and yielded a hundredfold." As he said this, he called out, "He who has ears to hear, let him hear."

⁹And when his disciples asked him what this parable meant, ¹⁰he said, "To you it has been given to know the secrets of the kingdom of God; but for others they are in parables, so that seeing they may not see, and hearing they may not understand. ¹¹Now the parable is this: The seed is the word of God. ¹²The ones along the path are

those who have heard; then the devil comes and takes away the word from their hearts, that they may not believe and be saved. [13]And the ones on the rock are those who, when they hear the word, receive it with joy; but these have no root, they believe for a while and in time of temptation fall away. [14]And as for what fell among the thorns, they are those who hear, but as they go on their way they are choked by the cares and riches and pleasures of life, and their fruit does not mature. [15]And as for that in the good soil, they are those who, hearing the word, hold it fast in an honest and good heart, and bring forth fruit with patience.

[16]"No one after lighting a lamp covers it with a vessel, or puts it under a bed, but puts it on a stand, that those who enter may see the light. [17]For nothing is hid that shall not be made manifest, nor anything secret that shall not be known and come to light. [18]Take heed then how you hear; for to him who has will more be given, and from him who has not, even what he thinks that he has will be taken away."

[19]Then his mother and his brothers came to him, but they could not reach him for the crowd. [20]And he was told, "Your mother and your brothers are standing outside, desiring to see you." [21]But he said to them, "My mother and my brothers are those who hear the word of God and do it."

The missionary community included Jesus, the Twelve and a number of women (8:1-3). Luke now situates it in the midst of a great crowd and indicates that such gatherings were a recurrent phenomenon. Jesus' teaching with a parable is consequently presented not as an isolated event, but as one which has general and quasi-universal significance (8:4).

The parable of the sower focuses the reader's attention not on the sower himself but on the seed which was being sowed and what happened to it (8:5-8a). It concludes with

Jesus' challenge to the great crowds which were coming to him from town after town: let anyone whose ears are open to hearing this parable hear it (8:8b).In the unit's conclusion, Jesus would indicate that truly hearing the word of God included doing that word, and that those who both heard and did the word were Jesus' true family (8:21).

By Luke's time, christian tradition had long shown that Jesus' parable fell on deaf ears (Mk 4:1-20). While the parable may have been quite clear when Jesus first spoke it, the crowds had not really heard it (8:21). In the succeeding decades, its implications had become unclear even to the disciples who were ever called to discern the meaning of it for changing concrete situations. Hence the disciples' request for an explanation (8:9). In his response, Jesus first accounts for the deafness of the crowd. This he does in terms which were largely taken from Mk 4:11-12 and which had been inspired by Is 6:9-10. The crowd's lack of understanding should consequently come as no surprise: it was according to the scriptures (8:10-11). Having distinguished the disciples from the crowd (8:10a), Jesus then interprets the parable for them (8:11-15).

It does not suffice to point out that the seed is the word of God (8:11). That word could be viewed from the point of view of its divine source. In that case, the hearers would correspond to the kind of soil which receives the word. Luke's allegory of Jesus' parable, however, is quite other. Along with the other synoptics (Mk 4:14-20; Mt 13:18-23), the word which has been sowed is viewed from the standpoint of the hearers who have internalized it in varying degrees or who have rejected it. The word is thus seen as operative in the believers, and the kind of ground merely describes the quality of its internalization. This traditional view of the word corresponds to Paul's theology of the word of God as working in the believers (1 Th 2:13).

While the word's meaning may have been enveloped in God's mystery (8:9; 9:45), however, it would be revealed

(8:17). Such is the purpose of divine communication, which is like the lighting of a lamp. The latter is pointless unless it serves to enlighten those who enter into its light (8:16).

While describing the unfolding of understanding and accounting for the previous lack of it, Luke enlarges the theme to challenge the disciples in their mission. The disciples must reveal the light and share the word. They must consequently be very careful to hear that through them others might hear. Discipleship is thus apostolic. Should the disciples fail to assume their apostolic mission, their own hearing as disciples would be dulled, and they themselves would no longer understand the word (8:18). The author thus applies the basic christian paradox that it is in giving that the Christians receive.

A similar development of the symbol of the lamp and of the constitutive nature of the word in discipleship will be presented in 11:33-36 and 27-28 in relation to the christian journey to God.

3. c. Jesus' Identity and the Gentile Mission.
   *Where is your faith?*
   8:22-39.

> [22]One day he got into a boat with his disciples, and he said to them, "Let us go across to the other side of the lake." So they set out, [23]and as they sailed he fell asleep. And a storm of wind came down on the lake, and they were filling with water, and were in danger. [24]And they went and woke him, saying, "Master, Master, we are perishing!" And he awoke and rebuked the wind and the raging waves; and they ceased, and there was a calm. [25]He said to them, "Where is your faith?" And they were afraid, and they marveled, saying to one another, "Who then is this, that he commands even wind and water, and they obey him?"

²⁶Then they arrived at the country of the Gerasenes, which is opposite Galilee. ²⁷And as he stepped out on land, there met him a man from the city who had demons; for a long time he had worn no clothes, and he lived not in a house but among the tombs. ²⁸When he saw Jesus, he cried out and fell down before him, and said with a loud voice, "What have you to do with me, Jesus, Son of the Most High God? I beseech you, do not torment me." ²⁹For he had commanded the unclean spirit to come out of the man. (For many a time it had seized him; he was kept under guard, and bound with chains and fetters, but he broke the bonds and was driven by the demon into the desert.) ³⁰Jesus then asked him, "What is your name?" And he said, "Legion"; for many demons had entered him. ³¹And they begged him not to command them to depart into the abyss. ³²Now a large herd of swine was feeding there on the hillside; and they begged him to let them enter these. So he gave them leave. ³³Then the demons came out of the man and entered the swine, and the herd rushed down the steep bank into the lake and were drowned.

³⁴When the herdsmen saw what had happened, they fled, and told it in the city and in the country. ³⁵Then people went out to see what had happened, and they came to Jesus, and found the man from whom the demons had gone, sitting at the feet of Jesus, clothed and in his right mind; and they were afraid. ³⁶And those who had seen it told them how he who had been possessed with demons was healed. ³⁷Then all the people of the surrounding country of the Gerasenes asked him to depart from them; for they were seized with great fear; so he got into the boat and returned. ³⁸The man from whom the demons had gone begged that he might be with him; but he sent him away, saying, ³⁹"Return to your home, and declare how much God has done for you." And he went away, proclaiming throughout the whole city how much Jesus had done for him.

In Mark's gospel, Jesus spoke his discourse on the meaning of the parables from a boat on the water (Mk 4:1-34). Once the discourse was over, he moved off toward the farther shore with his disciples. During the crossing, Jesus stilled a storm at sea. At his destination in Gerasene territory, he expelled an unclean spirit from an unfortunate man, and the unclean spirit took possession of a herd of swine which plunged to watery destruction (Mk 4:35-5:20).

Luke follows the same sequence of events. However, the discourse was given in the cities, villages and towns, that is in the urban environment of the Lukan communities. The boat context is consequently limited to the sea-crossing and the Gerasene event (8:22-39). As in Mk, the crossing raises the question of Jesus' identity (8:25; see Mk 4:41) and the Gerasene, a Gentile, goes about proclaiming what Jesus had done (8:39b; see Mk 5:20). The episode thus reveals the implications of Jesus' identity for the gentile mission, which Jesus himself sets in motion (8:39a; see Mk 5:19). Unlike Mk, however, Luke does not restrict the gentile's mission to specific cities, the Ten Cities or Decapolis. Instead he broadens the scope of the mission to the city as such, that is to the urban world in general.

The passage parallels 7:1-10, where Luke showed how the new Israel included the gentiles. The subsequent and final unit in this section deals with the cure and resurrection of Jews (8:40-56). It parallels 7:11-17, where Jesus cured the only son of a jewish widow. The formation of the new Israel thus corresponds to its basic nature as outlined in 6:12-7:50 (see also 8:4-21 and 6:46-49).

The sea journey is a crossing from jewish to gentile territory (8:22-25). For Luke's readers it must consequently have evoked Christianity's movement from the jewish to the gentile world. Occasioned and marked by persecution and internal turmoil in the community (Acts 6:8-8:3; 8:4; 9:1-2; 11:19-26), this movement is symbolically represented by the storm which overtook Jesus and his disciples (8:23b).

While the boat moved through the storm, however, and was filling with water, Jesus was sleeping through the danger (8:23a). In the same way, the christian community felt abandoned by Jesus, who was already with his Father (2:49) in glory (24:26). Ascended from history (24:51), Jesus seemed to be sleeping through the community's troubles.

In their plight the disciples went to awaken Jesus with cries that they were perishing. Jesus did awake, and he rebuked the winds and the raging waters into quiet and calm (8:24). Luke's storm-tossed and fearful readers are thus taught to turn to Jesus who will surely come to their distress. Although Jesus is ascended to God, he still comes to the community's assistance. In the story, he rebukes the disciples concerning their lack of faith, and through the disciples he rebukes Luke's readers (8:25a).

Jesus' demonstration of power over the elements raises the question of his identity (8:25b). The disciples' question constitutes the episode's climax and provides a transition to the second episode, which again dwells on Jesus' identity (8:28) in relation to a manifestation of power (8:26-39).

The second episode is situated in the country of the Gerasenes opposite the lake from Galilee (8:26). There among the gentiles, Jesus effectively banishes demons from a man (8:27-33). By joining 8:26-39 into one unit with 8:22-25, Luke shows how Jesus' power over the demonic is grounded in his relationship to creation (see 3:38; 4:1-13). The one who stills the winds and calms the waters has mastery over the humanly uncontrollable and destructive forces which attack human life and propel human beings away from their normal social environment or home into the desert regions and among the tombs where all is death. As Luke would show, however, the living one was not to be sought at the tomb among the dead (24:5). In the same way, Jesus' disciples were not to be sought among the tombs. Jesus consequently cured the posssessed man of the demons of death, drew him into his company (8:35; see 10:38-42) and sent him on mission (8:39).

As Jesus stepped on land, the possessed man, who was from the city, saw him and fell before him with a question and a plea (8:27-28). Recognizing that Jesus is the Son of the Most High God, he asks what Jesus has to do with him. What possible relationship could the Son of God have to this poor man who was torn by the demonic? As the story shows, Jesus does indeed have something to do with the man. As Son of Adam and Son of God (see 3:38), he was there to destroy the power of evil (see 4:1-13). Awed by Jesus' divine sonship, however, the man was unaware of its implications for salvation and he begged Jesus not to torment him.

Jesus then confronts the demons directly and asks that they reveal their identity. Speaking through the man, they declare themselves to be Legion. Unmasked, they then ask Jesus not to banish them into the abyss (8:30-31), a term which evokes the depths of the primaeval waters of the universe before creation (Gen 1:2). As we see in the story of the flood, these waters threatened to overwhelm the order which God had established by his word (Gen 6:11-9:29). They represented the depths where death ruled, the netherworld into which Jonah had been cast (Jon 1:11-2:10).

For the sea to be calmed, evil had to be plunged into the netherworld where it belonged (see 8:22-25; Jon 1:11-12). Jesus did banish the demons into the abyss. At their own request, the demons were sent into a herd of swine who rushed into the lake and drowned (8:32-33). The lake is thus a symbol for the abyss, and in retrospect the storm (8:22-25) takes on a deeper significance. As in Jonah, it represents the forces of evil unleashed by the difficulties connected with the mission to the gentiles.

Brilliantly told, the story contains a dual irony. Given Christianity's origins in the jewish world, Luke's gentile readers must have been keenly sensitive to Jesus' sending of unclean spirits into unclean animals. They must also have enjoyed the fact that the demons unwittingly invited their own banishment into the abyss.

News of the event spread. Filled with fear, the gentiles asked that Jesus depart from them (8:34-37). Within the general flow of the narrative, this provides Luke with the occasion to bring Jesus back into jewish territory. The man who had been healed, however, asked to remain with Jesus (8:38a), a reaction not unlike that of the apostles on the mount of transfiguration (9:33). This, however, could not be. The man had to move away from Jesus' company (8:38b). As a disciple (8:35b), he was commissioned to go home (see 8:27) and to declare how much God had done for him (8:39a). The man did so, proclaiming what God had accomplished on his behalf through Jesus (8:39b). Cured, the gentile had become an evangelist. Here was the sign of Jonah and the response of the men of Nineveh (see 11:29-32).

3. d. Jesus and the Jewish Mission.
   *Your faith has made you well.*
   8:40-56.

> ⁴⁰Now when Jesus returned, the crowd welcomed him, for they were all waiting for him. ⁴¹And there came a man named Jairus, who was a ruler of the synagogue; and falling at Jesus' feet he besought him to come to his house, ⁴²for he had an only daughter, about twelve years of age, and she was dying.
>
> As he went, the people pressed round him. ⁴³And a woman who had had a flow of blood for twelve years and could not be healed by any one, ⁴⁴came up behind him, and touched the fringe of his garment; and immediately her flow of blood ceased. ⁴⁵And Jesus said, "Who was it that touched me?" When all denied it, Peter said, "Master the multitudes surround you and press upon you!" ⁴⁶but Jesus said, "Some one touched me; for I perceive that power has gone forth from me."

⁴⁷And when the woman saw that she was not hidden, she came trembling, and falling down before him declared in the presence of all the people why she had touched him, and how she had been immediately healed. ⁴⁸And he said to her, "Daughter, your faith has made you well; go in peace."

⁴⁹While he was still speaking, a man from the ruler's house came and said, "Your daughter is dead; do not trouble the Teacher any more." ⁵⁰But Jesus on hearing this answered him, "Do not fear; only believe, and she shall be well." ⁵¹And when he came to the house, he permitted no one to enter with him, except Peter and John and James, and the father and mother of the child. ⁵²And all were weeping and bewailing her; but he said, "Do not weep; for she is not dead but sleeping." ⁵³And they laughed at him, knowing that she was dead. ⁵⁴But taking her by the hand he called, saying, "Child, arise." ⁵⁵And her spirit returned, and she got up at once; and he directed that something should be given her to eat. ⁵⁶And her parents were amazed; but he charged them to tell no one what had happened.

At the end of the previous unit (8:22-39), Jesus had returned from gentile to jewish territory (8:37). The concluding unit in the section on the formation of the new Israel now tells of a resurrection and a cure (8:40-56). Although the story parallels 7:11-17 within the structure of the gospel, its scope is broader and its emphasis on the christian mission to the Jews greater. In 7:11-17, Jesus raised the only son of a jewish widow. In 8:40-56, a woman is healed by Jesus' power, but the one who is raised is the twelve-year old daughter of a ruler of the synagogue. The ruler's status and important function in the synagogue draws attention to Jesus' efforts on behalf of the synagogue and Judaism in general.

Structurally, the story of the woman (8:43-48) is sandwiched between that of the ruler and his daughter (8:40-42,

49-56). They thus serve to interpret one another. The resurrection story (8:40-42, 49-56) draws out the deeper implications of Jesus' cure (8:43-48), and the latter shows how Jesus' salvific power responds to a human being's turning to Jesus in faith. When Jesus heals, he thus grants life (8:55-56), and his granting of life is a response to faith and a source of peace (8:48). This relationship is also indicated stylistically by the fact that the ruler's daughter was about twelve years of age (8:42) and the woman had had a flow of blood for twelve years (8:43). The stories' emphasis on women had been prepared by the section's introductory summary, in which the author referred to women whom Jesus had healed (8:1-3).

When Jesus returned from the other side of the lake, he was welcomed by the crowd awaiting him (8:40). It is in this setting that Jairus comes to Jesus and falls at his feet with the insistent request that the latter come to his house, where his twelve-year old daughter lay dying (8:41-42).

The cure of the woman with a twelve-year flow of blood takes place while Jesus accompanies Jairus to his home. She was one of many who pressed round Jesus. The narrator points out that no one was able to heal this woman. He thus brings out the singular nature of the cure when she does no more than touch Jesus' garment (8:43). At this point, the account focuses on Jesus' knowledge of what had taken place, on Peter's lack of understanding and on the woman's need to publicly proclaim what had been done for her (8:45-47; see 8:39). Her cure stems from faith. Healed, she is sent in peace (8:48; see 7:50).

As the journey continues, a man arrives from the ruler's house with the message that the girl is dead and that he need not trouble Jesus, the Teacher, any longer (8:49). Jesus then reveals himself to be no ordinary teacher. The faith which healed the woman (8:48) can also make the dead girl well (8:50). The object of Jesus' teaching is faith.

Together with the girl's father and mother, only Peter and John and James (see 5:1-11; 9:28-36) are allowed into the house (8:51). As in 5:1-11 and 9:28-36, Peter's unique position among the three has been indicated in 8:45. Called by Jesus (5:1-11), the three would now witness his life-giving power (8:52-55) before being introduced into the mystery of his *exodos* (9:31). Jesus' intention is greeted by the mocking laughter of those who were gathered in the house, an attitude of unbelief which evokes the response of many to Jesus' own resurrection. As in the case of Jesus who demonstrated his risen presence in a meal (24:13-35, 36-43), the girl was to eat after her spirit had been restored (8:55).

Jesus' mission to the Jews does not end like that to the gentiles. Whereas the latter were to proclaim what God had done for them through Jesus (8:39-40), the girl's parents were not to reveal what had happened (8:56). Unlike the gentile who had been cured of a demon, they had not taken a position at the Teacher's (8:49) feet (see 8:35; 10:38-42). Their proclamation would not have disclosed Jesus' true identity as the Son of the Most High God (see 8:28). Luke thus reflects the christian historical situation in which the Jews, unlike the gentiles have not received Jesus in faith. Efforts such as this resurrection would be recalled in the journey narrative, when Jesus exclaims that he had so often tried to gather Jerusalem's children together, but to no avail (13:34).

## B. 4. JESUS AND THE MISSION OF THE NEW ISRAEL.
### 9:1-50.

Jesus had already called a number of associates to apostolic discipleship (5:1-6:11), established the foundations of the new Israel (6:12-7:50), and formed it as an apostolic community (8:1-56). In a fourth and final section on the life and mission of the disciples and apostles, he now sends the new Israel on mission (9:1-50). As in the previous stages in this development, the mission is intimately bound up with the identity and mission of Jesus himself (4:14-44).

The section includes three closely related literary units. The first narrates the actual missioning of the Twelve, explicitly raises the question of Jesus' identity, and develops the mission in terms of the community's breaking of bread (9:1-17). In this unit, focus is on the twelve apostles. The second unit reiterates the question of Jesus' identity, responds to it through Peter's faith confession and Jesus' own announcement of the passion-resurrection, spells out its consequences for missionary discipleship (9:18-27), and presents the ultimate manifestation of Jesus' identity, the transfiguration (9:28-36). Its focus is on the disciples as well as on Peter, John and James (see 5:1-11) and the community's continuing apostolic role in history. The third unit draws attention to three major problems which the community experienced in the exercise of its mission and how the disciples were to respond to these (9:37-50). Its focus is on the crowd.

The singling out of Peter, John and James (9:28-36) recalls the call of the first disciples (5:1-11). As in the latter, the author is careful to show Peter's preeminent role in this inner circle of three. The distinction between the twelve apostles (9:1-17), the disciples (9:18-27) and the crowd (9:37-50) recalls Jesus' discourse on the plain, where the same distinction is maintained (6:17-49). In his treatment of the mission of the new Israel, Luke is thus sensitive to distinct historical phases of the life of the Church as well as to the basic continuity which links the Church of his addressees to their remotest origins. The disciples and the crowds belong to every period including Luke's own. In their mission to the vast numbers gathering about them, the Lukan disciples stand in continuity with the twelve apostles, the inner circle of three, Peter, and Jesus himself.

## 4. a. The Mission of the Twelve.
### *You give them something to eat.*
### 9:1-17.

**9** And he called the twelve together and gave them power and authority over all demons and to cure diseases,

²and he sent them out to preach the kingdom of God and to heal. ³And he said to them, "Take nothing for your journey, no staff, nor bag, nor bread, nor money; and do not have two tunics. ⁴And whatever house you enter, stay there, and from there depart. ⁵And wherever they do not receive you, when you leave that town shake off the dust from your feet as a testimony against them." ⁶And they departed and went through the villages, preaching the gospel and healing everywhere.

⁷Now Herod the tetrarch heard of all that was done, and he was perplexed, because it was said by some that John had been raised from the dead, ⁸by some that Elijah had appeared, and by others that one of the old prophets had risen. ⁹Herod said, "John I beheaded; but who is this about whom I hear such things?" And he sought to see him.

¹⁰On their return the apostles told him what they had done. And he took them and withdrew apart to a city called Bethsaida. ¹¹When the crowds learned it, they followed him; and he welcomed them and spoke to them of the kingdom of God, and cured those who had need of healing. ¹²Now the day began to wear away; and the twelve came and said to him, "Send the crowd away, to go into the villages and country round about, to lodge and get provisions; for we are here in a lonely place." ¹³But he said to them, "You give them something to eat." They said, "We have no more than five loaves and two fish—unless we are to go and buy food for all these people." ¹⁴For there were about five thousand men. And he said to his disciples, "Make them sit down in companies, about fifty each." ¹⁵And they did so, and made them all sit down. ¹⁶And taking the five loaves and the two fish he looked up to heaven, and blessed and broke them, and gave them to the disciples to set before the crowd. ¹⁷And all ate and were satisfied. And they took up what was left over, twelve baskets of broken pieces.

In this first unit, Luke discloses the relationship between the mission of the Twelve (Lk 9:1-6; see 8:1) and that of

Jesus (Lk 9:10-11), a relationship which is intimately bound up with the question of Jesus' identity (Lk 9:7-9). He then interprets the apostolic mission in terms of table fellowship (Lk 9:12-17), where the Twelve are asked to assume Jesus' role in nourishing the crowds. He thus presents the Eucharist as an epitome or capsule of the Church's missionary challenge and situates pastoral service to Jesus' followers within the primary apostolic mission to extend Jesus' welcome beyond the existing communities.

*The Mission of the Twelve.*
*9:1-6.*

The missioning of the Twelve (Lk 9:1-6) departs from Mark's account on several significant points which draw attention to Luke's own specific message.

First, Jesus does not send the Twelve out two by two (Mk 6:7). This aspect of the mission is reserved for the seventy-two (Lk 10:1), an expansion of the core apostolic community which plays no part in Mark. For Luke, the pairing of apostles is thus an enduring characteristic of the christian mission and a symbol of its continuity through history. Luke's handling of tradition in this matter is a good example of how he reserves some elements from his literary source for a new and distinct context.

Second, greater emphasis is placed on the healing mission than in Mark, where it is appended as an aspect of the apostles' authority over unclean spirits (Mk 6:7,13). In Luke's world of gentile Christianity, illness may not have been so closely associated with the demonic as in the Jewish context which Mark seeks to interpret. Healing is thus a distinct aspect of the mission and directly grounded in the explicit command of Jesus (Lk 9:1).

Third, Jesus' demands with regard to what the disciples should not take with them are more radical in Luke, where even the staff is excluded and no mention is made of sandals (Lk 9:2; Mk 6:8-9). It should be noted, however, that these demands are somewhat softened in the missioning of the

seventy-two (Lk 10:4) and actually reversed in Jesus' farewell discourse (Lk 22:25-36). The triple development, in
which the original demands of the Palestinian mission are
adapted to the physical exigencies of the vastly expanded
mission to the Greco-Roman world, reveals Luke's sensitivity to the need for adaptability in Christianity's mission
style. At this point in the Gospel, his retention of the
demands in their starkest expression speaks to the kind
of commitment which must accompany every missionary
adaptation.

Taken together, these three observations concerning the
account's relationship to Mark and its place in the greater
Lukan context highlight Luke's focus on the apostles and
their relationship to the christian communities which
succeeded them. Dealing with the past, Luke's message is
clearly for the present.

*Herod's Perplexity.*
*9:7-9.*

Herod's perplexity is the vehicle for raising the question
of Jesus' identity (Lk 9:7-9; Mk 6:14-16). The difference
between Mark and Luke again proves enlightening. In
Mark, Herod maintains that Jesus is actually John who has
been raised from the dead (Mk 6:16). Luke, on the other
hand, credits some with this position, but carefully distances
it from Herod's own view. John has been beheaded; the
question of Jesus' identity remains (Lk 9:9). There was
consequently no point in including Mark's flashback concerning the Baptist's death (Mk 6:17-29). As we have
already noted, Luke was more concerned with showing how
Jesus' mission transcended that of John (see Lk 1:5-2:52;
3:21-22). This interest is now reflected in the way he has
revised Mark's account. Choosing not to anticipate Peter's
confession by means of a John the Baptist typology, Luke
affirms that the nature and meaning of the mission hinge
on the unique identity of Jesus. Precisions concerning
that identity are left aside for a later development.

## A Sharing Mission.
### 9:10-17.

The nourishing of the five thousand (9:10-17) follows the return of the apostles from the mission (Lk 9:10a). As with the call of Simon and his partners, the missioning of the new Israel is thus associated with an experience of abundance mediated by Jesus. In Lk 5:1-11, however, the abundant fish focused attention on the extraordinary growth of the future community. In the present case, it refers to the nourishment needed to serve this community.

Unlike Mark, who followed tradition and situated the sharing event in the desert, Luke transferred the whole episode to a city (Lk 9:10b). He thus adapted the account to the urban context of his intended readers. The same sensitivity is revealed in Lk 9:14, where Jesus orders that the crowd be divided in table-companies and made to recline on dining couches. Unfortunately, English versions of the Greek New Testament fall short at this point. Although Luke has not transformed and assimilated Mark's desert context in every respect (Lk 9:12), we must take careful note of the editorial adaptations which he did make. In the present case, the matter is particularly important due to the historic episode's narrative interpretation as a eucharistic account (Lk 9:16). Luke presents the sharing event as the community's own eucharistic challenge.

As in Mark 6:34-36, but unlike Mark 8:1-3, it is the disciples who take the initiative concerning the crowd (Lk 9:12). Jesus, however, does not accept their suggestion that he send them away but orders that they give the crowd to eat, at which they object that their five loaves and two fish would hardly be adequate (Lk 9:13). Jesus' persistence (Lk 9:14b) underlines the apostles' ongoing responsibility in nourishing the christian communities. The followers whom Jesus had welcomed, taught and cured (Lk 9:11) were not to be dismissed. Rather the apostles themselves were to give food to the crowd. In no way were they allowed to desist from the mission on which they had embarked with Jesus. The growth and development of the communities and the ever-expanding scope of the mission did not provide grounds for capitulation but a problem to be overcome (see Acts 6:1-6).

The paradox of radical poverty (Lk 9:3) and apostolic munificence (Lk 9:13-14) in the mission is resolved by the nature of the bread which the apostles are ordered to give. Having no bread of their own (Lk 9:3), the apostles are missioned to give the bread which Jesus himself gave to the crowds. Hence the significance of the twelve baskets (Lk 9:17) of the leftover bread which Jesus had broken. In the context of Lk 9:1-17, they correspond to the twelve apostles (Lk 9:1). As leftovers from an episode in which marvelous sharing had been inspired and mediated by Jesus, they emphasize the historical continuity between Jesus and his apostles as well as the latter's relative position in christian history.

Within the narrative's eucharistic context, the expression "You give them something to eat" (Lk 9:13) constitutes the equivalent of the liturgical expression "Do this in remembrance of me" (Lk 22:19). By sharing and leading others to share, the apostles fulfilled the promise of Jesus' ministry as well as God's own promise of abundant nourishment (2 Kgs 4:42-44). In and through their efforts, the risen Lord continues to nourish the crowds and the latter have a living memorial of his abundant generosity.

4. b. The Nature of the Mission.
   *This is my Son, my Chosen.*
   9:18-36.

> [18]Now it happened that as he was praying alone the disciples were with him; and he asked them, "Who do the people say that I am?" [19]And they answered, "John the Baptist; but others say, Elijah; and others, that one of the old prophets has risen." [20]And he said to them, "But

who do you say that I am?" And Peter answered, "The Christ of God." [21]But he charged and commanded them to tell this to no one, [22]saying, "The Son of man must suffer many things, and be rejected by the elders and chief priests and scribes, and be killed, and on the third day be raised."

[23]And he said to all, "If any man would come after me, let him deny himself and take up his cross daily and follow me. [24]For whoever would save his life will lose it; and whoever loses his life for my sake, he will save it. [25]For what does it profit a man if he gains the whole world and loses or forfeits himself? [26]For whoever is ashamed of me and of my words, of him will the Son of man be ashamed when he comes in his glory and the glory of the Father and of the holy angels. [27]But I tell you truly, there are some standing here who will not taste death before they see the kingdom of God."

[28]Now about eight days after these sayings he took with him Peter and John and James, and went up on the mountain to pray. [29]And as he was praying, the appearance of his countenance was altered, and his raiment became dazzling white. [30]And behold, two men talked with him, Moses and Elijah, [31]who appeared in glory and spoke of his departure, which he was to accomplish at Jerusalem. [32]Now Peter and those who were with him were heavy with sleep, and when they wakened they saw his glory and the two men who stood with him. [33]And as the men were parting from him, Peter said to Jesus, "Master, it is well that we are here; let us make three booths, one for you and one for Moses and one for Elijah"—not knowing what he said. [34]As he said this, a cloud came and overshadowed them; and they were afraid as they entered the cloud. [35]And a voice came out of the cloud, saying, "This is my Son, my Chosen; listen to him!" [36]And when the voice had spoken, Jesus was found alone. And they kept silence and told no one in those days anything of what they had seen.

Although Jesus' personal identity had been left in abeyance in Lk 9:7-9, the apostles' faith in him is obviously a key element for understanding their mission and the nature of the nourishment they are to provide. The question is thus reiterated, but this time it is addressed to the apostles (9:18-20) and the author spells out the implications of faith in Jesus, the Christ of God, for the life of Jesus (9:21-22) and the apostles (9:23-27). In order to fulfill their mission the apostles must share Jesus' own commitment unto death. Jesus' identity is then manifested to the three whom he had first called, Peter, and his partners James and John (Lk 9:28-36; see 5:1-11).

Luke has thus established a literary link between the apostolic mission and three important gospel themes: Jesus' identity as defined by the passion-resurrection, the conditions of discipleship, and the transfiguration experience. In Mark the latter are given a distinct and more elaborate development (Mk 8:27-9:29) in the first section (Mk 8:27-10:52) of the gospel's second major unit (Mk 8:27-16:8). The result of Luke's transposition is that Jesus' teaching on discipleship is immediately directed to the christian life attitudes required of those engaged in the apostolic mission.

*Jesus' Identity.*
*9:18-22.*

Jesus raised the question of his identity while alone at prayer with his disciples (9:18-20; compare Mk 8:27). Prayer is the ordinary Lukan context for disclosures of Jesus' identity (3:21-22; 9:28) and divine commissions. The opening section of the dialogue (9:18b-19) recalls Herod's earlier questioning (9:7-8; see Mk 6:14-16). However, as in Mk 8:29, the dialogue suddenly focuses on the disciples, and it is Peter who responds (9:20). His response expands Mark's "You are the Christ" (Mk 8:29) to "the Christ of God" and provides a christological link between Peter's faith proclamation (9:20) and the heavenly manifestation of Jesus as God's Son at the end of the transfiguration scene (9:35).

Jesus' charge that the disciples not speak of his identity (9:21) is related to the first prediction of the passion and resurrection (9:22) but the precise nature of the relationship is not taken up until 9:45. As in the case of Jesus' identity (9:7-9, 18-20), Luke thus develops this second issue in gradual narrative stages. For the present, it sufficed to affirm that the Christ of God (9:20) is also the Son of man who must suffer, be rejected and killed and on the third day be raised. As we shall see, the necessity in question is relative to both the word of Jesus and the biblical word of God.

## Conditions of Missionary Discipleship.
9:23-27.

Luke's insistence on the necessity of Jesus' suffering death is not a purely christological issue. The same necessity defines the life of those who would be Jesus' followers. Unlike Mark, however, who transmits the saying concerning self-denial and the assumption of the cross in the absolute terms of a radical challenge (Mk 8:34), Luke calls for a "daily" taking up of one's cross (Lk 9:23). The christian life is thus lived in the every-day of on-going history.

Further sayings present the most fundamental paradox of Jesus' teaching: a life bent on personal survival is a life lost, but a life lost for Jesus' sake is a life saved (9:24). Such indeed is the message of the death and resurrection of Jesus whose steps the Christians must follow (9:22-24). Nothing else can be counted for gain (9:25). With Mk 8:38, Luke then announces the fate of those who would be ashamed of Jesus' paradox and of its manifestation in Jesus' own life, which led to death and resurrection. Hope is then held out in the promise that some of Jesus' hearers would not die before seeing the reign of God (9:27). However, whereas Mk 8:38-9:1 refers to Jesus' ultimate eschatological return, Luke adapts the saying to Jesus' post-Easter presence, an outlook consistent with his view of Christianity's commitment to the daily life of history.

*Full Manifestation.*
*9:28-36.*

The ensuing narrative of Jesus' transfiguration (9:28-36) recalls the heavenly revelation of Jesus' divine sonship after his baptism (3:21-22). As in the latter instance, the event takes place while Jesus is at prayer. In the present case, however, the first three disciples, Peter, John and James (see 5:1-11) have joined Jesus at prayer, and it is they who are addressed by the voice from the cloud (9:34-35). In the context of 9:1-36, the voice represents the final manifestation of Jesus' identity, affirming the divine sonship and divinely chosen status of the suffering Son of man. The apostles are consequently to listen to him (9:35) as he sets forth the conditions for the following of Christ in the apostolic mission (9:21-27). Just as the question of Jesus' identity had been raised in the context of prayer, so also its revelation (9:28). For Luke, prayer is thus the experiential setting for the quest and discovery of the meaning of Jesus.

Even as he affirms the divine sonship of the Son of man who must suffer and be put to death, Luke never loses sight of the cross. For the disciples and Luke's readers, that cross entails the departure or *exodos* of Jesus (9:31), which is the subject of the conversation between Jesus, Moses and Elijah. In jewish thought, these two biblical figures, who had been mysteriously taken up into the heavens, were expected to return at the end of time. In keeping with the tradition, Mark had introduced them as symbols of Christ's return (Mk 9:2-8). In Luke, however, the symbolism is reversed, and they serve to emphasize the necessity of Jesus' death-resurrection-ascension, which is here designated as Jesus' *exodos*.

The apostles must consequently understand and accept that Jesus' identity requires his departure and that their apostolic mission must be fulfilled in his historical absence. The transfiguration event thus counters expectations that Jesus would soon return and helps Christians to cope with the seeming meaninglessness of life in Jesus' absence (see 2:41-51; 4:16-44). It also prepares the reader for Jesus' great journey to Jerusalem, which is framed by the ascension theme (9:51; 24:50-53), as well as for Acts' narrative of the foundations of the apostolic mission (Acts 1:6-11; 3:19-21).

After the transfiguration, Jesus does not command silence. Rather, the disciples themselves are said to have remained silent and to have told no one of what they had seen (9:36; see 9:21,45).

## 4. c. Problems in the Mission.

*The Son of man is to be delivered into the hands of men.* 9:37-50.

[37]On the next day, when they had come down from the mountain, a great crowd met him. [38]And behold, a man from the crowd cried, "Teacher, I beg you to look upon my son, for he is my only child; [39]and behold, a spirit seizes him, and he suddenly cries out: it convulses him till he foams, and shatters him, and will hardly leave him. [40]And I begged your disciples to cast it out, but they could not." [41]Jesus answered, "O faithless and perverse generation, how long am I to be with you and bear with you? Bring your son here." [42]While he was coming, the demon tore him and convulsed him. But Jesus rebuked the unclean spirit, and healed the boy, and gave him back to his father. [43]And all were astonished at the majesty of God.

But while they were all marveling at everything he did, he said to his disciples, [44]"Let these words sink into your ears; for the Son of man is to be delivered into the hands of men." [45]But they did not understand this saying, and it was concealed from them, that they should not perceive it; and they were afraid to ask him about this saying.

[46]And an argument arose among them as to which of

them was the greatest. [47]But when Jesus perceived the thought of their hearts, he took a child and put him by his side, [48]and said to them, "Whoever receives this child in my name receives me, and whoever receives me receives him who sent me; for he who is least among you all is the one who is great."

[49]John answered, "Master, we saw a man casting out demons in your name, and we forbade him, because he does not follow with us." [50]But Jesus said to him, "Do not forbid him; for he that is not against you is for you."

The final section of 9:1-50 focuses on key problems and difficulties in the apostolic mission (9:37-50). The disciples' inability to cast out evil (9:37-40) like Jesus had done (9:41-43a; see 4:1-13) stems from their failure to grasp the implications of Jesus' passion for the life of his followers (9:43b-44). What had been concealed from the apostolic community (9:45) is now revealed by the narrator who spells out the demands of apostolic discipleship in relation to the community's internal (9:46-48) and external relationships (9:49-50).

The section opens with a dramatic confrontation (9:37-43a), in which an unclean spirit's action (9:42) enables us to grasp the deeper pervasive reality which Jesus confronted and which his followers must confront. This singular incident, which concerns an epileptic boy, is consequently symbolic of the general power of evil which finds concrete expression in the various struggles of daily life. The author thus moves us to penetrate beneath the surface of particular challenges and to recognize that the ultimate issue in the christian life and mission is evil itself.

Correlatively, Jesus' cure of the epileptic boy manifests his victory over evil and its destructive effects on human life. Like the boy's seizure, Jesus' action reveals a deeper reality which is the majesty of God (9:43a; see 24:19; Acts 2:22). Luke thus presents this particular incident, in which Jesus cures an epileptic, as God's victorious confrontation with evil.

The Lukan narrative follows the general pattern first set by Mk 9:14-29 but as traditionally interpreted and abbreviated in the communities of both Luke and Matthew (Mt 17:14-20). Unlike Mark and Matthew, however, who emphasize the role of faith in those who seek healing (Mk 9:23-24) and of prayer (Mk 9:29) or faith (Mt 17:20) in the healer, Luke views the incident from the point of view of God's action (9:43a) in overcoming evil through the work of Christ (9:21), his Son and Chosen (9:35).

In both Mark and Matthew, the disciples inquired into the reason for their inability to cast out the evil spirit. As we have indicated, Jesus answered them in terms of faith and prayer. Luke retained neither the disciples' question nor the answers provided by the other synoptics. Instead, he associated the apostles' failure with Jesus' passion and death (9:43b-44). While granting that Jesus' cure was astonishing (9:43a) and marvelous (9:43b), Luke asks the followers to recognize the coming passion as the source of power over evil (see 24:19-21,26). At that point in history, however, they were unable to perceive what Jesus meant and they feared to ask (9:45). Only later would their minds be opened to understanding (24:45) what for the present was concealed from them (9:45).

In Luke, Jesus' second prediction of the passion (9:44), which unlike Mk 9:30-31 and Mt 17:22-23 makes no mention of the resurrection, has been incorporated into an account of Jesus' victory over evil. The incident with the epileptic must consequently be seen in relation to the over-all mission of Jesus. His cure of the epileptic can only be understood as an expression of a fundamental intention which would be fulfilled in Jesus' death and its ultimate overcoming of evil.

Unable to understand Jesus' word concerning the passion and the source of all power over evil (9:45), the disciples begin to argue as to who was the greatest among them. Reading their hearts, Jesus placed a child by his side (9:47) and declared that whoever received the child in his name received him and whoever received him received the one who sent him (9:48a; see 10:16). He who is the least among the disciples is the one who is great (9:48b; see 22:24-27).

Paradoxically, the child is thus the model for discipleship and christian greatness, and becoming like a child is a condition for understanding what was now concealed from the disciples. What this implied would be revealed in the resurrection, an aspect of Jesus' mystery which was omitted from the passion prediction (9:44). In 10:16, 21-24, the author would pursue this theme in relation to the disciples' mission, which was the original context of 9:48a. As supplemented by 9:48b, however, the mission statement is used to define the attitudes of disciples within the mission community. Further elaboration in Jesus' farewell discourse at the last supper (22:24-27) indicates that in Luke's estimation the question of human status and greatness was an important problem in the communities for which he wrote.

Luke then turns to the matter of other followers who cast out demons in Jesus' name. The disciples in the Lukan communities rejected the mission of those who were followers of Jesus but who were not of their own communities (9:49). Jesus responds with a simple principle that whoever is not against them is for them (9:50). Prepared by the general statement concerning whoever receives a child in Jesus' name, this brief concluding unit brings us back to the basic issue in the christian mission, that is victory over evil (9:37-43a). Success in this mission called for a faith-understanding of Jesus' passion and death, an understanding which would be revealed only to those who accepted to be the least (9:46-48) and who remained open to the work of christian communities other than their own (9:49-50). While we cannot name which communities Luke had in mind, the affirmation is an indication of growing awareness that communities which had originated from different missions were now interrelated in Christ's victory over evil.

## C. The Journey.
## *Jesus and the Destiny of the Church.*
## *9:51-24:53.*

The story of Jesus, a narrative of the human life and message of the Son of God, began with an introductory unit (4:14-44) and moved into an account of his mission (5:1-9:50). In that account Luke showed how the Church originated in the life and work of Jesus.

The story of Jesus now takes up his great journey to Jerusalem, a journey which would lead him out of history into the heavenly sphere (9:51-24:53). This journey is also that of the Church, which accompanies Jesus on his way to God. Thematically, it points to the Church's destiny and shows how the christian life-mission derives meaning and energy from its fulfillment in God. Literarily, the journey provides the entire section with a strong sense of movement and direction. Moved by its past and building on its origins in the historical life of Jesus, the Church is drawn by its future and that ultimate moment when it will join the ascended Lord.

In terms of christian tradition, the Lukan journey narrative represents a major development of Mark's journey motif (Mk 10:32-11:11) and of Jesus' challenge that the disciples follow him and assume his way of life (Mk 8:34; 10:52). In terms of Jesus' life, it was inspired by the historic ascent to Jerusalem which climaxed in his death and new life. In scriptural terms, the journey theme had long roots in the sapiential imagery of walking in the way of the Lord and in the account of Israel's exodus from Egypt (see 9:31).

While Luke's development of the journey motif is related to Mark, however, it also is quite different. In Mark, the journey focused on the disciples' need to accept and assume Jesus' way of the cross. While this is not absent in Luke (see 9:23), emphasis is on Jesus' departure from history (9:31), a divinely ordained event, whose acceptance was absolutely essential for assuming the universal mission.

Within Luke's gospel, the journey and its necessity had been prepared in the conclusion of the prologue (2:41-51), in the programmatic presentation of Jesus' life and mission (4:30, 42-43), and in the transfiguration narrative (9:31). The events of Jesus' exodus had also been outlined in two predictions of the passion (9:22,44). Until now, however, the significance of all these things had remained hidden (2:50; 9:45). The journey narrative describes the process through which the meaning of Jesus' exodus was revealed to those who accompanied him and remained faithful to the end. A further journey narrative, in which Paul proceeds through Jerusalem to the gentile world of Rome (Acts 19:21-28:31) will provide a more specific and historically oriented paradigm for the christian journey of those who accepted Jesus' exodus-ascension.

The journey includes four stages, which correspond to the four major sections of the narrative. These stages are geographical, but only in the broadest terms. Primary emphasis is on the various aspects of christian life.

In the first stage, Jesus expands the core group of apostles and disciples to include the seventy or seventy-two and presents the basic attitudes required to pursue Jesus' way to God. It is situated in the villages of Galilee (9:51-13:21).

In the second stage, he shows how the journey is a way of salvation and develops its implications for table fellowship, for family, economic and political relationships and for the course of christian history, which entailed Jerusalem's rejection of Jesus and God's rejection of Jerusalem. Geographically, it moves from Galilee to Jerusalem (13:22-19:48).

In the third stage, Jesus teaches the various groups which participated in the gospel story and which either rejected or struggled with his challenge. In each of its units, Jesus addresses the specific issue which deterred a particular group from joining him on the way (20:1-21:38). It is situated in the temple of Jerusalem.

In the fourth and final stage, Luke presents the journey's definitive fulfillment in the passion, crucifixion, resurrection and ascension of Jesus. Jesus' journey involves betrayal, condemnation and death. However, it is not a way of despair. Accepted as inevitable and divinely ordained, Jesus' death is a gift of life. As an ascension to God in which all are blessed, Jesus' journey is a way of hope. Theologically, the journey now moves from Jerusalem to God (22:1-24:53).

## C. 1. IN THE VILLAGES OF GALILEE.
## DISPOSITIONS AND ORIENTATION
## FOR THE CHRISTIAN JOURNEY.
## 9:51-13:21.

The first section of the journey narrative (9:51-13:21) opens with a long introductory unit which sets the christian journey in the fundamental context of mission (9:51-10:37). It then takes up various life contexts, activities and relationships and develops the basic dispositions necessary for those who join Jesus in the missionary journey (10:38-11:54). Its third long unit provides a general orientation for the journey's final crisis and judgment (12:1-13:21).

Throughout the section, the author is extremely sensitive to the life and attitudes of his addressees and to their particular moment of history. However, he is also careful to situate that moment within the greater patterns of the history of salvation.

Structurally, the introductory unit (9:51-10:37) is framed by the Samaritan question. During Jesus' historical journey, the Samaritans had rejected Jesus because of his Jerusalem destination (9:52-53). However, they were not to be condemned (9:54-56). The time would come when they would transcend their long-standing antipathy for the Jews, reveal themselves true neighbors, and challenge the Jews who failed to love their neighbor (10:30-37; Acts 1:8; 8:4-25).

The unit is also structured in parallel fashion (9:51-62; 10:1-37). Both the story of the first messengers (9:51-56) and that of the seventy (10:1-24) include a commissioning statement (9:52; 10:1-16), an indication of the missionaries' reception (9:53; 10:17b), their reaction (9:54; 10:17a), and Jesus' teaching relative to their failure or success (9:55; 10:18-24). Similarly, both of these stories are followed by important teaching on the response of those who encounter Jesus and the disciples on the way (9:57-62; 10:25-37).

The difference between the two parallel units is extremely significant. First there was the mission of those who accompanied Jesus to the ascension (9:51-62). This mission, however, was followed by that of the enlarged community which pursued Jesus' work from the ascension to the Lord's final judgment (10:1-37). The more extensive treatment given the latter is indicative of Luke's primary concern with the ongoing mission journey to the Church. By presenting that journey within the gospel narrative as well as in Acts, he also shows how the missions of Jesus and the Church are interrelated and continuous.

In general, the first part of the introduction looks to the first part of the body, whose four units focus on the Lord's word (10:38-42), prayer (11:1-13), power (11:14-36), and authenticity (11:37-54). The second part of the introduction (10:1-37) orients the reader toward the second part of the body, which deals with the final crisis and judgment (12:1-13:21). Its five units relate to persecution (12:1-12), possessions, security and readiness (12:13-40), service and retribution (12:41-53), interpreting the signs of the times (12:54-13:9), and the distinction between the development of the kingdom and the life of the Pharisees (13:10-21).

1. a. Introduction: the Missionary Journey.

    i. The Journey Begins.
    *He sets his face to go to Jerusalem.*
    9:51-56.

        51When the days drew near for him to be received up, he set his face to go to Jerusalem. 52And he sent messengers ahead of him, who went and entered a village of

> the Samaritans, to make ready for him; [53]but the people would not receive him, because his face was set toward Jerusalem. [54]And when his disciples James and John saw it, they said, "Lord, do you want us to bid fire come down from heaven and consume them?" [55]But he turned and rebuked them. [56]And they went on to another village.

Luke 9:51 introduces the journey which underlies the remainder of the gospel and defines that journey in terms of its destination, namely Jerusalem. Jerusalem, however, is no mere geographical locus. Luke presents the city which in fact marked the journey's end as the place where Jesus would "be received up," an expression which refers to the ascension. Jesus' journey is thus a journey to God, and Jerusalem is both a geographical point and a symbol of the journey's heavenly fulfillment beyond every earthly reality.

By referring to the ascension, the journey's opening verse also indicates the literary limits of the journey narrative, which extends to the very end of the gospel (9:51-24:53). This is corroborated by the fact that although Luke repeatedly refers to the journey to Jerusalem (9:51-56,57; 10:38; 13:22; 17:11; 18:31; 19:11,28,37,41), he never indicates that Jesus has actually arrived. At the point when such an indication would have been appropriate, he simply states that Jesus entered the temple (19:45), and the journey appears incomplete.

In his reference to Jesus' ascension, Luke uses a noun which is based on the passive form of the verb. Jesus is consequently not viewed as the agent of his own ascension but as its beneficiary. The agent, who remains implicit, is God. The event, however is fully accepted by Jesus, who deliberately "set his face to go to Jerusalem."

After introducing the journey, Luke draws attention to the disciples, messengers sent ahead of Jesus to prepare the way (9:52). The messengers thus recapitulate the role of John the Baptist. However, whereas John had been sent to prepare the way for Jesus' advent (Lk 3:4), the messengers were commissioned to prepare his exodus-ascension. Accordingly, their attitude could not be that of John and his proclamation of apocalyptic judgment (Lk 3:16-17; 9:53-56). While the theme of consuming fire was associated with the Lord's definitive coming (10:10-15) after Christianity's movement from Jerusalem to the ends of the earth (Acts 1:6-8), it had to be divorced from Jesus' departure and the beginnings of the christian community's mission in history. Fire would indeed follow the ascension, but it would be the transforming, sanctifying and empowering fire of the promised Spirit (Lk 3:16; Acts 1:5,8; 2:3-4).

Rejected by the Samaritans because Jesus set his face toward Jerusalem, the messengers ask the Lord if he wants them to invoke destructive fire upon them (9:53-54). Rebuked by Jesus, they went on to another village, and the narrative is set for the first stage of the journey which is situated in the villages of Galilee (9:55-56).

Since Jerusalem is a symbol for the ascension, the Samaritan rejection of Jesus and his messengers is grounded in their refusal to accept Jesus' departure from history as an event integral to the history of salvation and the christian mission. The event thus points to a major problem in the Lukan communities, which suffered from Jesus' absence.

i. (cont.) The Following of Jesus.
*The Son of man has nowhere to lay his head.*
9:57-62.

[57]As they were going along the road, a man said to him, "I will follow you wherever you go." [58]And Jesus said to him, "Foxes have holes, and birds of the air have nests; but the Son of man has nowhere to lay his head." [59]To another he said, "Follow me." But he said, "Lord, let me first go and bury my father." [60]But he said to him, "Leave the dead to bury their own dead; but as for you,

> go and proclaim the kingdom of God." [61]Another said,
> "I will follow you, Lord; but let me first say farewell to
> those at my home."[62]Jesus said to him, "No one who puts
> his hand to the plow and looks back is fit for the kingdom
> of God."

In 9:51-56, the disciples had been sent ahead as messengers to prepare Jesus' way. In 9:57-62, they proceed in his company (see 9:56). Luke's concern, however, is not so much with the actual disciples as with those whom they encountered along the way. As so often happened in the story of the mission (5:1-9;50), Jesus himself responds to problems which arose in the life of the missionary community. Christian attitudes and policy are thus endowed with the authority of Jesus, the Son of man (9:58) who is Lord (9:59,61).

Three anonymous figures emerge as types of every person who considers following Jesus on his journey. Those who wish to join Jesus must disengage themselves from any earthly home (9:57-58), from former responsibilities (9:59-60) and from past relationships (9:61-62). Those who proclaim the kingdom of God must live in a manner befitting the kingdom (9:60,62) and bid farewell to their historical past. Setting out on the journey to Jerusalem and the ascension, Jesus had demonstrated a singular detachment from earthly matters. That detachment must now be reflected in the way of life of his first disciples and of all who would join them on the journey.

### ii. The Mission of the Seventy.
*He who hears you hears me.*
10:1-24.

> **10** After this the Lord appointed seventy others, and
> sent them on ahead of him, two by two, into every town
> and place where he himself was about to come. [2]And he
> said to them, "The harvest is plentiful, but the laborers

are few; pray therefore the Lord of the harvest to send out laborers into his harvest. ³Go your way; behold, I send you out as lambs in the midst of wolves. ⁴Carry no purse, no bag, no sandals; and salute no one on the road. ⁵Whatever house you enter, first say, 'Peace be to this house!' ⁶And if a son of peace is there, your peace shall rest upon him; but if not, it shall return to you. ⁷And remain in the same house, eating and drinking what they provide, for the laborer deserves his wages; do not go from house to house. ⁸Whenever you enter a town and they receive you, eat what is set before you; ⁹heal the sick in it and say to them, 'The kingdom of God has come near to you.' ¹⁰But whenever you enter a town and they do not receive you, go into its streets and say, ¹¹'Even the dust of your town that clings to our feet, we wipe off against you; nevertheless know this, that the kingdom of God has come near.' ¹²I tell you, it shall be more tolerable on that day for Sodom than for that town.

¹³"Woe to you, Chorazin! woe to you, Bethsaida! for if the mighty works done in you had been done in Tyre and Sidon, they would have repented long ago, sitting in sackcloth and ashes. ¹⁴But it shall be more tolerable in the judgment for Tyre and Sidon than for you. ¹⁵And you, Capernaum, will you be exalted to heaven? You shall be brought down to Hades.

¹⁶"He who hears you hears me, and he who rejects you rejects me, and he who rejects me rejects him who sent me."

¹⁷The seventy returned with joy, saying, "Lord, even the demons are subject to us in your name!" ¹⁸And he said to them, "I saw Satan fall like lightning from heaven. ¹⁹Behold, I have given you authority to tread upon serpents and scorpions, and over all the power of the enemy; and nothing shall hurt you. ²⁰Nevertheless do not rejoice in this, that the spirits are subject to you; but rejoice that your names are written in heaven."

²¹In that same hour he rejoiced in the Holy Spirit and said, "I thank thee, Father, Lord of heaven and earth,

that thou hast hidden these things from the wise and understanding and revealed them to babes; yea, Father, for such was thy gracious will. [22]All things have been delivered to me by my Father; and no one knows who the Son is except the Father, or who the Father is except the Son and any one to whom the Son chooses to reveal him."

[23]Then turning to the disciples he said privately, "Blessed are the eyes which see what you see! [24]For I tell you that many prophets and kings desired to see what you see, and did not see it, and to hear what you hear, and did not hear it."

Once Jesus had set his face toward Jerusalem (9:51), sent messengers on ahead (9:52-56), and challenged those who would follow him on the journey (9:57-62), he enlarged the mission group of the Twelve (9:1-6) by appointing an additional seventy (10:1-16) from among those who accepted to follow him (9:57-62). Like the messengers in 9:52-56, they too are sent on ahead of Jesus (10:1). Their function, however, looks beyond Jesus' departure and is seen as a preparation for the eventual day of judgment (10:12-14). Hence the text's hard-headed emphasis on eschatological judgment (10:10-15), an attitude which contrasts sharply with that of the messengers in 9:52-56. Hence also the account's preoccupation with establishing a clear line of continuity between Jesus, the earliest disciples and the seventy (10:16-20) as well as with the revelation of what had formerly been hidden (10:21-24; see 9:45).

Living in Jesus' absence, the seventy actualize the presence of the Lord (see 10:1) in the historical years between his ascension and the definitive consummation of history (10:16). Jesus' journey thus provides the community with a pattern for its eschatological mission as well as for its journey to God.

In relation to tradition, the first part (10:1-12) of the mission of the seventy (10:1-24) is a creative Lukan composition based on Mark's account of the mission of the

Twelve (Mk 6:7-13), which also underlies Lk 9:1-6. The latter, however, made no mention of the apostles' being sent out two by two (Mk 6:7). This element had been reserved for the mission of the seventy, whose roots lay in the story of Jesus but which was deployed in the community's post-ascension history. While it may appear as a relatively minor detail, the journeying in pairs provides an important element for understanding Lk 24:13-35, a story concerning one of the pairs which Jesus had sent on mission (24:13). It also provides an element of continuity with the mission of John the Baptist, who also sent his disciples out in pairs (7:19).

Within the basic narrative structure provided by Mk 6:7-13, Luke introduced a number of significant elements. The injunction to pray that additional laborers be sent to work in the plentiful harvest (10:2; see Mt 9:37-38) corresponds to the vastly expanded scope of the Church's post-ascension mission. The peace greeting (10:5) which points to the proximity of the kingdom of God (10:9,11) evokes the characteristic greeting of the risen Lord in the assembled community (Jn 20:19,21,26; see Lk 7:50).

The most significant Lukan addition, however, is the seventy themselves. Like the Twelve, the seventy are related to the origins of Israel. In Num 11:16-25, we read that Moses was ordered to gather seventy men of the elders of Israel. These men would receive some of the spirit which God had given to Moses, and they would assist him in leading the people. The fact that two further men, who stayed behind in the camp, would also receive that spirit, which was a spirit of prophecy (Num 11:26-30), may account for the variant reading "seventy-two" which appears in some important manuscripts. In light of Num 11, the seventy whom Jesus commissioned prefigure the elders who lead the Lukan communities (see Acts 14:23). Like Jesus and the Twelve, the seventy were endowed with the Spirit and their role was to prophetically strengthen the souls of the disciples (Acts 14:22).

Supplementing Mk 6:7-13, Luke then expands Jesus' teaching concerning the mission. Beginning with a "woe" (10:13-15) and concluding with a beatitude (10:23-24), the additions provide a rich and concise expression of the theological basis of the christian mission during the post-ascension era.

First, a "woe" anticipates the Jews' future rejection of those commissioned by Jesus as well as the gentile world's openness to them (10:13-15). The passage thus sets the stage for the story of the good Samaritan (10:25-37). The reason for Jesus' judgment is then outlined. Since the missionaries represent Jesus in history, to hear or reject them is to hear or reject Jesus as well as him who had sent Jesus (10:16). Like 10:2, both of these additions are drawn from a tradition of Jesus' sayings (see Mt 11:21-23; 10:40). Rejection is then transposed from the sphere of ordinary history to the deeper level of the community's encounter with evil itself (10:17-20; see 9:37-43a). Just as demons had been subject to Jesus, so now to those who continue to speak in his name (10:17) and whose authority they enjoy (10:19). Associated with demons, Satan and the enemy, the serpents evoke Gen 3 and prepare the reader for Paul's episode with a symbolic serpent in Acts 28:1-6.

The account then turns to the theme of revelation (10:21-22) and manifestation (10:23-24). Those who continue Jesus' historical mission and speak in his name (10:16-20) may be mere babes (see 9:46-48), but it was to these that the Father revealed these things through the Son (10:21-22). The object of this revelation is precisely what had been set forth in 10:16 and 17-20. Cast in the form of a prayer, this same teaching (Mt 11:25-27) received a distinct setting in Matthew's long discussion concerning John the Baptist (Mt 11:2-30).

By contrast with Chorazin, Bethsaida and Capernaum (10:13-15), the seventy are consequently truly blessed. Even prophets and kings had not seen and heard what they see and hear (10:23-24).

ii. (cont.)    The Way to Eternal Life.
*Do this, and you will live.*
10:25-37.

[25]And behold, a lawyer stood up to put him to the test, saying, "Teacher, what shall I do to inherit eternal life?" [26]He said to him, "What is written in the law? How do you read?" [27]And he answered, "You shall love the Lord your God with all your heart, and with all your soul, and with all your strength, and with all your mind; and your neighbor as yourself." [28]And he said to him, "You have answered right; do this, and you will live."

[29]But he, desiring to justify himself, said to Jesus, "And who is my neighbor?" [30]Jesus replied, "A man was going down from Jerusalem to Jericho, and he fell among robbers, who stripped him and beat him, and departed, leaving him half dead. [31]Now by chance a priest was going down the road; and when he saw him he passed by on the other side. [32]So likewise a Levite, when he came to the place and saw him, passed by on the other side. [33]But a Samaritan, as he journeyed, came to where he was; and when he saw him, he had compassion, [34]and went to him and bound up his wounds, pouring on oil and wine; then he set him on his own beast and brought him to an inn, and took care of him. [35]And the next day he took out two denarii and gave them to the innkeeper, saying, "Take care of him; and whatever more you spend, I will repay you when I come back.' [36]Which of these three, do you think, proved neighbor to the man who fell among the robbers?" [37]He said, "The one who showed mercy on him." And Jesus said to him, "Go and do likewise."

The introduction (9:51-10:37) to the first section of the journey narrative (9:51-13:21) ends with a dialogue between Jesus and a lawyer who wished to put him to the test (10:25-37). Structurally and functionally, the unit is parallel to 9:57-62. The latter had focused on Jesus' challenge to those among whom he travelled with his disciples. The present unit dwells on those who responded to the mission of the seventy. As in 9:57-62, Luke invokes Jesus' authoritative word to resolve a difficult question in the gospel mission. The dialogue is developed in two stages (10:25-28, 29-37), of which the second includes Jesus' parable concerning a Samaritan who was a true neighbor (10:30-35).

The first stage in the dialogue opens with the lawyer's question as to what he must do to inherit eternal life (10:25). Recognizing the test, Jesus responds with a further question concerning what is written in the law and the lawyer's reading of it (10:26). He thus leads the lawyer to furnish his own answer in terms which were familiar and acceptable, especially for one who specialized in legal matters. The answer comes in the words of Dt 6:5 and Lv 19:18, and Jesus considers the response adequate. If the lawyer does indeed love the Lord and his neighbor, he will live (10:27-28). While the passage was inspired by Mk 12:28-33, Luke has transformed it by requiring that the lawyer and not Jesus answer the fundamental question.

In the first stage, Luke provided the context for the second, which brings us to the heart of the matter. What had begun as a lawyer's test of Jesus now becomes Jesus' test of the lawyer. Placed on the defensive, the latter returns to the charge with a further question. In an effort to justify his personal behavior in the matter of loving his neighbor, the lawyer inquires concerning his neighbor's identity (10:29).

Earlier Jesus had responded to the lawyer's questions with questions of his own. He now answers with a story in which three men came upon someone who had been robbed, beaten and abandoned half dead along the road from Jerusalem to Jericho (10:30-35). Of these three, a priest and a levite both saw the man, but they crossed over to the other side of the road and continued on their way. Both of these men represented respected and religiously honorable positions, and the lawyer no doubt would have been eager to include them among his neighbor. The third, however, was a Samaritan. As such he was mistrusted and despised by the Jews. However, it is he who cared for the stricken Jew, and he did so in a manner which far surpassed ordinary obligation and sense of fraternal decency. This Samaritan, whom the lawyer would probably have excluded from his neighbor, is thus presented as one who was fully worthy of being considered such and to whom the law of love consequently extended.

Having told the parable, Jesus again calls on the lawyer to answer his own questions (10:36; see 10:26). In so doing, however, he also transformed the question. For Jesus, the real question is not who is my neighbor but how does one prove oneself a true neighbor to others. The lawyer's question allowed for a distinction between those who are neighbor to us and those who are not and placed all responsibility for this distinction on others. Jesus' question places the responsibility for being a neighbor on the inquirer who must then be neighbor to all without distinction. The lawyer is then told to act like the Samaritan in showing mercy even to one who was foreign to his community (10:37).

## 1. b. Basic Dispositions.

### i. The Lord's Word.
*One thing is needful.*
10:38-42.

> [38]Now as they went on their way, he entered a village; and a woman named Martha received him into her house. [39]And she had a sister called Mary, who sat at the Lord's feet and listened to his teaching. [40]But Martha was distracted with much serving; and she went to him and said, "Lord, do you not care that my sister has left me to serve alone? Tell her then to help me." [41]But the Lord answered her, "Martha, Martha, you are anxious and troubled about many things; [42]one thing is needful. Mary has chosen the good portion, which shall not be taken away from her."

The body of the first stage in the journey narrative includes two sections (10:38-11:54; 12:1-13:21). The first opens with the story of Martha and Mary (10:38-42). This simple story, whose immediate setting is a meal in the home of Martha, draws attention to the most fundamental value in the lives of those who join Jesus on the great christian journey and receive him in the cities and villages which dot its way to God. That value is the very person of Jesus, the Lord, and the teaching or word which he imparts. The other episodes included in 10:38-11:54 develop various aspects of that word and prepare the reader for the body's second section, which deals with preparedness for the final crisis (12:1-13:21). The passage thus contributes to the historical theology of the word which was a major concern in the previous sections of the gospel.

The beginning of the section is marked by a reference to the journey (10:38; see 9:51-56,57). As in 9:57, the journey is not that of Jesus alone, but of Jesus together with those who have joined him (10:38a). In the actual account, however, those who accompany Jesus remain in the background and the whole action and dialogue focuses on Jesus, who acts as Lord and is recognized as such (10:38b-42; see 9:58-62). The episode thus addresses the day when Christians would look back to the historical Jesus to articulate the demands made on them by the presence of the risen Lord.

Prescinding from Jesus, who is the main personage in the entire gospel, Martha is the principal personage. It is she who receives Jesus into her home, who joins Jesus in dialogue, who presents a problem and whose problem is resolved. Mary, on the other hand is simply Martha's sister and an important source of Martha's problem, at least as she sees it.

From Martha's point of view, the problem is threefold: the demands of hospitality or table service are too great, she is alone in fulfilling them, and the Lord fails to note her plight (10:40). Her solution to the problem is that Jesus recognize her situation and take action by ordering her sister to help her in fulfilling her many tasks (10:40). The narrator had already indicated that Mary was sitting at the Lord's feet and listening to his word (10:39).

In his reponse, the Lord does not accept Martha's solution. Indeed, he does not accept her assessment of the problem. As in the story of the Samaritan who showed himself a true neighbor (10:30-37), he goes to the heart of the matter and tells Martha that her real problem is that she is anxious and troubled (10:41). As the narrator had indicated, she was "distracted with much serving" (10:40a). Consequently, it is not that Martha had too much to do but that she was making herself too busy with matters which were secondary and unneeded. The Lord's solution is that "one thing is needful," and that thing is exemplified by her sister who is attending to his person and listening to his word (10:42).

The unit thus points to the primacy of Jesus and his word in table fellowship and in the christian life which it epitomizes. Apart from these basic values, nothing else matters. A similar problem occurs in the life of the Jerusalem community, when the Twelve find themselves unable to cope with the demands of an expanding and increasingly diversified community. Overwhelmed by service at tables, they must expand the community's leadership structure in order to devote themselves to prayer and the ministry of the word (Acts 6:1-6). After the taking of appropriate action, the word of God continued to increase among the people (Acts 6:7).

ii. The Lord's Prayer.
*Lord, teach us to pray*.
11:1-13.

**11** He was praying in a certain place, and when he ceased, one of his disciples said to him, "Lord, teach us to pray, as John taught his disciples." [2]And he said to them, "When you pray, say:

"Father, hallowed be thy name. Thy kingdom come. [3]Give us each day our daily bread; [4]and forgive us our sins, for we ourselves forgive every one who is indebted to us; and lead us not into temptation."

[5]And he said to them, "Which of you who has a friend will go to him at midnight and say to him, 'Friend, lend me three loaves; [6]for a friend of mine has arrived on a journey, and I have nothing to set before him'; [7]and he will answer from within, 'Do not bother me; the door is now shut, and my children are with me in bed; I cannot get up and give you anything'? [8]I tell you, though he will not get up and give him anything because he is his friend, yet because of his importunity he will rise and give him whatever he needs. [9]And I tell you, Ask, and it will be given you; seek, and you will find; knock, and it will be opened to you. [10]For every one who asks receives, and he who seeks finds, and to him who knocks it will be opened. [11]What father among you, if his son asks for a fish, will instead of a fish give him a serpent; [12]or if he asks for an egg, will give him a scorpion? [13]If you then, who are evil, know how to give good gifts to your children, how much more will the heavenly Father give the Holy Spirit to those who ask him!"

In Luke-Acts, prayer is intimately associated with the word, common life, table fellowship and hospitality (see Lk 10:38-42; Acts 2:42; 6:1-7). Accordingly, the section moves from a unit on the word (10:38-42) to one on prayer (11:1-13). Like the story of Martha and Mary, the passage on prayer is related to christian sharing and common nourishment. The unit includes an introduction (11:1), the Lord's prayer (11:2-4), and a brief discourse on perseverance in prayer and on the grounds of hope (11:5-13).

In 3:21-22, Luke had distinguished Jesus from John the Baptist and showed how he received the Holy Spirit while he was praying. Endowed with the Spirit, Jesus was God's beloved Son. By implication, God was consequently Jesus'

Father. In the introduction to the present passage, we once again find Jesus at prayer. This time, however, he is in the company of his disciples. Once Jesus had ceased praying, the latter ask that he teach them "to pray, as John taught his disciples" (11:1). John's prayer does not express the identity of Jesus' disciples before God. The latter need a prayer which is adequate to their own specific identity as disciples of the Lord, and it is with the title Lord that they address Jesus (see 10:40). According to the prayer which Jesus imparts (11:2-4), they are to address God as Father. By implication, they consequently share in the Lord's divine life or sonship. Like Jesus (3:21-22), they too will receive the Holy Spirit, if they pray for it (11:13). The passage on prayer (11:1-13) thus distinguishes Jesus' disciples from those of John, just as 3:21-22 distinguished Jesus himself from John.

In the introduction to this section of the journey, Jesus had joyfully prayed in the Holy Spirit to the Father, the Lord of heaven and earth, who had delivered all things to him. As the Son and the human expression of the Father's lordship, Jesus reveals what is hidden concerning his identity to those whom he chooses (10:21-22). In the present passage, he now reveals how those whom he has chosen are related to the Father, what this relationship demands of them and what they can expect from it. The whole unit, including the Lord's prayer, develops the implications of the one thing that is needful (10:42) for the prayer life of those who have embarked on the christian journey.

The Lord's prayer (11:2-4) is the prayer of those who accept to follow Jesus on his journey to God, who recognize that it is necessary that he be with the Father (2:49) and that they too must press on in the christian mission toward the Father. It is the prayer of those who have received the promise of the Holy Spirit (11:13; Acts 1:4-5). As such it is truly the Lord's prayer and not merely the prayer of Jesus. Inspired by the prayer of the historical Jesus, it is the prayer of those who have been taught by the experience of the risen Lord and who know that they are God's sons and daughters. Before his death, Jesus had only begun to act and teach (Acts 1:1). After his resurrection, when God made him Lord (Acts 2:36), he continued to do so. The Lord's prayer reflects the fullness of that teaching, and its petitions reflect the challenges of the post-ascension Church, a Church which has been enriched by the fulfillment of all that had been divinely ordained in his regard.

In view of the nature of the Lord's prayer, the differences between the Lukan (11:2-4) and the Matthean (6:9-13) traditions appear extremely significant. The main problem, however is not to find the prayer's original wording as it sprang from Jesus, but to explore the rich potential which Jesus' prayer held for historically distinct communities. That potential, at least in part, is revealed by the two gospel traditions.

The authenticity of the Lord's prayer does not hinge on what Jesus might have taught during his historical life but on how the prayer articulates the identity of a particular christian community with the specific challenges thrust upon it by its stance in history. It also hinges on how its formulation has integrated the passion and resurrection events which provide Jesus' historical teaching with its ultimate meaning.

The Matthean and Lukan communities were both profoundly christian and rooted in Jesus' life, death and resurrection. Their respective versions of the Lord's prayer are consequently very similar in their basic elements. However, since these communities were also quite different with regard to their historical development, ethnic composition and position vis-à-vis Judaism and the Greco-Roman world, their statement of the Lord's prayer was also bound to reflect these differences within a common Christianity.

The Lukan tradition of the Lord's prayer is markedly shorter than Matthew's. Structurally, it includes a simple address and two sets of petitions, of which the first presents two petitions and the second presents three. In the Matthean tradition, the address and the two sets of petitions have all been amplified by material which extends the prayer's three structural units. These "additions" reflect the Matthean community's on-going rootedness in jewish tradition.

At various points, and in particular in the second set of petitions, the Lukan wording is quite different from that of Matthew. These differences reflect the gentile world of Luke and the stance which he and his communities have taken with regard to history and their role in it.

In the following analysis of the prayer's structure, the specifically Matthean elements or additions are given in italics, and other textual differences are added in parenthesis and in italics. The wording follows the order of the Greek text.

Address
    Father *our, who art in heaven,*
First Set of Petitions
    hallowed be thy name.
    Thy kingdom come.
    *Thy will be done, on earth as it is in heaven.*
Second Set of Petitions
    Our daily bread, give us each day (*today*);
    and forgive us our sins (*debts*)
        for (*as*) we also forgive (*we have forgiven*)
        everyone who is indebted to us (*our debtors*);
    and lead us not into temptation
    *but deliver us from evil.*

An additional difference appears in the petition for bread. Whereas Matthew's form of the verb (aorist) presupposes a single action, Luke's form (present) calls for repeated action.

In order to appreciate the import of the address and of the individual petitions, we should first see how they are dynamically related to one another. All five petitions are addressed to the Father, the source of life as it historically unfolds. The two sets, however, are quite different. In the first, Christians formulate their essential vision for life and history and ask that it be fulfilled. In the second, they ask for the means to take part in its fulfillment. The second set of petitions thus pertains to the christian mission, while the first looks to the goal which draws it forward.

By addressing God as Father, Christians acknowledge their divine filiation. The basis of their prayer is thus a life which together they share in the Lord. God may be Father of all, but for those who have experienced the risen Lord and received the Holy Spirit, he is Father in a special way. It is specifically as Christians that those who have joined Jesus on the journey address God as Father.

God is holy. Since his name is his manifestation in human life and history, Christians pray that the Father's self-manifestation be truly reflected in their own lives as well as in those of all to whom they are sent. In the first petition, they consequently pray that God's holiness be revealed and communicated in the holiness of men and women.

God is Lord of history. Since his lordship requires that all subject themselves to his dominion, Christians pray that God's universal dominion be concretely reflected in human life and society. In the second petition, they consequently pray that God's dominion vanquish the dominion of evil (see 4:5-8) as history moves toward its fulfillment when all shall serve him alone (see 4:8).

God is the source of bread and christian fellowship. In the second set of petitions Christians consequently pray that their Father provide them with a truly christian meal, the meal which is characteristic of their life relationships and which is open to all. Through this meal which transcends all ethnic, social and economic differences, they will bring about the kingdom of God (14:15). The prayer for bread is thus a prayer for the breaking of bread (see 24:13-35; Acts 2:42-47), the Lukan term for the Eucharist.

God is the one who forgives sins. In the fourth petition, Christians consequently pray that their Father forgive them their sins. At the same time, however, they recognize their own responsibility in expressing his forgiveness to others (17:3-4). In the prayer for forgiveness, they thus pray that God's forgiveness be extended to them through their very act of extending it to others. In forgiving, they are forgiven, and this is manifested especially in their breaking of bread, when like Jesus they express solidarity with all who repent (5:27-32; 7:36-50).

God is one who protects and strengthens. In the fifth and final petition, the Christians consequently ask that he assist them in order that when tempted they might never give in or enter into temptation. By responding to temptation as Jesus had done (4:1-13), their lives will contribute to the hallowing of the Father's name and the full manifestation of his kingdom or dominion.

After teaching his disciples to pray as John had taught his disciples, the Lord Jesus added a brief discourse on how the heavenly Father responds without fail to those who are persistent in prayer (11:5-13). Luke thus buttresses faltering communities, which do not see their prayer answered, by calling them to fidelity.

First we have a parable, a hypothetical situation in the life of the community in which someone goes to a friend who has already retired for the night with a request for bread that he might extend hospitality to another friend. In the parable, persistence finally overcomes resistance, and the request is granted (11:5-8).

The parable is then applied to the christian situation. Like the man who goes to his friend and who perseveres in his request until it is granted, Christians must not desist from prayer until it is answered, for it surely will be (11:9-10). The image of bread (11:5) develops one of the petitions in the Lord's prayer (11:3) and helps us to appreciate its nature. The christian prayer for bread is not a prayer for individual or personal sustenance but for a meal in which Christians share the bread which comes from the Father.

A second parable or hypothetical situation, which also focuses on nourishment, develops another aspect of prayer (11:11-12). Setting aside the relationship which obtains between friends (11:5-8), Luke takes up the familial father-son relationship and applies it to Christians who turn to their heavenly Father (11:13). The point of the parable is that a father responds to his son's request in a manner which corresponds to his genuine need. If a human father, who after all is part of sinful humanity, does not seek his son's destruction, how could anyone think that the heavenly Father will do otherwise?

It would thus appear that some members of the Lukan churches had given up hope that their prayer would be answered, or worse had concluded that God was responding to their prayer in a negative and destructive manner. For such Christians, who failed to understand the various forces which were assailing them from within and from without, Luke turned to Jesus' teaching and assembled the elements of an adequate attitude. Their prayer will be answered if they persevere, and the most fundamental answer will be in the form of the Holy Spirit (11:13), the energizing personal force in their christians life and mission. "Man shall not live by bread alone" (4:4).

iii. The Lord's Power.
   *Your eye is the lamp of your body.*
   11:14-36.

   [14]Now he was casting out a demon that was dumb; when the demon had gone out, the dumb man spoke, and the people marveled. [15]But some of them said, "He casts out demons by Beelzebul, the prince of demons"; [16]while others, to test him, sought from him a sign from heaven. [17]But he, knowing their thoughts, said to them, "Every kingdom divided against itself is laid waste, and a divided household falls. [18]And if Satan also is divided against himself, how will his kingdom stand? For you say that I

cast out demons by Beelzebul. [19]And if I cast out demons by Beelzebul, by whom do your sons cast them out? Therefore they shall be your judges. [20]But if it is by the finger of God that I cast out demons, then the kingdom of God has come upon you. [21]When a strong man, fully armed, guards his own palace, his goods are in peace; [22]but when one stronger than he assails him and overcomes him, he takes away his armor in which he trusted, and divides his spoil. [23]He who is not with me is against me, and he who does not gather with me scatters.

[24]"When the unclean spirit has gone out of a man, he passes through waterless places seeking rest; and finding none he says, 'I will return to my house from which I came.' [25]And when he comes he finds it swept and put in order. [26]Then he goes and brings seven other spirits more evil than himself, and they enter and dwell there; and the last state of that man becomes worse than the first."

[27]As he said this, a woman in the crowd raised her voice and said to him, "Blessed is the womb that bore you, and the breasts that you sucked!" [28]But he said, "Blessed rather are those who hear the word of God and keep it!"

[29]When the crowds were increasing, he began to say, "This generation is an evil generation; it seeks a sign, but no sign shall be given to it except the sign of Jonah. [30]For as Jonah became a sign to the men of Nineveh, so will the Son of man be to this generation. [31]The queen of the South will arise at the judgment with the men of this generation and condemn them; for she came from the ends of the earth to hear the wisdom of Solomon, and behold, something greater than Solomon is here. [32]The men of Nineveh will arise at the judgment with this generation and condemn it; for they repented at the preaching of Jonah, and behold, something greater than Jonah is here.

[33]"No one after lighting a lamp puts it in a cellar or under a bushel, but on a stand, that those who enter may

see the light. ³⁴Your eye is the lamp of your body; when your eye is sound, your whole body is full of light; but when it is not sound, your body is full of darkness. ³⁵Therefore be careful lest the light in you be darkness. ³⁶If then your whole body is full of light, having no part dark, it will be wholly bright, as when a lamp with its rays gives you light."

After treating of the Lord's word (10:38-42) and the Lord's prayer (11:1-13), the narrative focuses on the Lord's power (11:14-36), a power which springs from the Spirit (4:14) in whose fulness Jesus overcomes the forces of evil (4:1) as he effectively proclaims the good news to those in need of healing (4:18). In 11:14-36, Luke responds to those who no longer attribute the deployment of the Lord's power to the Spirit. Since its fruits appear to be evil (see 11:11-13), its source must be demonic.

The unit includes an introductory episode (11:14-16) and two sub-units in which Jesus responds to the reactions of two anonymous groups (11:17-28, 29-36). Its basic theme is the interpretation of Jesus' power in terms of its source, revelation and faith-acceptance.

The introductory episode shows Jesus casting out a demon from a dumb man (11:14a). The Lord thus vanquishes the evil which prevents a man from speaking. Those who attend to the Lord's word and have been taught to pray must also be able to speak that word. Three reactions to the Lord's act are noted. While the people in general marvel (11:14b), there are those who say that he casts out demons by the prince of demons (11:15), and there are others who seek a heavenly sign that Jesus' power is not demonic (11:16). In the two sub-units, Jesus takes up the latter two reactions in turn.

The Lord knows the thoughts of those around him. There is consequently no need for them to express their reaction to him (11:17a). In the first sub-unit, the Lord addresses those who have concluded that his power is from the prince of demons (11:15). First he responds directly to their evaluation of his power and challenges them to align themselves with him (11:17b-23). Having done so, he unveils the demonic source of their reaction (11:24-26) and affirms the conditions for divine blessedness (11:27-28). In the Lukan context, this teaching is addressed to faltering Christians who are out of step with Jesus' message in 10:38-42 (11:27-28). Like 11:5-13, the passage also focuses on themes included in the Lord's prayer, in particular the petition for the coming of the kingdom, for forgiveness, and for protection from succumbing to temptation.

Good cannot be the work of the evil one. From Satan's point of view, such activity would be self-destructive. What has been observed is not the power of Satan's kingdom but the superior power of God's kingdom. Those who do not recognize the true source of this power and accept it are against the Lord and unfaithful to their christian identity as expressed in the Lord's prayer (11:17b-23). In their reaction, those who think Jesus' power is demonic are themselves succumbing to evil. The simple fact that the Lord had cured them from the unclean spirit does not guarantee future freedom from its power (11:24-26). It is not enough to declare the human source of Jesus' life blessed. Rather the truly blessed are those who hear the word of God and keep it (11:27-28). In the second sub-unit, Luke takes up the matter of hearing the word of God (11:29-36). In the last unit of this section, he will deal with the question of keeping that word (11:37-54).

The second sub-unit (11:29-36) opens with the remark that the crowds around Jesus were increasing (11:29a). For Luke's readers, these crowds were meant to evoke the growing numbers who were gathering to hear the christian message.

Drawing on the tradition of Jesus' teaching, the author then challenges those community members who need a sign that Jesus' power is not demonic (11:29b-32). Like the Jews in Jesus' environment, they would receive none other than the sign of Jonah. They would see Jesus' power, faith and repentance move away from them to others who were far off. On the day of judgment, these new Ninivites, who recognized in Jesus something greater than Jonah, would arise to condemn them (11:29b-30,32). Just as a foreigner had recognized the wisdom of Solomon, foreigners would recognize the wisdom of the Lord's teaching, which transcended that of Solomon, and would arise to condemn them on the day of judgment (11:31). Jesus' message to the Nazareth synagogue (4:25-27) is thus re-addressed to the Lukan communities.

Those who thought Jesus' power was demonic had been healed of the unclean spirit only to fall into a worse state (11:24-26). In the same way, those who sought a sign had been illuminated by the lamp of faith, only to place it under a bushel and be once again filled with darkness. In this they contravene what the Lord had done on their behalf and what he intended to achieve through their mission (11:33-34). They must therefore take care not to mistake darkness for light but allow the light to fill their whole person, that they in turn might be a source of light for all who enter into their company (11:35-36,33b). This concluding emphasis on the interiority and fullness of light sets the stage for the next unit, where authenticity in the christian mission is related to interior darkness (11:37-54).

iv. The Lord's Authenticity.
*The key of knowledge.*
11:37-54.

[37]While he was speaking, a Pharisee asked him to dine with him; so he went in and sat at table. [38]The Pharisee was astonished to see that he did not first wash before dinner. [39]And the Lord said to him, "Now you Pharisees cleanse the outside of the cup and of the dish, but inside you are full of extortion and wickedness. [40]You fools! Did not he who made the outside make the inside also?

⁴¹But give for alms those things which are within; and behold, everything is clean for you.

⁴²"But woe to you Pharisees! for you tithe mint and rue and every herb, and neglect justice and the love of God; these you ought to have done, without neglecting the others. ⁴³Woe to you Pharisees! for you love the best seat in the synagogues and salutations in the market places. ⁴⁴Woe to you! for you are like graves which are not seen, and men walk over them without knowing it."

⁴⁵One of the lawyers answered him, "Teacher, in saying this you reproach us also." ⁴⁶And he said, "Woe to you lawyers also! for you load men with burdens hard to bear, and you yourselves do not touch the burdens with one of your fingers. ⁴⁷Woe to you! for you build the tombs of the prophets whom your fathers killed. ⁴⁸So you are witnesses and consent to the deeds of your fathers; for they killed them, and you build their tombs. ⁴⁹Therefore also the Wisdom of God said, 'I will send them prophets and apostles, some of whom they will kill and persecute,' ⁵⁰that the blood of all the prophets, shed from the foundation of the world, may be required of this generation, ⁵¹from the blood of Abel to the blood of Zechariah, who perished between the altar and the sanctuary. Yes, I tell you, it shall be required of this generation. ⁵²Woe to you lawyers! for you have taken away the key of knowledge; you did not enter yourselves, and you hindered those who were entering."

⁵³As he went away from there, the scribes and the Pharisees began to press him hard, and to provoke him to speak of many things, ⁵⁴lying in wait for him, to catch at something he might say.

The last unit (11:37-54) in this section (10:38-11:54) is thematically related to the preceding unit. They are blessed who not only hear the word of God but keep it (11:28). Luke now shows what it means to keep the word of God. Enlightened, the disciples had been told to raise their light on a stand that all might see it (11:33-36). Luke now shows how keeping the word calls for an inner attitude, without which external practices lose their authenticity in the mission. These thematic relationships are literarily indicated by the introductory phrase, "While he was speaking."

Like 11:14-36, the unit includes an introductory event or episode (11:37-38) and two sub-units (11:39-44, 45-52). To these Luke added a conclusion for the entire section (11:53-54).

In the introductory episode, a Pharisee invites Jesus, the Lord, to dine with him, and the Lord accepts his invitation (11:37). The setting thus evokes 7:36-50 (see 7:36). However, whereas the latter dealt with Jesus' relationship to a sinner, the present issue is Jesus' own behavior at table. The Pharisee is astonished that Jesus did not first wash (11:38). This abandonment of a particular accepted practice is the point of departure for the Lord's discourses in 11:39-44, 45-52.

The first discourse begins by addressing the point at issue and by justifying Jesus' behavior (11:39-41). First we have a judgmental observation on the Pharisees in general, who are careful about external observances but pay no attention to their inner attitudes (11:39). Bent on extortion and full of inner wickedness, they are fools (11:40a). This exclamation leads to a question: did not God create the inside as well as the outside? (11:40b), and the question leads to a command to give for alms those things which are within (11:41a). Unless almsgiving expresses the gift of themselves, it does not fulfill the intention of the divine maker. Finally, we have a declaration that with the inner gift all is clean (10:41b). It is on this basis that Jesus can dispense with ritual washing before dining.

In his response to the matter of washing, the Lord's primary concern was not so much with his own behavior as with that of the Pharisees. Nor was his concern limited to ritual washing. The latter merely represented a symptom of a far broader problem and an occasion for addressing social issues such as extortion and genuine almsgiving.

The second part of the discourse challenges the Pharisees directly on various aspects of their dealings and relationships with others and on the consequences of their behavior. It is presented in the form of three "woes" (see 6:24-26) which contrast the Pharisees with the blessedness of those who hear the word of God and keep it (see 11:28; 6:20-23). First the Pharisees neglect justice and the love of God. Without these their tithing is reprehensible (11:42). Second they seek honored places and public acclaim (11:43). As such, they are like hidden graves, personally full of death, and unnoticed, they are of no use to others (11:44). Without justice and love, their quest for honor and recognition is groundless and their mission empty. They are like those whose light has become darkness, whose lamp is under a bushel, and who shed no light on those who come to them (11:33-36).

The first brief discourse ended by showing how the religious leadership of the Pharisees was frustrated (11:44). The second focuses altogether on this issue of leadership. It is occasioned by the questioning response of a lawyer who points out that Jesus' message to the Pharisees applies equally to the lawyers (11:45). Structurally, it includes three "woes" (see 11:42-44).

First, the lawyers do not themselves assume the legal burdens which they impose on others (11:46). Second, they persecute and kill the prophets and apostles which God was sending to them. In so doing, they are like men building the tombs of the prophets whom their fathers had killed before them. In view of this solidarity with their history, the blood of all the prophets would be required of them (11:47-51). Third, although God's word had been active among them, they rejected its efforts by not keeping it (11:46); by failing to live according to that word, they rejected the key of knowledge and personally remained outside (see 11:9-10). By killing and persecuting the prophets and apostles (11:47-51), they also withheld the key of knowledge from others and hindered them from entering (11:52).

Having concluded the second discourse, Jesus went away, and the scribes and the Pharisees intensified their efforts to trap him in his speech (11:53-54; see 6:11). The conclusion of this section thus sets the stage for the second section, which deals with the community's response to persecution and judgment (12:1-13:21).

## 1. c. The Final Crisis.

### i. Persecution and the Lord's Reassurance.
*Beware of the leaven of the Pharisees.*
12:1-12.

**12** In the meantime, when so many thousands of the multitude had gathered together that they trod upon one another, he began to say to his disciples first, "Beware of the leaven of the Pharisees, which is hypocrisy. ²Nothing is covered up that will not be revealed, or hidden that will not be known. ³Therefore whatever you have said in the dark shall be heard in the light, and what you have whispered in private rooms shall be proclaimed upon the housetops.

⁴"I tell you, my friends, do not fear those who kill the body, and after that have no more that they can do. ⁵But I will warn you whom to fear: fear him who, after he has killed, has power to cast into hell; yes, I tell you, fear him! ⁶Are not five sparrows sold for two pennies? And not one of them is forgotten before God. ⁷Why, even the hairs of your head are all numbered. Fear not; you are of more value than many sparrows.

⁸"And I tell you, every one who acknowledges me before men, the Son of man also will acknowledge before the angels of God; ⁹but he who denies me before men will be denied before the angels of God. ¹⁰And every one who speaks a word against the Son of man will be forgiven; but he who blasphemes against the Holy Spirit will not be forgiven. ¹¹And when they bring you before

the synagogues and the rulers and the authorities, do not be anxious how or what you are to answer or what you are to say; [12]for the Holy Spirit will teach you in that very hour what you ought to say."

The second part (12:1-13:21) of the journey's first stage (10:38-13:21) begins with a unit on persecution and its relationship to the final crisis (12:1-12). Since the judgment on Christians will correspond to the way they react to persecution, they must live and witness in a manner which will bring a favorable judgment. The unit both warns the disciples against inappropriate behavior and reassures them concerning the outcome of a genuinely christian response.

Jesus' address to his disciples (12:1b) takes place in the midst of a vast crowd (12:1a). Luke had frequently mentioned the presence of such a crowd. The crowds, however, had been increasing (11:29), and it has now become so great that those present are treading upon one another. The description suggests that the crowds are eager to hear what Jesus and his disciples have to say. For the disciples, this underscores the urgency of the mission. The crowds' size emphasizes the enormous scope of their challenge.

Jesus' message to the disciples is consequently not meant for their benefit alone but in view of their relationship to those for whom they were sent and in whose interest they had embarked on Jesus' journey. This purpose is reflected in the unit's content, which focuses on the relationship between the disciples' personal life and their responsibility toward others. In times of persecution, this responsibility is not diminished but intensified.

First, we have a warning concerning hypocrisy, a characteristic attitude of the Pharisees which is compared to leaven. By their hypocrisy, the disciples would influence the vast crowds which come to them in the same way that the Pharisees influenced the synagogue (12:1b). The warning refers to Jesus' discourse to the Pharisees and the lawyers in

11:37-52 and to the way their hypocritical attitude had resulted in an antagonistic search to trap Jesus in his words (11:53-54). The very need for such a warning shows that in Luke's estimation some Christians were at least in danger of assuming pharisaic attitudes. Jesus' word to the Pharisees (11:37-52) is thus relevant to the disciples.

The warning continues with a traditional saying (12:2) which Luke had already used in a variant form (8:17) and further developed in 11:33-36. In the present context, the future revelation of what is now covered up refers to the unmasking of hypocrisy at the final judgment. The warning against the leaven of the Pharisees is thus supported by a statement concerning its ultimate futility. Finally, Jesus applies the saying to the word or teaching of the disciples. Words spoken in hypocritical darkness or privately whispered away from the crowds will one day be heard in the light and proclaimed for all to hear (12:3).

After this general warning (12:1-3), Jesus issues a new warning and complements it with a word of reassurance (12:4-7). The basic theme is fear, who is to be feared, and who is not. Luke thus attributes the danger of hypocrisy (12:1-3) to the disciples' fear, a fear which is occasioned by persecution but which is misdirected and groundless. The only one who should be feared is God, who not only has the power to kill but also to cast into hell (12:4-5). After refocusing the grounds of fear, however, Luke proceeds to show how the disciples' attitude toward God need not be governed by fear in the first place. If God's care extends to the least significant things in the universe, how much more does it extend to them (12:6-7). The passage recalls Jesus' teaching on prayer (11:11-13). The avoidance of hypocrisy should consequently stem not from fear but from trust in God.

Having dealt with hypocrisy (8:1-3) and the fear which occasioned it (8:4-7), Luke takes up the matter of christian witness in a time of persecution (8:8-12). The sub-unit includes two antitheses (12:8-9,10) and a concluding statement on the proper attitudes and behavior of those being persecuted (12:11-12).

The antitheses contrast the behavior which calls for fear of God and that which calls for confidence. The first antithesis deals with the acknowledgment and denial of Jesus, two responses to persecution which will bring on a corresponding acknowledgment or denial by the Son of man on the day of judgment (12:8-9). The second contrasts those who speak against the Son of man with those who blaspheme against the Holy Spirit (12:10). The former speak out of ignorance, recognizing in Jesus no more than a human created reality, however significant. They will be forgiven. The latter, however, speak out of christian knowledge and attack Jesus in the source of his divine existence. Since they thereby deny the source of their own divine existence, their blasphemy is a radical rejection of their christian life, and they will not be forgiven. Such forgiveness would be contradictory and is consequently impossible.

The disciples need not be anxious about how to acknowledge Jesus when they are brought before their persecutors. The Holy Spirit will teach them what to say (12:11-12). This presupposes, however, that they have not blasphemed against the Holy Spirit (12:10). Again the passage recalls Jesus' teaching on prayer, which concluded with the Father's promise of the Holy Spirit (11:13).

ii. Possessions, Security and Readiness.
*Where your treasure is.*
12:13-40.

> [13]One of the multitude said to him, "Teacher, bid my brother divide the inheritance with me." [14]But he said to him, "Man, who made me a judge or divider over you?" [15]And he said to them, "Take heed, and beware of all covetousness; for a man's life does not consist in the abundance of his possessions." [16]And he told them

a parable saying, "The land of a rich man brought forth plentifully; [17]and he thought to himself. 'What shall I do, for I have nowhere to store my crops?' [18]And he said, 'I will do this: I will pull down my barns, and build larger ones; and there I will store all my grain and my goods. [19]And I will say to my soul, Soul, you have ample goods laid up for many years; take your ease, eat, drink, be merry.' [20]But God said to him, 'Fool! This night your soul is required of you; and the things you have prepared, whose will they be?' [21]So is he who lays up treasure for himself, and is not rich toward God."

[22]And he said to his disciples, "Therefore I tell you, do not be anxious about your life, what you shall eat, nor about your body, what you shall put on. [23]For life is more than food, and the body more than clothing. [24]Consider the ravens; they neither sow nor reap, they have neither storehouse nor barn, and yet God feeds them. Of how much more value are you than the birds! [25]And which of you by being anxious can add a cubit to his span of life? [26]If then you are not able to do as small a thing as that, why are you anxious about the rest? [27]Consider the lilies, how they grow; they neither toil nor spin; yet I tell you, even Solomon in all his glory was not arrayed like one of these. [28]But if God so clothes the grass which is alive in the field today and tomorrow is thrown into the oven, how much more will he clothe you, O men of little faith! [29]And do not seek what you are to eat and what you are to drink, nor be of anxious mind. [30]For all the nations of the world seek these things; and your Father knows that you need them. [31]Instead, seek his kingdom, and these things shall be yours as well.

[32]"Fear not, little flock, for it is your Father's good pleasure to give you the kingdom. [33]Sell your possessions, and give alms; provide yourselves with purses that do not grow old, with a treasure in the heavens that does not fail, where no thief approaches and no moth destroys. [34]For where your treasure is, there will your heart be also.

35"Let your loins be girded and your lamps burning, 36and be like men who are waiting for their master to come home from the marriage feast, so that they may open to him at once when he comes and knocks. 37Blessed are those servants whom the master finds awake when he comes; truly, I say to you, he will gird himself and have them sit at table, and he will come and serve them. 38If he comes in the second watch, or in the third, and finds them so, blessed are those servants! 39But know this, that if the householder had known at what hour the thief was coming, he would not have left his house to be broken into. 40You also must be ready; for the Son of man is coming at an unexpected hour."

Like the first (12:1-12), the second unit looks to the final judgment (12:13-40). In the first, Jesus' teaching contrasted what was expected of his disciples with the hypocrisy of the Pharisees. In the second, he contrasts the proper attitude toward possessions and security with the worldly avarice of the multitudes (12:13-21; see 12:1).

The unit opens with a parable addressed to a spokesman for the multitudes (12:13-21). The conclusions to be drawn from this parable, however, are directed to Jesus' disciples (12:22-40). The need for such teaching indicates that in many respects the christian communities were at least in danger of assuming the attitude which was characteristic of the multitudes to which they were sent. Jesus' message to the multitudes has consequently become relevant to the disciples.

The occasion for the parable is a request that Jesus bid a man's brother to divide the inheritance with him (12:13). Like Martha in 10:38-42, the man thus expects Jesus to intervene with a relative. The request is dismissed with a question. It is not for Jesus to judge in such matters (12:14). Rather, Jesus' concern is with the covetousness which gave rise to the request. Such covetousness springs from the tendency to identify life itself with the abundance of possessions (12:15). As in the case of Martha (10:38-42), Jesus thus responds to the underlying problem rather than to the man's surface perception of his problem. The problem does not reside in his brother's presumed refusal to divide the inheritance, but in his own attitude toward that inheritance.

The parable shows the futility of amassing material stores for the future when that future could be cut off at any time (12:16-20). In the application, Jesus points out that self-serving riches is worthless when compared with being rich toward God (12:21). The problem is not the mere possession of riches but the selfishness which governs their use. In his address to the disciples, Jesus will show how one becomes rich for God by sharing one's earthly riches.

Jesus' teaching to the disciples (12:22-40) includes three basic points, all of which are related to the introductory parable (12:13-21). First they must not be anxious over material security (12:22-31). Second they must be generous in giving alms (12:32-34). Third, with regard to these matters, they must be always ready for the coming of the Son of man (12:35-40).

Since life does not consist in the abundance of possessions (see 12:15), the disciples must not be anxious about what they shall eat or how they shall clothe their bodies (12:22-23). Jesus then points to the ravens and how God feeds them (12:24a). Later he points to the lilies and the worthless grass and how God clothes them (12:27). *A fortiori*, will not God nourish and clothe the disciples who are of much greater value (12:24b,28a)? Besides, of what good is anxiety when they are actually unable to do the least thing about lengthening their span of life (12:25-26; see 12:20)? How little is their faith! Anxious concerns belong to the nations of this world. The disciples' concern must be with the kingdom of God. If they seek his kingdom, the Father, who knows their earthly needs, will see to it that they are met (12:28b-31). The discourse develops and applies Jesus' earlier and more general teaching on prayer (11:1-13).

It is not enough to place one's security in the kingdom which the Father willingly offers (12:32; see 12:31). Disciples who work at the coming of the kingdom must sell their possessions and give alms. They thus extend the implications of table fellowship into daily life, which calls for both the breaking of bread and communal sharing (Acts 2:42). It is in this way that they truly accept the characteristic christian bread for which they pray (11:3; see Acts 2:42). By reaching out to others, the disciples also provide themselves with an ageless and imperishable treasure, their own place in the kingdom's fulfillment (12:33). The section concludes with a brief saying, reminding the disciples that their heart is where their treasure is (12:34). Their heart is set upon the kingdom when they selflessly devote themselves to its coming.

The third and final unit deals with readiness for the coming of the Son of man (12:35-40). False anxiety and lack of generosity (12:22-31, 32-34) are urgent matters which cannot be put aside for the future. In their attitudes and relationships, the disciples must have their loins girt (12:35a), as is appropriate for those who have embarked on Jesus' journey. Participating in Jesus' *exodos* (9:31), their attitude corresponds to that of the Israelites in their departure from slavery (Ex 12:11). The disciples must also keep their lamps burning (12:35b). This second metaphor is associated with the parable of the servants who await their master's return from a wedding feast (12:36-38). The metaphor of the lamp (11:33-36) is thus applied to the need for constant watchfulness during the historical era of the Church. The Son of man is already at the wedding feast. When he returns at an unexpected hour he will introduce the disciples into his banquet, provided they are awake and ready (12:40).

The passage also includes a warning to unfaithful servants, who are like thieves. A householder who is aware of their presence in his house returns to catch them. The Son of man is indeed aware (12:39-40). Like God in the parable (12:16-20), he will catch thieving disciples unprepared for the banquet.

iii. The Responsibility of the Disciples.
*The faithful and wise steward.*
12:41-53.

41Peter said, "Lord, are you telling this parable for us or for all?" 42And the Lord said, "Who then is the faithful and wise steward, whom his master will set over his household, to give them their portion of food at the proper time? 43Blessed is that servant whom his master when he comes will find so doing. 44Truly, I say to you, he will set him over all his possessions. 45But if that servant says to himself, 'My master is delayed in coming,' and begins to beat the menservants and the maidservants, and to eat and drink and get drunk, 46the master of that servant will come on a day when he does not expect him and at an hour he does not know, and will punish him, and put him with the unfaithful. 47And that servant who knew his master's will, but did not make ready or act according to his will, shall receive a severe beating. 48But he who did not know, and did what deserved a beating, shall receive a light beating. Every one to whom much is given, of him will much be required; and of him to whom men commit much they will demand the more.
49"I came to cast fire upon the earth; and would that it were already kindled! 50I have a baptism to be baptized with; and how I am constrained until it is accomplished! 51Do you think that I have come to give peace on earth? No, I tell you, but rather division; 52for henceforth in one house there will be five divided, three against two and two against three; 53they will be divided, father

against son and son against father, mother against daughter and daughter against her mother, mother-in-law against her daughter-in-law and daughter-in-law against her mother-in-law."

The third unit (12:41-53) in this section (12:1-13:21) deals with the disciples' responsibility in the missionary journey. Responding to a question raised by Peter (12:41), Jesus first tells a parable (12:42-48a) which he applies to his addressees (12:48b). Focusing on final retribution, he presents the disciples' historical responsibility in light of the Lord's return at the journey's end. Jesus then adds a number of considerations on the purpose of his life mission and how it affects the disciples' social and familial relationships (12:49-53). Awareness of the journey's ultimate goal ought to strengthen the disciples in the conflicts and divisions which they are experiencing.

Peter's question whether Jesus' previous parable (12:35-40) was intended for the disciples (see 12:22) or for all (12:41) parallels the reply of a lawyer who had indicated that Jesus' harsh word to the Pharisees (11:39-44) applied to the lawyers as well (11:45). Like the lawyer's reply, Peter's question introduces a clear and explicit statement concerning the scope of those to whom Jesus' message applies. The point of Peter's question, however, is not whether Jesus' parable applies to the disciples as well as to the multitudes (see 12:13). This had been made abundantly clear in 12:22. Rather, Peter asks whether the parable was relevant exclusively for those who were associated with the historical Jesus and who continued his work immediately after his death-resurrection. Did it also apply to all, that is to the original disciples as well as to those who later would join in Jesus' journey to God? Did it also apply to Luke's readers?

In his response to Peter, Jesus indicates that the parable applies to all, but according to the degree of responsibility which each one has been given in the community (12:48b).

Jesus' answer thus goes beyond the point of Peter's question and shows how the parable is relevant for all. To this end, the parable which prompted Peter's question (12:35-40) is complemented by a related parable (12:42-48a).

Both parables deal with the attitude and role of the disciples as servants. However, the previous parable focused almost exclusively on the servants' readiness for the master's return. The second parable draws attention to their responsibilities in the christian community. Readiness for the Lord's return (12:35-40) is consequently not a purely personal matter but one which is inseparable from the servants' responsibility in the community.

While the parable applies to all, it is especially relevant to those who have been given roles of leadership and special service in the community. In terms of Luke's message to his readers, we must assume that many christian leaders were proving unfaithful to their commitment as servants.

In 12:49-53, the communities' struggles and christian challenge become even clearer. Many must have expected that the journey would be untroubled and peaceful. However, it had become clear that fidelity to the christian mission frequently resulted in painful conflicts and divisions even in the same family. In the face of these, Christians needed to maintain a clear sense of values and priorities. Had not Jesus taught them that the only kinship which ultimately mattered was that which sprang from the hearing and doing of God's word (8:19-21; 11:27-28)?

Jesus' response to this situation refers to the purpose of his mission, which is symbolically expressed as a baptism. That baptism, which is with fire (see 3:16), must be accomplished (12:49-50). For Jesus' addressees, the fulfillment of his baptism implies a separation of wheat from chaff and the burning of the latter in unquenchable fire (3:17).

Since the Church was not founded on existing human and family relationships but on Christ's baptism, Christians must be prepared for divisive struggles at the earthly level.

Christ's peace is not ordinary human peace. It is not inconsistent with social divisiveness. On the contrary, it frequently occasions or creates such divisions (12:51-53). The greater attention which Luke accords to divisions among women indicates that the latter had assumed prominent roles in the mission of the early Church.

iv. Repentance.
*How to interpret the present time.*
12:54-13:9.

54He also said to the multitudes, "When you see a cloud rising in the west, you say at once, 'A shower is coming'; and so it happens. 55And when you see the south wind blowing, you say, 'There will be scorching heat'; and it happens. 56You hypocrites! You know how to interpret the appearance of earth and sky; but why do you not know how to interpret the present time?

57"And why do you not judge for yourselves what is right? 58As you go with your accuser before the magistrate, make an effort to settle with him on the way, lest he drag you to the judge, and the judge hand you over to the officer, and the officer put you in prison. 59I tell you, you will never get out till you have paid the very last copper."

13 There were some present at that very time who told him of the Galileans whose blood Pilate had mingled with their sacrifices. 2And he answered them, "Do you think that these Galileans were worse sinners than all the other Galileans, because they suffered thus? 3I tell you, No; but unless you repent you will all likewise perish. 4Or those eighteen upon whom the tower in Siloam fell and killed them, do you think that they were worse offenders than all the others who dwelt in Jerusalem? 5I tell you, No; but unless you repent you will all likewise perish."

> 6And he told this parable: "A man had a fig tree planted in his vineyard; and he came seeking fruit on it and found none. 7And he said to the vinedresser, 'Lo, these three years I have come seeking fruit on this fig tree, and I find none. Cut it down; why should it use up the ground?' 8And he answered him, 'Let it alone, sir, this year also, till I dig about it and put on manure. 9And if it bears fruit next year, well and good; but if not, you can cut it down.'"

Beset by persecution (12:4) which frequently stems from their own earthly families (12:52-53), the Christians have been reassured, exhorted and warned to remain faithful in their christian journey. The pressure of the times and false expectations, however, had led many astray. Christian leaders in particular had assumed the attitude of Pharisees and become self-serving and domineering, abandoning the ideal of christian service. In many ways, they have rejoined the multitudes from which they had been called and which they were now called to serve. In 12:54-13:9, Jesus confronts this situation with a new address to the multitudes (see 12:1, 13-21). The purpose of the unit, which includes two sub-units, is to awaken christian sinners to repentance.

First, Jesus attacks the multitudes' hypocrisy. Endowed with a natural wisdom which enables them to predict future developments in the weather from present conditions, they ought to see how the Church's historical experience is related to its ultimate fulfillment (12:54-56). Appealing to their self-interest, Jesus compares the multitudes to people accompanying their accuser to the magistrate. While they still have the opportunity, they should settle their differences and be reconciled. Otherwise, when they come before the magistrate, they will surely pay to the full (12:57-59; see 12:42-48). Such is the meaning of the present time, which is clearly moving toward God's judgment. However, whereas the multitudes are powerless to change the weather patterns, which they can only predict, they can do something about their infidelity and avoid ultimate condemnation.

Second, Jesus shows how the punishment of the multitudes is related to two historical events, one involving Pilate and the other the collapse of a tower in Siloam. The death of many who perished on those two occasions does not prove that they were worse sinners than those who remained alive. Consequently, Jesus' addressees have no grounds to pride themselves on their comparative righteousness. On the contrary, like those who died, they too will surely perish if they do not repent (13:1-5). Their survival up to this point springs from the Lord's hope that they will yet do so.

A parable concerning a man who wants to cut down a fig tree which has been fruitless for three years makes this point extremely effectively. The vinedresser asks for an additional year during which he will provide the tree with special care. If, at the end of that year, the tree is again fruitless, then it should be cut down (13:6-9). Perhaps the vinedresser's intervention has prevented the multitudes from grasping their situation in the present time. Let them not err, however. If they have not perished or been cut down, it is in view of their possible repentance and not of their righteousness.

v. Healing and the Kingdom of God.
*All his adversaries were put to shame.*
13:10-21.

> [10]Now he was teaching in one of the synagogues on the sabbath. [11]And there was a woman who had had a spirit of infirmity for eighteen years; she was bent over and could not fully straighten herself. [12]And when Jesus saw her, he called her and said to her, "Woman, you are freed from your infirmity." [13]And he laid his hands upon her, and immediately she was made straight, and she praised God. [14]But the ruler of the synagogue, indignant because Jesus had healed on the sabbath, said to the people, "There are six days on which work ought to be done; come on those days and be healed, and not on the

sabbath day." ¹⁵Then the Lord answered him, "You hypocrites! Does not each of you on the sabbath untie his ox or his ass from the manger, and lead it away to water it? ¹⁶And ought not this woman, a daughter of Abraham whom Satan bound for eighteen years, be loosed from this bond on the sabbath day?" ¹⁷As he said this, all his adversaries were put to shame; and all the people rejoiced at all the glorious things that were done by him.

¹⁸He said therefore, "What is the kingdom of God like? And to what shall I compare it? ¹⁹It is like a grain of mustard seed which a man took and sowed in his garden; and it grew and became a tree, and the birds of the air made nests in its branches."

²⁰And again he said, "To what shall I compare the kingdom of God? ²¹It is like leaven which a woman took and hid in three measures of flour, till it was all leavened."

The final unit (13:10-21) in this section pursues the theme of repentance which was introduced in 12:54-13:9. In the latter, emphasis was on the need for repentance in light of the journey's end. In the present unit, it is on how Jesus extends healing reconciliation over the objections of a ruler of the synagogue (13:10-17). Jesus' healing is a manifestation of the kingdom which develops gradually to its ultimate fulfillment (13:18-21).

The setting for this last unit is one of the synagogues, where Jesus was teaching on the sabbath (13:10). The end of the journey's first stage (9:51-13:21) thus corresponds to that of the mission (5:1-6:11). In both instances, the episode represents a definitive confrontation and marks the last time that Jesus sets foot in a synagogue. The journey narrative thus takes up the story of Jesus and the origins of the Church and refocuses it in light of its destiny. As in 6:6-11, the episode is a healing story. While teaching in the synagogue, Jesus heals one of those present and challenges those who object to such activity on the sabbath.

In 13:10-17, Jesus' antagonist is a ruler of the synagogue. Unlike the scribes and the Pharisees in 6:5-11, however, he does not challenge Jesus directly but addresses the people in his role as ruler (13:14). The synagogue and Jesus thus stand in sharp contrast precisely in their function as teachers and religious leaders.

Jesus, the Lord, accuses the ruler and those who are associated with him of hypocrisy (13:15). It is altogether appropriate to free a daughter of Abraham from a satanic bond on the sabbath (13:16). Do not the rulers of the synagogue free an ox or an ass on the sabbath to water it? Why should they not do likewise when the Lord's freedom and life are at stake?

Shamed as teachers, the rulers of the synagogue are ineffective and the people rejoice at all the glorious things done by Jesus (13:17). Some christian leaders may share in attitudes analogous to those of the synagogue, but this should not be a source of dismay for the Christians. The kingdom of God was never intended to be fully manifest from the start. Rather, its beginnings are very small. However, like the mustard seed, it holds the full potential for gradual development (13:18-19). Like leaven, which is hidden in the flour, it will eventually influence the entire loaf (13:20-21).

## C. 2. FROM GALILEE TO JERUSALEM. SOCIAL AND HISTORICAL IMPLICATIONS OF THE CHRISTIAN JOURNEY. 13:22-19:48.

The second section of the journey narrative (13:22-19:48) is structured very much like the first. After an introductory unit (13:22-35; see 9:51-10:37), it includes two major units. In the first, the author's focus is on table fellowship, the sharing of goods, and their relationship to salvation and the kingdom (14:1-17:10; see 10:38-11:54). In the second, his concern is more with Jesus' ascent to Jerusalem, the city's rejection of Jesus and its approaching destruction (17:11-19:48; see 12:1-13:21). As in the first section of the journey, these two large units correspond to the two sub-units which comprise the introduction (13:23-30; 31-35; see 9:51-62; 10:1-37).

While the two sections or stages are similar in their movement from immediate concerns to eschatological considerations, they are also markedly different. The first section dealt mainly with the personal dispositions required for the christian journey and its orientation (9:51-13:21). The second, on the other hand, deals primarily with social and historical implications of the journey (13:22-19:48). At its conclusion, Jesus has arrived at the geographical goal of his journey, and everything has been prepared for the final two stages, which present the immediate context and conflicts (20:1-21:38) through which Jesus' journey to Jerusalem would become a journey to God (22:1-24:53).

The first major unit (14:1-17:10) includes four sub-units. First the author presents the radical demands of discipleship in relation to the christian meal, relationships and possessions in the kingdom of God (14:1-35). Second he deals with the problems of reconciliation and the need to joyfully receive those who have been lost and were dead but are now found and living (15:1-32). Third he takes up the important matter of wealth and the need to share with the needy (16:1-31). Fourth and finally, he again turns to the issue of sin and reconciliation (17:1-10). The latter has obviously become a pressing concern in the Lukan communities.

The second major unit (17:11-19:48) is directly concerned with historical rather than social questions. To appreciate the unfolding of salvation history, one must distinguish between the presence of the kingdom and its full manifestation when the faithful will enter into the kingdom on the day of the Son of man. One must also situate the rejection of many who had first been called to the kingdom and the opening of the kingdom to the Gentiles.

The section includes six sub-units. The first begins with the story of a Samaritan whom Jesus cured and who, unlike nine others, was saved by reason of his grateful faith, and continues with warnings and teaching on the presence of the kingdom and the future day of the Son of man (17:11-37). The second seeks to reassure the faithful and takes up the question of constancy and humility in prayer (18:1-17). In the third, Luke shows how riches and merely human relationships obstruct entry into the kingdom and how God can overcome such an obstruction for those who follow Christ (18:18-30). The fourth deals with the matter of understanding the passion and its necessity, the need to have one's eyes opened to faith, to be converted and to accept Jesus' salvific presence (18:31-19:10). The fifth sub-unit deals directly with Jesus' departure in the ascension and the responsibilities of those who are entrusted with stewardship during his absence (19:11-27). The sixth and final unit focuses on Jesus' royal entry into Jerusalem and on how the kingdom is not of this world (19:28-48). At its conclusion, a summary prepares the reader for the journey's next stage which is situated in the temple at Jerusalem (19:47-48).

2. a. Introduction.
The Journey of Salvation.
*And the third day I finish my course.*
13:22-35.

> 22He went on his way through towns and villages, teaching, and journeying toward Jerusalem. 23And some one said to him, "Lord, will those who are saved be few?" And he said to them, 24"Strive to enter by the narrow door; for many,I tell you, will seek to enter and will not be able. 25When once the householder has risen up and shut the door, you will begin to stand outside and to knock at the door, saying, 'Lord, open to us.' He will answer you, 'I do not know where you come from.' 26Then you will begin to say, 'We ate and drank in your presence, and you taught in our streets.' 27But he will say, 'I tell you, I do not know where you come from; depart

from me, all you workers of iniquity!' [28]There you will weep and gnash your teeth, when you see Abraham and Isaac and Jacob and all the prophets in the kingdom of God and you yourselves thrust out. [29]And men will come from east and west, and from north and south, and sit at table in the kingdom of God. [30]And behold, some are last who will be first, and some are first who will be last."

[31]At that very hour some Pharisees came, and said to him, "Get away from here, for Herod wants to kill you." [32]And he said to them, "Go and tell that fox, 'Behold, I cast out demons and perform cures today and tomorrow, and the third day I finish my course. [33]Nevertheless I must go on my way today and tomorrow and the day following; for it cannot be that a prophet should perish away from Jerusalem.' [34]O Jerusalem, Jerusalem, killing the prophets and stoning those who are sent to you! How often would I have gathered your children together as a hen gathers her brood under her wings, and you would not! [35]Behold, your house is forsaken. And I tell you, you will not see me until you say, 'Blessed is he who comes in the name of the Lord!'"

The second section of the journey to Jerusalem opens with an introductory unit (13:22-35), which includes two chronologically related encounters situated somewhere along the journey. The first of these encounters deals with salvation and focuses on its relationship to eating with Jesus (13:23-30). As such, it prepares the reader for the section's first major unit, all of which concerns table fellowship and its relationship to salvation (14:1-17:10). The second encounter deals with the necessity that Jesus pursue his journey to Jerusalem and the forsaking of that city (13:31-35). It prepares the reader for the section's second major unit, which concerns Jesus' ascent to Jerusalem, that city's rejection of Jesus, and its coming destruction (17:11-19:48).

Literarily, the two encounters are extremely closely related. In the context of 13:22-35, the first encounter, which concerns salvific entry into the house of God's kingdom (13:23, 24-25,28), announces the abandonment of the house of Jerusalem (13:35). In spite of Jesus' efforts (13:34), the forsaking of Jerusalem is inseparable from the end of Jesus' course in that city (13:32-33) and the universalization of salvation in the kingdom (13:29-30).

Even as they challenge the reader to a personal response, the introductory unit's two encounters comment on the history of salvation. In their few verses, Luke refers to Abraham, Isaac, Jacob and all the prophets (13:29), to Jesus' historical life (13:26,34), to his passion (13:33) and resurrection (13:32), to the forsaking of Jerusalem (13:35) and to the positive response of many who had not orginally been invited to feast in the kingdom but who now take the place of many who had been first called (13:29-30). We are thus given a synthesis of salvation history in terms of Jesus' great journey. The reader is enlightened concerning the journey to salvation, asked to situate himself or herself within its course and to respond according to Jesus' intention.

*Admission to Salvation.*
*13:22-30.*

The first encounter opens with an introductory summary (13:22), similar to that found in 4:14-15 and 8:1, but altogether colored by Jesus' orientation toward Jerusalem (see 9:51-56,57; 10:38). Unlike 4:14-15, however, Jesus' work is not associated with the synagogue. After the first section of the journey, which climaxed in Jesus' teaching in one of the synagogues (13:10-21), Jesus never again enters the synagogue. In this respect, the structure of the journey parallels that of Jesus' mission, whose first section also ended with a definitive synagogue episode (6:6-11). Unlike 8:1, Jesus' teaching is marked by a strong sense of his personal destiny, a major theme in 13:31-36.

In the first encounter, someone approaches Jesus and asks whether those who are saved will be few (13:23). As so often happens in Luke's gospel, however, Jesus does not answer the question which has been asked. Instead he tells a parable concerning the effort required for salvation and how those who were first invited will in fact be passed by, while others from all parts of the world will gain entry (13:24-30). Responding to the question which should have been asked, Jesus outlines the course of christian history. The religious Jews, who had formed part of Jesus' environment and who should normally have inherited salvation, will be replaced in the kingdom by large numbers who could not have forseen such a blessing. He thus announces the salvation of Jews and gentiles who had no recognized place in synagogue righteousness. This theme, which had already been adumbrated in earlier portions of the gospel, will be greatly elaborated in the following chapters.

In the parable, Jesus uses the image of the narrow door through which one must enter (13:24), an image which also figures in Mt 7:13-14. In Luke, however, it is wed to the image of the door which has been shut against those who knock after the master of the house has risen (13:25). This second image proves jarring to the attentive reader who expects that the door would be shut against outsiders either while the master of the house has retired (see 11:5-10) or while a banquet is already in progress (see Mt 25:10-12). The anomaly of the door's being closed when the master rises, however is extremely significant. By referring to the master's rising, Luke draws attention to the decisive moment of Jesus' resurrection (13:25) on the third day, when he will have finished his course (13:32) and when an unresponsive Jerusalem will have been forsaken (13:34-35a).

Once Jesus is risen, it will prove of no avail that one has eaten or drunk in his presence or that he taught in their streets (13:26). Eating and drinking alongside of Jesus or in Jesus' presence is not the same as eating and drinking with Jesus and being present to him in a meal. Jesus' teaching in their midst does not necessarily mean that they have heard his teaching. Many Jews will consequently be thrust out and separated from the patriarchs and the prophets and from the many who will join them in the kingdom of God (13:27-39). Unresponsive Jews will thus be cut off from their roots and others will take their place in the fulfillment of biblical promise. Some of those who are last, including many gentiles, will be first and some of the first will be last in the kingdom (13:30).


*Salvation and the Forsaking of Jerusalem.*
*13:31-35.*

The second part of 13:22-35 is a direct encounter with the Pharisees (13:31-35). Jesus rejects their suggestion that he should desist from his journey because Herod wants to kill him. All of Jesus' work is ordained to the completion of his course on the third day (13:31-32). It is in this larger context that his death must be seen. Further, Jesus must die a prophet's death in Jerusalem (13:33; see 4:24, 29-30; 24:19-20), and Herod's cunning cannot interfere with the fulfillment of prophetic tradition (13:32; see 24:25-27). Finally, prior to his death Jesus must repeatedly try to gather Jerusalem's children like a hen gathers her brood beneath her wings (13:34b). In no way can Herod the fox interrupt that mission (13:32).

The unit ends with an apostrophe to Jerusalem (13:34-35), the killer of prophets and the stoner of those sent to her (13:34a; see 24:19b-20; Acts 6:8-7:60). Grieving over Jerusalem's rejection of his salvific efforts (13:34b), Jesus sees her house already forsaken and announces that the city would not see him until that moment when she would herald his coming in the name of the Lord (13:35).

The apostrophe thus looks to the 19th chapter when Jesus' entry into Jerusalem would be acclaimed as the advent of the king who comes in the name of the Lord (19:28-40; see esp. v.38) and when Jesus would announce the desolation of Jerusalem (19:41-44) and its temple, which no longer could be considered a house of prayer

(19:45-46). Indeed all of 13:22-35 is related to 19:1-48, the conclusion of this section of the journey narrative. The various themes of 13:22-30 are developed in the story of Zacchaeus with its challenge of open hospitality and Jesus' identification of a true son of Abraham (19:1-10). The relationship between Jesus' death and access to the kingdom (13:28-29, 32-33) is discussed in the parable concerning the place of christian history in the kingdom's definitive advent (19:11-27).

## 2. b. The House of God's Kingdom.

### i. Discipleship and the Journey of Salvation.
*Whoever does not bear his own cross and come after me, cannot be my disciple.*
14:1-35.

Chapter 14 develops the radical demands of discipleship for those who have joined Jesus on the way to Jerusalem. The first part of the narrative presents discipleship in terms of the challenges of the christian banquet and in relation to the history of salvation (14:1-24). The second part focuses on the total renunciation required in a christian mission which intends to follow through to the end (14:25-35).

As the first unit in this segment (14:1-17:10) of the journey narrative's second section (13:22-19:48), 14:1-35 sets forth Jesus' fundamental challenge concerning table fellowship and total renunciation of the relationships and goods of this world. The same double challenge will be further developed and applied to concrete situations in the subsequent units of this segment (15:1-17:10). Together with 15:1-17:10, the unit focuses on the various themes introduced in 13:22-30.

*The Meal in the Kingdom of God.*
*14:1-24.*

**14** One sabbath when he went to dine at the house of a ruler who belonged to the Pharisees, they were watching him. ²And behold, there was a man before him who had dropsy. ³And Jesus spoke to the lawyers and Pharisees, saying, "Is it lawful to heal on the sabbath, or not?" ⁴But they were silent. Then he took him and healed him, and let him go. ⁵And he said to them, "Which of you, having a son or an ox that has fallen into a well, will not immediately pull him out on a sabbath day?" ⁶And they could not reply to this.

⁷Now he told a parable to those who were invited, when he marked how they chose the places of honor, saying to them, ⁸"When you are invited by any one to a marriage feast, do not sit down in a place of honor, lest a more eminent man than you be invited by him; ⁹and he who invited you both will come and say to you, 'Give place to this man,' and then you will begin with shame to take the lowest place. ¹⁰But when you are invited, go and sit in the lowest place, so that when your host comes he may say to you, 'Friend, go up higher'; then you will be honored in the presence of all who sit at table with you. ¹¹For every one who exalts himself will be humbled, and he who humbles himself will be exalted."

¹²He said also to the man who had invited him, "When you give a dinner or a banquet, do not invite your friends or your brothers or your kinsmen or rich neighbors, lest they also invite you in return, and you be repaid. ¹³But when you give a feast, invite the poor, the maimed, the lame, the blind, ¹⁴and you will be blessed, because they cannot repay you. You will be repaid at the resurrection of the just."

¹⁵When one of those who sat at table with him heard this, he said to him, "Blessed is he who shall eat bread in the kingdom of God!" ¹⁶But he said to him, "A man once gave a great banquet, and invited many; ¹⁷and at the time for the banquet he sent his servant to say to those who had been invited, 'Come; for all is now ready.' ¹⁸But they all alike began to make excuses. The first said to him, 'I have bought a field, and I must go out and see it; I pray you, have me excused.' ¹⁹And another said, 'I have

bought five yoke of oxen, and I go to examine them; I pray you, have me excused.' [20]And another said, 'I have married a wife, and therefore I cannot come.' [21]So the servant came and reported this to his master. Then the householder in anger said to his servant, 'Go out quickly to the streets and lanes of the city, and bring in the poor and maimed and blind and lame.' [22]And the servant said, 'Sir, what you commanded has been done, and still there is room.' [23]And the master said to the servant, 'Go out to the highways and hedges, and compel people to come in, that my house may be filled. [24]For I tell you, none of those men who were invited shall taste my banquet."

While on his way to Jerusalem, Jesus paused for a sabbath meal in the home of a leading Pharisee (14:1a). On two previous occasions (7:36-50; 11:37-44), such meals had developed into confrontative situations, with the result that the Pharisees had been pressing and provoking Jesus to speak that they might eventually find justifiable grounds for accusing him (11:53-54; see 6:11). Cast against this background and in light of Jesus' announcement that he would perish in Jerusalem (13:33), the deceptively casual observation that they were now watching him (14:1b) introduces an ominous note. Their silent response (14:4a) and subsequent inability to respond (14:6) to his questions reveal further deterioration in a relationship which would lead to Jesus' death.

This first section (14:1-24) of the unit is a dramatic presentation of the characteristic demands of table fellowship in the kingdom of God (14:15) and of the kingdom's historical movement away from those who had first been invited to those who had been considered as outsiders. Both of these themes had been carefully introduced in 13:22-30 in Jesus' response to the question of who can be saved. A story in the life of Jesus is thus presented as a reflection on the post-Easter christian meal and the latter is viewed in its creative relationship to the eschatological banquet of the kingdom.

Structurally, the section consists of an introductory statement which presents the meal setting (14:1) and four distinct but closely related sub-units in which Jesus confronts the various participants at the meal (14:2-6, 7-11, 12-14, 15-24).

One of the dinner guests, a man suffering from dropsy, provides an occasion for challenging the lawyers and the Pharisees on the issue of healing and sabbath observance (14:2-6; see 6:6-11; 13:10-17). Jesus himself raises the question (14:3). With silence for an answer, he proceeds to cure the man (14:4). A further question forces the Pharisees and lawyers to confront the issue in terms of what they themselves would do in an emergency (14:5). Healing on the sabbath is thus de-absolutized and related to their own hypothetical behavior. Assuming that the Pharisees' practical course of action would be inconsistent with their theoretical stand on the matter, Jesus thus places his addressees in a position where they cannot reply and his accusers thereby become the accused (14:6).

The remainder of the segment consists of three parables directed in turn to the guests (14:7-11), to the host (14:12-14) and to an anonymous participant (14:15-24).

In the first two parables, Jesus departs from the ordinary form of parables and presents the addressees themselves as the protagonists in the story (see 15:3-7, 8-10). By addressing the guests and the host in the second person, these parables possess a high degree of immediacy, involving the listeners in situations which correspond to their respective positions as guest or host. Formally, they had been prepared by Jesus' question to the Pharisees and lawyers concerning what they would do if a son or an ox fell into a well on the sabbath (14:5). Together these two parables introduce the third, which concerns a man who once gave a great banquet (14:15-24). In this final parable, the protagonist remains anonymous and the story is cast in the third person narrative which we normally associate with the parable form (see 15:11-32). The concluding verse, however, reintroduces the second person plural as Jesus personally addresses all the participants (14:24).

Maintaining the initiative which he assumed in 14:1-6, Jesus addresses the guests concerning their choice of places of honor at table (14:7). The story concerns a hypothetical marriage feast to which the addressees, including the lawyers and Pharisees, have been invited (14:8a). Using their observed behavior at the sabbath meal as a springboard, Jesus then confronts them with two alternative situations in which personally assumed positions are reversed. Those who seek an honored place are shamed in favor of one more eminent than they (14:8b-9), and those who take the lowest place are honored in the presence of all (14:10). Thus it is that the self-exalted will be humbled and the truly humble will be exalted (14:11), as Mary had sung in her canticle (1:52). The guests are asked to be attitudinally last if indeed they wish to be first among the saved (see 13:30).

Turning next to his host, Jesus presents a second parable in which he abandons every hypothetical guise. When the latter gives a dinner, he is not to invite his friends, relatives and the rich of his own social class in view of being invited in return (14:12). Rather, he must invite the poor and disadvantaged who cannot reciprocate. The good host must not look to repayment in this life but in the resurrection of the just (14:13-14). Indirectly, the parable reflects on the status of those who were present at the sabbath meal. Literarily, it also prepares the reader for the second part of this unit, where family relationships and material goods will be the primary concern (14:25-35).

When one of the participants recognizes that Jesus has been describing the attitudes and the status of the guests and of the host at the messianic banquet (14:15), Jesus responds with a third parable, in which the story of a man who once gave a great banquet (14:16-23) is transformed into a story concerning Jesus' banquet (14:24). It now becomes clear that all are not able to accept an invitation to the meal in which God truly rules. Rejecting the demands of humility (14:7-11), those who were first invited seek excuses not to attend (14:16-20) and the host recognizes that those closest to him (14:12) will in fact cede their place to strangers (14:13-14, 21-23). Like the man afflicted with dropsy (14:2-4), the latter will be healed and nourished at Jesus' banquet. The third parable thus builds on foundations established in 14:1-6, 7-11, 12-14 and situates these encounters in the christian history of salvation which had been introduced earlier in 13:22-30.

The sabbath meal in 14:1-24 presents table sharing and fellowship in the kingdom of God (14:15) as Jesus' banquet (14:24), a healing and salvific banquet in which humility is exalted (14:7-11) and to which the poor, the maimed, the lame and the blind must be invited (14:12-14). It is they in fact who have accepted and who will accept the invitation (14:15-24), contrary to the hypocritical expectations and observances of those who share the attitudes of the lawyers and the Pharisees (14:2-6). The meal in the kingdom is thus associated with Jesus' fulfillment of messianic prophecy as presented in his inaugural statement at Nazareth (4:18-21) and in his response to the disciples of John the Baptist (7:22).

In 14:1-24, the author has redirected the question of who will be saved (13:23) to how can one be saved (see 13:24). He thus addressed what had been required of the jewish leaders and their communities and what was now demanded of those who formed the Church and joined in the meal which symbolized its entire life. So conceived, the unit enabled the christian communities and their leaders to situate themselves in relation to their jewish origins, and it challenged them to resist any tendencies which were or which might have been surfacing, contrary to Jesus' teaching and intention.

## Relationships and Possessions in the Kingdom of God. 14:25-35.

²⁵Now great multitudes accompanied him; and he turned and said to them, ²⁶"If any one comes to me and does not hate his own father and mother and wife and children and brothers and sisters, yes, and even his own life, he cannot be my disciple. ²⁷Whoever does not bear his own cross and come after me, cannot be my disciple. ²⁸For which of you, desiring to build a tower, does not first sit down and count the cost, whether he has enough to complete it? ²⁹Otherwise, when he has laid a foundation, and is not able to finish, all who see it begin to mock him, ³⁰saying, 'This man began to build, and was not able to finish.' ³¹Or what king, going to encounter another king in war, will not sit down first and take counsel whether he is able with ten thousand to meet him who comes against him with twenty thousand? ³²And if not, while the other is yet a great way off, he sends an embassy and asks terms of peace. ³³So therefore, whoever of you does not renounce all that he has cannot be my disciple.

³⁴"Salt is good; but if salt has lost its taste, how shall its saltness be restored? ³⁵It is fit neither for the land nor for the dunghill; men throw it away. He who has ears to hear, let him hear."

In his treatment of discipleship in the journey of salvation, Luke now turns his attention to the multitudes and the requirements for ultimate perseverance (14:25-35). Thematically, the passage is clearly an extension of 14:1-24. In order to broaden the scope of the addressees to include the multitudes, however, the meal setting is put aside and its imagery temporarily abandoned, to be once again assumed in chapter 15. In 14:25-35, the banquet symbol thus cedes to the reality of church life which it symbolized, as the author focuses on the challenge of christian life in history.

The conditions for discipleship are radical. Any one who comes to Jesus without hating every human family relationship and his own personal life cannot be his disciple (14:26). This traditional hyperbole (see Mt 10:37), which further specifies the call issued at the beginning of the journey narrative (9:57-62), is then symbolically reinterpreted as the bearing of one's cross in the following of Jesus (14:27; see Mt 10-38). To appreciate its significance, one must recall 8:19-21 and 11:27-28, where Jesus' true relatives are described as those who hear the word of God and keep it.

The christian journey is patterned on Jesus' way of the cross (14:27), a journey which calls for total renunciation (14:33). Apart from this attitude, the christian mission becomes like salt which has lost its taste, which is no longer able to flavor those in need of it, which is itself unable to be restored, and which is consequently worthless (14:34-35). In the christian mission as in the christian meal, the followers must consequently share Jesus' attitude of total self-giving, placing the life of others ahead of their own from every point of view.

Two comparisons, given in 14:28-30 and 31-32, situate Jesus' challenge in relation to the personal history of the addressees. Unless they accept Jesus' challenge, they are like someone who intends to build a tower or a king who sets out for war without taking the means to bring these projects to completion. So it is with Christians who have come to Jesus but have failed to assume the radical challenge of discipleship and the way of the cross. Their mission is frustrated. They will not enjoy the christian meal's fulfillment in the kingdom.

ii. The Lost and the Found.
*Rejoice with me.*
15:1-32.

In 14:1-35, Luke set forth the general attitude required to take part in the kingdom of God. In doing so, he insisted on the community's need for humility and openness to the economically and physically poor as well as on the radical commitment needed to accompany Jesus to the end of the mission journey. In 15:1-32, he now addresses the particular question of those who have wandered away and were lost and how the communities must rejoice when they return and are found. Openness to the poor, the maimed, the lame and the blind (14:13,21) applies to Christians who have fallen away as well as to those who had not yet ap-proached the Lord's table. Luke thus continues to apply the teaching of Jesus to the concrete historical situation of the Church in the mid-eighties.

*The Setting.*
*15:1-2.*

> **15**  Now the tax collectors and sinners were all drawing near to hear him. ²And the Pharisees and the scribes murmured, saying, "This man receives sinners and eats with them."

Chapter 15 consists of a brief narrative introduction (15:1-2) and three parables (15:3-7, 8-10, 11-32). Prescinding from all accidentals of time and space, the setting focuses altogether on two important groupings or categories in the human environment of Jesus.

First there were the tax collectors and sinners, a category well-known from earlier parts of the gospel. Representing all religious outcasts, their symbolic role is emphasized in Luke's statement that they *all* drew near to hear Jesus (15:1). In verse 2, they are referred to more simply as sinners.

Second there were the Pharisees and the scribes, equally well-known as symbols for the self-righteous. Jesus, be it recalled, was a welcome guest in the homes of both cate-gories (5:29; 7:36; 11:37; 14:1), a situation which proved intolerable for the religiously exclusive Pharisees and their scribes. Accordingly, the latter protested against Jesus' attitude toward sinners (15:2). Note, however, that they murmured not at Jesus' acceptance of hospitality but at his granting of it. Jesus is consequently viewed as a welcoming host who receives sinners at his table rather than as a guest welcomed at theirs.

Luke has thus adapted the historical setting to evoke the fellowship of early Christians gathered at the table of the Lord. As in Jesus' day, the openness and universality of that fellowship was being challenged by the self-righteous who protested the presence of sinners. Such is the context which called forth three parables of Jesus concerning rejoicing over the recovery of what had been lost.

*The Three Parables.*
*15:3-32.*

³So he told them this parable: ⁴"What man of you, having a hundred sheep, if he has lost one of them, does not leave the ninety-nine in the wilderness, and go after the one which is lost, until he finds it? ⁵And when he has found it, he lays it on his shoulders, rejoicing. ⁶And when he comes home, he calls together his friends and his neighbors, saying to them, 'Rejoice with me, for I have found my sheep which was lost.' ⁷Just so, I tell you, there will be more joy in heaven over one sinner who repents than over ninety-nine righteous persons who need no repentance.

⁸"Or what woman, having ten silver coins, if she loses one coin, does not light a lamp and sweep the house and seek diligently until she finds it? ⁹And when she has found it, she calls together her friends and neighbors, saying, 'Rejoice with me, for I have found the coin which I had lost.' ¹⁰Just so, I tell you, there is joy before the angels of God over one sinner who repents."

¹¹And he said, "There was a man who had two sons; ¹²and the younger of them said to his father, 'Father, give me the share of property that falls to me.' And he divided his living between them. ¹³Not many days later, the younger son gathered all he had and took his journey

into a far country, and there he squandered his property in loose living. [14]And when he had spent everything, a great famine arose in that country, and he began to be in want. [15]So he went and joined himself to one of the citizens of that country, who sent him into his fields to feed swine. [16]And he would gently have fed on the pods that the swine ate; and no one gave him anything. [17]But when he came to himself he said, 'How many of my father's hired servants have bread enough and to spare, but I perish here with hunger! [18]I will arise and go to my father, and I will say to him, "Father, I have sinned against heaven and before you; [19]I am no longer worthy to be called your son; treat me as one of your hired servants."' [20]And he arose and came to his father. But while he was yet at a distance, his father saw him and had compassion, and ran and embraced him and kissed him. [21]And the son said to him, 'Father, I have sinned against heaven and before you; I am no longer worthy to be called your son.' [22]But the father said to his servants, 'Bring quickly the best robe, and put it on him; and put a ring on his hand, and shoes on his feet; [23]and bring the fatted calf and kill it, and let us eat and make merry; [24]for this my son was dead, and is alive again; he was lost, and is found.' And they began to make merry.

[25]"Now his elder son was in the field; and as he came and drew near to the house, he heard music and dancing. [26]And he called one of the servants and asked what this meant. [27]And he said to him, 'Your brother has come, and your father has killed the fatted calf, because he has received him safe and sound.' [28]But he was angry and refused to go in. His father came out and entreated him, [29]but he answered his father, 'Lo, these many years I have served you, and I never disobeyed your command; yet you never gave me a kid, that I might make merry with my friends. [30]But when this son of yours came, who has devoured your living with harlots, you killed for him the fatted calf!' [31]And he said to him, 'Son, you are

always with me, and all that is mine is yours. [32]It was fitting to make merry and be glad, for this your brother was dead, and is alive; he was lost, and is found.'"

Thematically, all three of these parables focus on the joy that accompanies or should accompany the finding of what had been lost, and this theme is articulated in parallel stories concerning a lost sheep (15:3-7), a lost coin (15:8-10) and a lost son (15:11-32). Among these three parables, only the first can be found elsewhere in the synoptic tradition (Mt 18:10-14). In Mt, however, the lost sheep illustrates the position of the little ones (18:10; see 18:1-6) and the parable shows how the loss of one of these little ones is contrary to God's will (18:14). Luke's use of the parable is quite different.

The parallelism among the parables is especially evident in the first two, which are much shorter than the third. Both of these parables are introduced by a question in which the loss of a single sheep or coin draws one's whole attention and efforts away from the ninety-nine sheep or nine coins which remain in safe possession (15:3-4,8). Grammatically, the question is then abandoned in favor of a declarative statement concerning the activity of the one who has found the sheep or coin and who invites friends and neighbors to join in rejoicing over its recovery (15:5-6, 9). In this literary movement from a question to a descriptive declaration, the narrator assumes that the addressees, namely the Pharisees and scribes, have answered the question affirmatively. The declaration is then a good expression of their hypothetical attitude and behavior, and Jesus' addressees have an acceptable point of departure for grasping the situation of sinners who repent and the heavenly rejoicing which accompanies their repentance (15:7,10).

While parallel to one another in very significant respects, the parables of the lost sheep and the lost coin also constitute two distinct stages in a literary development. The first parable questions the Pharisees in the second person plural, implicating them directly in the story (15:3). The second, however, raises the question in the third person and broadens the scope of those to whom it can apply (15:8). Its concluding application to Jesus' immediate addressees suffices to establish its relevance to the Pharisees (15:10). Shorter than the parable of the sheep, that of the coin also complements the former by sharpening the reader's awareness of its key elements.

The first two parables have thus provided the grounds for Jesus' openness to tax collectors and sinners. Their drawing near to hear him is an expression of repentance (15:1). By receiving them, he accepts their repentance; and by hosting them at table, he communicates solidarity with them as they do with him (15:2). By implication, these parables also present the christian meal as a joyful celebration of salvation.

The parables of the lost sheep and the lost coin prepare the reader for that of the lost or prodigal son (15:11-32). This third and climactic parable consists of two long sections (15:11-24, 25-32), each of which concludes with a restatement of the author's main theme: joy at recovering what was lost. However, since the lost and found is now a human being, a father's son, the theme is also interpreted and articulated in terms of life and death: he who was dead is alive again, and his restored life must be celebrated (15:24-32).

Focusing on the experience of the younger or prodigal son and the father's welcome, the parable's first section corresponds to the parables of the lost sheep and the lost coin. It thus joins the latter in affirming the grounds for Jesus' fellowship with sinners. In the second section, however, the protagonists are the elder son who remained faithfully at home and the father. Luke thus moves the reader beyond the first two parables and focuses on the reaction of those who resent and resist Jesus' attitude toward repentant sinners and who refuse to rejoice at their return. The author's repeated emphasis on rejoicing (15:5-7, 9-10, 22-24, 25-32) is consequently intended as a challenge to the murmuring Pharisees and the scribes (15:2).

Unlike the parables of the lost sheep and the lost coin, that of the prodigal son does not open with a question. Plunging directly into the narrative of a man who had two sons, Jesus assumes that the Pharisees and the scribes will recognize how they are being addressed. Nor does the third parable end with a direct second-person address to Jesus' audience. Consequently, while the younger and the elder brother do correspond to the sinners and the Pharisees (15:1-2), the author's interest in their story is less historical than pastoral. Together the brothers and their father serve to dramatize and clarify situations in the Lukan communities which are struggling with the reconciliation of sinners.

The account of the younger son's experience of death away from his father's home draws sympathetic attention to the plight of those who have wandered away from life, to the experiential source of their decision to return, and to the attitude which they assume or should assume in approaching their father and renewed life. Recent experience has indeed affected their stance with regard to the community (15:13-19). Returning to their father's household, they consequently acknowledge their unworthiness. The father, however, rejoices at their return, ignores their protests of unworthiness and orders that a banquet be prepared to celebrate their return to life. Thus does God fill the hungry with good things (1:53). In their wandering, the younger sons were dead or lost; in their return, they live again and are found (15:20-24).

The reaction of the elder son is then told with equal understanding and sympathy. Those who have been faithful, however, must transcend all resentment against those who have abandoned the household and not be dismayed at the celebration which accompanies their return. The value of their abiding presence with the father whose life and possessions they enjoy is not diminished by the sinners' return and the celebration of their salvation. As members of the household they should rather be celebrating with the father at their brothers' return to life (15:25-32). Like the elder brother, the Pharisees and the scribes are not condemned but pastorally addressed. Luke's readers are thus made to confront any negative attitudes and behavior and to join in celebrating their brothers' salvation.

The banquet which accompanies the younger brother's return to life (15:22-24, 25-32) thus illumines Jesus' eating with sinners (15:2), and the latter provides a model for life in the christian communities. The christian meal is consequently an earthly reflection of the heavenly and angelic joy which accompanies the return of a repentant sinner (15:7,10).


### iii. The Proper Use of Wealth.
*Make friends for yourselves by means of unrighteous mammon.*
16:1-31.


Having dealt with reconciliation and its implications for table fellowship (15:1-32), Luke now turns to a second but closely related area of concern, namely right attitudes and behavior in the matter of wealth. First he presents Jesus' fundamental teaching on the sharing of wealth (16:1-13). Second he outlines his response to those who refuse to share (16:14-31). As in the introduction (13:22-30) and the first two units (14:1-35; 15:1-32), banquet imagery dominates the narrative (16:19-31). The sharing of wealth with the needy is thus inextricably bound to the implications of table fellowship (see Acts 2:42-47). Without sharing, the latter is vitiated and no longer constitutes a pledge of admission to the kingdom.

Literarily structured as Jesus' message to the disciples (16:1-13) and to the Pharisees (16:14-31), the unit includes two parables (16:1-8a, 19-31) joined by a number of Jesus' sayings (16:8b-13, 14-18). These parables and sayings had no doubt been spoken on different occasions and handed down independently of one another. In 16:1-31, Luke provides them with a new and coherent context and focuses them on the historical situation of his addressees. The parable of the unjust steward (16:1-8a) and of Abraham and Lazarus (16:19-31) and the sayings related to them (16:8b-13, 14-18) present a unified development closely related to the social problems of the Lukan communities.

## The Example of the Steward.
### 16:1-13.

**16** He also said to the disciples, "There was a rich man who had a steward, and charges were brought to him that this man was wasting his goods. [2]And he called him and said to him, 'What is this that I hear about you? Turn in the account of your stewardship, for you can no longer be steward.' [3]And the steward said to himself, 'What shall I do, since my master is taking the stewardship away from me? I am not strong enough to dig, and I am ashamed to beg. [4]I have decided what to do, so that people may receive me into their houses when I am put out of the stewardship.' [5]So, summoning his master's debtors one by one, he said to the first, 'How much do you owe my master?' [6]He said, 'A hundred measures of oil.' And he said to him, 'Take your bill, and sit down quickly and write fifty.' [7]Then he said to another, 'And how much do you owe?' He said, 'A hundred measures of wheat.' He said to him, 'Take your bill, and write eighty.' [8]The master commended the dishonest steward for his shrewdness; for the sons of this world are more shrewd in dealing with their own generation than the sons of light. [9]And I tell you, make friends for yourselves by means of unrighteous mammon, so that when it fails they may receive you into the eternal habitations.

[10]"He who is faithful in a very little is faithful also in much; and he who is dishonest in a very little is dishonest also in much. [11]If then you have not been faithful in the unrighteous mammon, who will entrust to you the true riches? [12]And if you have not been faithful in that which is another's, who will give you that which is your own? [13]No servant can serve two masters; for either he will hate the one and love the other, or he will be devoted to the one and despise the other. You cannot serve God and mammon."

The unit begins with a parable concerning a steward who was charged with wasting his rich master's goods (16:1-8a). Upon being dismissed, the steward called his master's debtors and instructed them to re-write their promissory notes to their own advantage. He would thus be cared for by his master's debtors. Taking stock of his threatening and critical situation, the steward thus drew on his worldly wisdom and acted cleverly and resolutely in providing for his future. In the conclusion, the master commends the steward for his prudence.

In its original context, this parable must consequently have been intended as a call to resolute action in a time of crisis. As such, it would normally have been addressed to the unheeding or wavering multitudes to whom Jesus preached the good news that the kingdom of God was at hand. In its present context, however, it is addressed to those who already are disciples (16:1,9), and the master's commendation provides a springboard for Jesus' contrast between the sons of this world and the sons of light (16:8b). Jesus' admonishment of the latter indicates that the Christians are failing in a manner somehow associated with the steward's behavior. Contextually, this contrast provides a literary transition to the sayings which follow.

First, Jesus asks that the disciples make friends by means of unrighteous mammon that when it fails these friends may receive them into the eternal habitations (16:9). In the Lukan context, the steward is still an example for the addressees, not however because of his prudent resolve in the face of crisis (16:8a), but in the way he has used money to help others. It is consequently in this respect that the sons of this world are wiser than the sons of light (16:8b).

Jesus' message, which addresses present behavior in the life of the community, is further developed in 16:10-11. Money, the unrighteous mammon, which will one day be useless (16:9b), is of little importance in comparison with true riches. However, if the disciples are unfaithful in this present matter and fail to give to others, they will not receive those true riches. Correct use of riches in the course of christian history is consequently a prerequisite for receiving the definitive riches of God's kingdom, when the disciples will be received in the eternal habitations (16:9). Drawing on the parable's pastoral potential, Luke has thus adapted its original eschatological perspective, which looked to the imminent coming of the kingdom, to the demands which the kingdom makes on life in the historical period of the Church.

Luke then reminds his readers that the wealth in question is not really their own. Indeed it belongs to the community which they serve (see Acts 2:42, 44-45; 4:32, 34-35). Unfaithful in this matter, they would not receive the true riches which awaited them (16:12). Failing to share their wealth, they would be serving mammon rather than God. In no way could they serve these two mutually exclusive masters (16:13). The failure to share one's goods with the needy is consequently incompatible with the service of God.

In its original context, the parable of the unjust steward could have been addressed to the rich and poor without distinction. Luke's reinterpretation, however, could hardly have been intended for the poor of the community, at least not directly. Addressing the wealthy, it presupposes that many of the latter have become unmindful of the poor and urges them to share their wealth with the needy. Since the wealthy corresponded to the leaders of the community, at least in large measure, it also calls for fidelity in the regular distribution to the poor (see Acts 4:35; 6:1). To the extent that Luke's readers included the poor, it reminded them of their rights as members of the community.

## Avoiding Love of Money.
## 16:14-31.

[14]The Pharisees, who were lovers of money, heard of this, and they scoffed at him. [15]But he said to them, "You are those who justify yourselves before men, but God knows your hearts; for what is exalted among men is an abomination in the sight of God.

[16]"The law and the prophets were until John; since then the good news of the kingdom of God is preached, and every one enters it violently. [17]But it is easier for heaven and earth to pass away, than for one dot of the law to become void.

[18]"Every one who divorces his wife and marries another commits adultery, and he who marries a woman divorced from her husband commits adultery.

[19]"There was a rich man, who was clothed in purple and fine linen and who feasted sumptuously every day. [20]And at his gate lay a poor man named Lazarus, full of sores, [21]who desired to be fed with what fell from the rich man's table; moreover the dogs came and licked his sores. [22]The poor man died and was carried by the angels to Abraham's bosom. The rich man also died and was buried; [23]and in Hades, being in torment, he lifted up his eyes, and saw Abraham far off and Lazarus in his bosom. [24]And he called out, 'Father Abraham, have mercy upon me, and send Lazarus to dip the end of his finger in water and cool my tongue; for I am in anguish

in this flame.' 25But Abraham said, 'Son, remember that you in your lifetime received your good things, and Lazarus in like manner evil things; but now he is comforted here, and you are in anguish. 26And besides all this, between us and you a great chasm has been fixed, in order that those who would pass from here to you may not be able; and none may cross from there to us.' 27And he said, 'Then I beg you, father, to send him to my father's house, 28for I have five brothers, so that he may warn them, lest they also come into this place of torment.' 29But Abraham said, 'They have Moses and the prophets; let them hear them.' 30And he said, 'No, father Abraham; but if some one goes to them from the dead, they will repent.' 31He said to him, 'If they do not hear Moses and the prophets, neither will they be convinced if some one should rise from the dead.'"

Although Jesus had been addressing his disciples (16:1-13), the Pharisees are now introduced as having heard all that Jesus said. Being lovers of money, they scoffed at him (16:14). While the sayings (16:15-18) and the parables which they introduce (16:19-31) could originally have formed part of Jesus' teaching to Pharisees, in the context of 16;1-31, the designation Pharisees clearly represents a category of Christians who had heard Jesus' message and rejected it.

Jesus accuses the christian Pharisees of self-justification in their refusal to share their wealth. God, however, knows their hearts, and what is exalted as righteous among men is an abomination before him (16:15). To justify themselves theologically, these christian Pharisees appealed to a theology of history which distinguished between the period of the law and the prophets and the period of the gospel. The former had ended with John the Baptist; the latter had begun with Jesus' proclamation of the kingdom of God which everyone enters violently (16:16; see 12:51-53). The Pharisees thus argued that the requirement to share with the needy had ceased with John and was no longer relevant now that the kingdom of God had been proclaimed.

While Luke accepted the major distinction between the old testament mission of John and the new testament mission of Jesus, he responds that this does not mean that the law and the prophets have been abrogated. Like creation itself, which endures in the new era, the law remains in full force (16:17). Luke thus reminds his readers that they have not yet entered into the eternal habitations (16:9) and received the true riches (16:11). The kingdom is a future eschatological reality open to those who use wealth rightly during the period of its emergence in the life of the Church. As an example of the law's relevance, Luke then cites the case of divorce and remarriage, an area of concern in which the christian Pharisees acknowledged the law's abiding value in the life of the community (16:18).

The sayings provided in 16:14-18 introduce the unit's second parable, which is that of a rich man and his relationship to a poor man named Lazarus (16:19-31). Having provided an example of behavior to be imitated in the story of the wise steward (16:1-8a), he now presents one of behavior to be avoided. This pattern corresponds to the positive example of Barnabas (Acts 4:36-37) and the negative example of Ananias and Sapphira (Acts 5:1-11) which illustrated the ideal of community sharing as presented in the summary statement of Acts 4:32-35.

The rich man, like the Pharisees, is a lover of money and of the good things of this life, and he refuses to share with the desperately poor, whom Lazarus represents. When the two men die, however, their lot is reversed. Lazarus is rich in the bosom of Abraham, and the rich man is poor in the torment of Hades (16:19-23). The story of these two men thus dramatizes the salvific reversal of which Mary had sung in her canticle (1:46-55).

Recognizing how his situation vis-à-vis Lazarus has been altered, the rich man appeals to Abraham. The dialogue proceeds in two stages. In the first, the rich man begs Abraham to send Lazarus to his aid. He is told, however, that in the afterlife this is impossible (16:24-26). In reference to the story of the wise steward and its application (16:1-9), the rich man is told that he should have made "friends for" himself "by means of unrighteous mammon, so that when it fails they" might receive him "into the eternal habitations" (16:9).

In the second stage of the rich man's dialogue with Abraham, the former asks that Lazarus be sent to warn his five living brothers. Abraham responds that they have Moses and the prophets precisely for this purpose. To a further appeal that his brothers would repent if someone returned to them from the dead, Abraham answers that those who do not hear Moses and the prophets will not be convinced by someone who is risen from the dead (16:27-31). Luke thus reinforces his earlier statements concerning the enduring value of the law and the prophets and how they are related to the good news of the kingdom of God (16:16-17). By implication, he also tells his readers that the word of Jesus the risen Lord falls on deaf ears when those who have ears to hear are unable to hear the law and the prophets. He thus helps them to understand why the word of the risen Lord in the community does not always result in the sharing which should characterize it.

iv. Sin and the Service of Reconciliation.
*We have only done what was our duty.*
17:1-10.

**17** And he said to his disciples, "Temptations to sin are sure to come; but woe to him by whom they come! [2]It would be better for him if a millstone were hung round his neck and he were cast into the sea, than that he should cause one of these little ones to sin. [3]Take heed to yourselves; if your brother sins, rebuke him, and if he repents, forgive him; [4]and if he sins against you seven times in the day, and turns to you seven times, and says, 'I repent,' you must forgive him.

⁵The apostles said to the Lord, "Increase our faith!" ⁶And the Lord said, "If you had faith as a grain of mustard seed, you could say to this sycamine tree, 'Be rooted up, and be planted in the sea,' and it would obey you.

⁷"Will any one of you, who has a servant plowing or keeping sheep, say to him when he has come in from the field, 'Come at once and sit down at table'? ⁸Will he not rather say to him, 'Prepare supper for me, and gird yourself and serve me, till I eat and drink; and afterward you shall eat and drink'? ⁹Does he thank the servant because he did what was commanded? ¹⁰So you also, when you have done all that is commanded you, say, 'We are unworthy servants; we have only done what was our duty.'"

The first major section (14:1-17:10) in the journey's second stage (13:22-19:48) concludes with a unit which contrasts those who tempt others to sin and those who are servants of reconciliation (17:1-10). Like 15:1-32, the unit realistically faces the fact of sin in the community and develops a concrete aspect of how those who have embarked on the journey should respond to one who sins. As in 14:1-35; 15:1-32; 16:1-31, the unit invokes meal imagery and relationships at table (17:8) as symbols of life itself together with its multiple challenges.

Within the unit, Luke does not indicate the specific attitudes and behavior included in the general term sin. However, from the previous units in this section, it becomes obvious that he is primarily concerned with social and economic concerns, both of which are intimately related to table fellowship. The christian meal context reflects the state of the community at large and calls for a way of life which is appropriate for the kingdom of God.

The unit unfolds in two sections. In the first, Jesus addresses the disciples concerning the inevitability of sin among them and on how they should deal with the sinner

(17:1-4). In the second he tells the apostles that what is expected of them is not extraordinary but the simple fulfillment of normal duty (17:5-10).

Temptations to sin are inevitable (17:1a). Since Jesus had foreseen and announced their coming, no one should be perturbed at the mere fact they are present. This, however, does not excuse one who would lead the community's little ones to sin. After accepting the fact of sin, the author issues a warning against leading someone to sin (17:1b-2). Jesus' hyperbolic language is intended as a pastoral deterrent rather than as a judgment. He then asks the community to forgive actual sinners as often as they repent (17:3-4). There is no limit to forgiveness.

The disciples find the Lord's message (17:1-4) too difficult for their present level of faith development. They consequently ask that he increase their faith (17:a). The Lord's answer is that even minimal faith should suffice (17:6). What he has asked of them is no more than should be expected of someone who has accepted to serve the community. When they fulfill their service, they should not seek special gratitude as though they had performed something extraordinary. They have merely done their duty as unworthy servants. Jesus thus reminds them that as unworthy servants they too are sinners (17:7-10).

## 2. c. The House of Jerusalem Forsaken.

### i. The Kingdom of God and the Day of the Son of Man.
*Now he was a Samaritan.*
17:11-37.

> [11]On the way to Jerusalem he was passing along between Samaria and Galilee. [12]And as he entered a village, he was met by ten lepers, who stood at a distance [13]and lifted up their voices and said, "Jesus, Master, have mercy on us." [14]When he saw them he said to them, "Go and show yourselves to the priests." And as they

went they were cleansed. [15]Then one of them, when he saw that he was healed, turned back, praising God with a loud voice; [16]and he fell on his face at Jesus' feet, giving him thanks. Now he was a Samaritan. [17]Then said Jesus, "Were not ten cleansed? Where are the nine? [18]Was no one found to return and give praise to God except this foreigner?" [19]And he said to him, "Rise and go your way; your faith has made you well."

[20]Being asked by the Pharisees when the kingdom of God was coming, he answered them, "The kingdom of God is not coming with signs to be observed; [21]nor will they say, 'Lo, here it is!' or 'There!' for behold, the kingdom of God is in the midst of you."

[22]And he said to the disciples, "The days are coming when you will desire to see one of the days of the Son of man, and you will not see it. [23]And they will say to you, 'Lo, there!' or 'Lo, here!' Do not go, do not follow them. [24]For as the lightning flashes and lights up the sky from one side to the other, so will the Son of man be in his day. [25]But first he must suffer many things and be rejected by this generation. [26]As it was in the days of Noah, so will it be in the days of the Son of man. [27]They ate, they drank, they married, they were given in marriage, until the day when Noah entered the ark, and the flood came and destroyed them all. [28]Likewise as it was in the days of Lot—they ate, they drank, they bought, they sold, they planted, they built, [29]but on the day when Lot went out from Sodom fire and sulphur rained from heaven and destroyed them all—[30]so will it be on the day when the Son of man is revealed. [31]On that day, let him who is on the housetop, with his goods in the house, not come down to take them away; and likewise let him who is in the field not turn back. [32]Remember Lot's wife. [33]Whoever seeks to gain his life will lose it, but whoever loses his life will preserve it. [34]I tell you, in that night there will be two in one bed; one will be taken and the other left. [35]There will be two women grinding together; one

will be taken and the other left." [37]And they said to him, "Where, Lord?" He said to them, "Where the body is, there the eagles will be gathered together."

Having dealt with the social questions confronting early Christianity (14:1-17:10), Luke focuses on historical questions (17:11-19:48). In this second part of Jesus' journey from Galilee to Jerusalem, his concern is with the unfolding of salvation history, the way it runs counter to human expectations, and the forsaking of a blind Jerusalem.

The section opens with a short episode in which Jesus cures ten lepers, but only one, a foreigner, returns to express his gratitude (17:11-19), and with two addresses, one to the Pharisees (17:20-21) and one to the disciples (17:22-37). Literarily, the triple unit is symbolic of the events and encounters which are narrated in 18:1-19:48, where selfish, exclusivistic and blind attitudes and expectations fail to appreciate the advent of the kingdom. On the day of the Son of man, the faithful will be saved, like the Samaritan foreigner who returned to praise God in faith.

The healing event is situated on the way to Jerusalem between Samaria and Galilee (17:11). Luke thus recalls the journey motif which governs this part of the gospel (9:51-56, 57; 10:38; 13:22). From this point on, the journey will be noted with increasing frequency as it moves toward its geographical climax (18:35,43; 19:1,11, 28-29,37,41,45).

Mention of Samaria is significant, since of the ten who were healed only the Samaritan responded with grateful faith and praise. At first, the Samaritans had rejected Jesus' disciples because he was going to Jerusalem (9:52-53). However, Jesus had not allowed his disciples to call down fire from heaven to destroy them (9:54-55). In actual fact a Samaritan would show the Jews how to be a good neighbor according to the law (10:30-37). By contrast with nine others, a Samaritan now embodies the conditions of salvation. In his going to Jerusalem, Jesus would confront the city and transcend its previous significance. The Samaritans in 9:52-55, however, had been in no position to appreciate this.

Healing is a requisite for salvation. For salvation to be actually realized, however, the person healed must respond in faith, a gift which is open to all. The grateful Samaritan in our story manifests the universality of faith and consequent salvation. Salvation is consequently not limited to the Jews, and the destruction of Jerusalem (19:41-44; see 13:34-35) does not frustrate the historical plan of salvation.

Like the nine lepers who did not return to praise God and Jesus (17:11-19), the Pharisees failed to recognize that the kingdom of God was already in their midst (17:20-21). It had been manifested in Jesus' healing, but in their blindness they continued to look for it elsewhere. Expecting a sign which would prove to them that the kingdom was present, they did not realize that faith alone would enable them to discern it. Without faith, Jesus' miracles remain opaque and non-revelatory.

The disciples and the Lukan communities may be like the Samaritan whose faith recognized the presence of the kingdom and responded with grateful praise, but with regard to the day of the Son of man they would have to resist that attitude of the Pharisees. In their struggles and persecutions, they would yearn to see one of the days of the Son of man. As in the case of the Pharisees, however, they would not see it (17:22; see 9:51-56). Contrary to what anyone might tell them (17:23), the day would eventually come with the speed, unexpectedness and unmistakable clarity of heavenly lightning (17:24). Consequently, they must not listen to those who think they have seen its signs (17:23b). Drawing on the authority of Jesus, Luke thus responds to any apocalyptic and vengeful tendencies which were surfacing among his intended readers.

Before the day of the Son of man comes, the latter must first suffer and be rejected (17:25). The disciples must expect the same for themselves. Simplistic and escapist efforts to gain or save their lives are of no avail. Only those who, like the Son of man, accept the necessity of suffering and rejection will preserve their lives and be saved (17:33). The others, those who seek their lives and continue to live as though the suffering and rejection of Jesus had made no difference (17:26-30) or who cling to earthly possessions (17:31-32) will be destroyed (17:33a). When the day does come, human associations and relationships will make no difference. Some will be taken and some will be left without regard for earthly values (17:34-35). The only criterion will be their acceptance of Christ's willingness to lose his life (17:25,33).

ii. Constancy and Humility in Prayer.
*To such belongs the kingdom of God.*
18:1-17.

**18**   And he told them a parable, to the effect that they ought always to pray and not lose heart. [2]He said, "In a certain city there was a judge who neither feared God nor regarded man; [3]and there was a widow in that city who kept coming to him and saying, 'Vindicate me against my adversary.' [4]For a while he refused; but afterward he said to himself, 'Though I neither fear God nor regard man, [5]yet because this widow bothers me, I will vindicate her, or she will wear me out by her continual coming.'" [6]And the Lord said, "Hear what the unrighteous judge says. [7]And will not God vindicate his elect, who cry to him day and night? Will he delay long over them? [8]I tell you, he will vindicate them speedily. Nevertheless, when the Son of man comes, will he find faith on earth?"

[9]He also told this parable to some who trusted in themselves that they were righteous and despised others: [10]"Two men went up into the temple to pray, one a Pharisee and the other a tax collector. [11]The Pharisee stood and prayed thus with himself, 'God, I thank thee that I am not like other men, extortioners, unjust,

adulterers, or even like this tax collector. [12]I fast twice a week, I give tithes of all that I get.' [13]But the tax collector, standing far off, would not even lift up his eyes to heaven, but beat his breast, saying, 'God, be merciful to me a sinner!' [14]I tell you, this man went down to his house justified rather than the other; for every one who exalts himself will be humbled, but he who humbles himself will be exalted."

[15]Now they were bringing even infants to him that he might touch them; and when the disciples saw it, they rebuked them. [16]But Jesus called them to him, saying, "Let the children come to me, and do not hinder them; for to such belongs the kingdom of God. [17]Truly, I say to you, whoever does not receive the kingdom of God like a child shall not enter it."

In the previous unit, Luke responded to false expectations concerning the kingdom of God and the day of the Son of man and indicated how the disciples were to ready themselves for the latter. His message concerning the day of the Son of man was somewhat terrifying, and by itself it could have led to discouragement. His teaching to the disciples is thus supplemented by two parables on prayer (18:1-8, 9-14) and a short unit which shows how the attitudes called for by the parables are concretely exemplified in those of children (18:15-17).

The coming day of the Lord and the sufferings which must precede it should not turn the Christians away from their commitment. In the midst of persecution, they "ought always to pray and not lose heart" (18:1). Such is the message of the first parable.

The story concerns a judge who neither fears God nor regards man and a widow who asks him to vindicate her against her adversary (18:2-5). In Jesus' application, God is contrasted with the unrighteous judge, and by implication the Christians stand in the position of the widow

(18:6-8). The judge finally vindicates the widow because of her incessant pleading. If this is true of an unrighteous judge, will not God vindicate his elect if they remain constant in prayer? The message parallels Luke's teaching on prayer in the parables (11:5-13) which follow the Lord's prayer (11:2-4).

However, it is not enough that the disciples persevere in prayer. They must look to the attitude which accompanies it. They may be persecuted, but this is no ground for self-righteous comparisons with others (18:9). Such is the message of the second parable.

The story concerns two men, a Pharisee and a tax collector, who pray in vastly different ways. The Pharisee thanks God for his righteousness. He sees himself as totally unlike the tax collector and others who are publicly recognized as unrighteous. The tax collector, on the other hand, prays humbly, recognizes his sinfulness and calls on God's mercy (18:9-13). Christians must pray like the tax collector and not like the Pharisee. Otherwise they shall not be justified (18:14a). The application ends with a favorite Lukan saying of Jesus: "Everyone who exalts himself will be humbled, but he who humbles himself will be exalted" (18:14b; see 1:52; 14:11).

After these two parables, an incident enables Jesus to concretize their teaching. The disciples rebuke those who are bringing infants to Jesus (18:15). Correcting them, Jesus points out that the kingdom of God belongs to children (18:16) and that the disciples must receive the kingdom like a child if they wish to enter it (18:17). To appreciate Jesus' message, we should recall that the kingdom already is in their midst (17:21). Like the grateful Samaritan (17:11-19), the widow (18:1-8) and the tax collector (18:9-14), they must receive the kingdom with the faith, grateful praise, persistence and unpretentiousness of a child (18:17a) if they wish to enter it (18:17b) on the day of the Son of man (17:22-37).

iii. Inheriting the Kingdom of God.
   *What is impossible with men is possible with God.*
   18:18-30.

> [18]And a ruler asked him, "Good Teacher, what shall
> I do to inherit eternal life?" [19]And Jesus said to him,
> "Why do you call me good? No one is good but God
> alone. [20]You know the commandments: 'Do not commit
> adultery, Do not kill, Do not steal, Do not bear false
> witness, Honor your father and mother.'" [21]And he said,
> "All these I have observed from my youth." [22]And when
> Jesus heard it, he said to him, "One thing you still lack.
> Sell all that you have and distribute to the poor, and you
> will have treasure in heaven; and come, follow me." [23]But
> when he heard this he became sad, for he was very rich.
> [24]Jesus looking at him said, "How hard it is for those who
> have riches to enter the kingdom of God! [25]For it is easier
> for a camel to go through the eye of a needle than for a
> rich man to enter the kingdom of God." [26]Those who
> heard it said, "Then who can be saved?" [27]But he said,
> "What is impossible with men is possible with God."
> [28]And Peter said, "Lo, we have left our homes and fol-
> lowed you." [29]And he said to them, "Truly, I say to you,
> there is no man who has left house or wife or brothers or
> parents or children, for the sake of the kingdom of God,
> [30]who will not receive manifold more in this time, and in
> the age to come eternal life."

In 17:11-37, Luke drew attention to the fulfillment of
history in the day of the Son of man. In 18:1-17, he then
showed how persistent and humble prayer would lead to
God's vindication of the elect. The disciples consequently
were not to look for an immediate manifestation of a day
of the Son of man in which their persecutors would be
destroyed (17:22; see 9:51-56). If they wish to enter the
kingdom of God (18:17), which already is in their midst
(17:21), their attitude must be like that of a child. Unlike

those who cling to earthly values, relationships and possessions (17:26-31), they must join the Son of man in accepting suffering, rejection and loss of life (17:25,33).

In 18:18-30, Luke now shows how riches and merely human relationships (see 17:26-31) can obstruct entry into the kingdom of God. Entry into the kingdom, an expression which is equivalent to eternal life in the age to come, is for those who leave all for the sake of the kingdom.

A ruler's question (18:18) recalls that of the lawyer in 10:25: "Teacher, what shall I do to inherit eternal life?" Unlike the lawyer, however, the ruler addresses Jesus as "Good Teacher," and Jesus asks why he calls him good, for no one is good but God alone (18:19). The reader, who knows that Jesus is the Son of God, recognizes the irony in Jesus' question. Had the ruler accepted Jesus' divine sonship, he could rightly have called him good. Without such faith, however, his address was objectively correct but subjectively inappropriate.

In his response to the lawyer, Jesus had asked that he spell out what is written in the law and the latter responded with the commandment of love of God and neighbor (10:26-27). To this Jesus had replied that his answer was correct, and that if he did this he would live (10:28). In his response to the ruler, on the other hand, Jesus himself cites a number of commandments, those concerning adultery, stealing, bearing false witness, and honoring one's father and mother (18:20). As in the encounter with the lawyer, the story has now reached the critical issue. The lawyer had tried to distinguish some who were not his neighbor from those who were, thus limiting the law's applicability and his own responsibility. The ruler states that he has observed all these commandments (18:21). Jesus then adds that only one thing is lacking for him to inherit eternal life. He must sell all he has and distribute to the poor. He will thus have treasure in heaven. Detached from earthly possessions, he is now enabled to come and follow Jesus on the way to God and eternal life in the kingdom (18:22). As in the case of the lawyer with whom Jesus shares the story of the good Samaritan (10:30-37), the main issue is thus selfless concern for the needy.

The ruler, who was very rich, was saddened by Jesus' challenging requirement for entry into the kingdom (18:23). Acknowledging the special difficulty created by riches, Jesus adds a startling hyperbole which places it in bold relief and shocks the reader into recognizing what ultimately is at stake: "It is easier for a camel to go through the eye of a needle than for a rich man to enter the kingdom of God" (18:24-25). The manifest impossibility elicited by Jesus' comparison leads those who heard the dialogue to ask: "Then who can be saved?" Jesus' answer is that it is humanly impossible but divinely possible for the rich to be saved (18:26-27). The example of Peter and Jesus' other followers is a visible sign of what God can do. Having left much to follow Jesus, all who imitate the latter are amply rewarded in the present life and will receive eternal life in the age to come (18:28-30).

iv. Lack of Understanding.
*Lord, let me receive my sight.*
18:31-19:10.

31And taking the twelve, he said to them, "Behold, we are going up to Jerusalem, and everything that is written of the Son of man by the prophets will be accomplished. 32For he will be delivered to the Gentiles, and will be mocked and shamefully treated and spit upon; 33they will scourge him and kill him, and on the third day he will rise." 34But they understood none of these things; this saying was hid from them, and they did not grasp what was said.

35As he drew near to Jericho, a blind man was sitting by the roadside begging; 36and hearing a multitude going by, he inquired what this meant. 37They told him, "Jesus of Nazareth is passing by." 38And he cried, "Jesus, Son of David, have mercy on me!" [39] And those who were in front rebuked him, telling him to be silent; but he cried out all the more, "Son of David, have mercy on me!" [40] And Jesus stopped, and commanded him to be brought to him; and when he came near, he asked him, [41] "What do you want me to do for you?" He said, "Lord, let me receive my sight." [42] And Jesus said to him, "Receive your sight; your faith has made you well." [43] And immediately he received his sight and followed him, glorifying God; and all the people, when they saw it, gave praise to God.

**19** He entered Jericho and was passing through. [2] And there was a man named Zacchaeus; he was a chief tax collector, and rich. [3] And he sought to see who Jesus was, but could not on account of the crowd, because he was small of stature. [4] So he ran on ahead and climbed up into a sycamore tree to see him, for he was to pass that way. [5] And when Jesus came to the place, he looked up and said to him, "Zacchaeus, make haste and come down; for I must stay at your house today." [6] So he made haste and came down, and received him joyfully. [7] And when they saw it they all murmured. "He has gone in to be the guest of a man who is a sinner." [8] And Zacchaeus stood and said to the Lord, "Behold, Lord, the half of my goods I give to the poor; and if I have defrauded any one of anything, I restore it fourfold." [9] And Jesus said to him, "Today, salvation has come to this house, since he also is a son of Abraham. [10] For the Son of man came to seek and to save the lost."

Once again Luke explicitly mentions the journey to Jerusalem (18:31b). Taking the Twelve with him (18:31a), Jesus announces the coming passion in great detail (18:32-33). Actually everything which would occur in Jerusalem was written of the Son of man by the prophets and it would now be accomplished (18:31c). Jesus himself draws the link

between the approaching Jerusalem events and the prophetic word. In itself, the promise-fulfillment relationship
was not obvious. Luke notes that the Twelve understood
none of what Jesus told them. The reason was that the
saying was hid from them (18:34). Their minds would have
to be opened to the understanding of the Scriptures (24:45)
once they had suffered the experience of Jesus' passion
and their eyes had been opened to recognize the risen Lord
in the breaking of the bread (24:13-35).

The account now focuses on Jericho, an oasis city in the
Jordan valley but a few miles from the northern end of the
Dead Sea, at the point where the Roman road began its
steep climb through the Judean desert to Jerusalem. As
Jesus draws near the city, he cures a blind beggar who was
sitting by the roadside (18:35-43). Having entered the city,
and while passing through it, he accepts the hospitality of
Zacchaeus, a rich tax collector (19:1-10).

The cure of the blind man prefigures the eventual opening
of the eyes of those who could not grasp Jesus' prediction
of the passion and the meaning of the Scriptures.

Hearing a multitude, the blind man inquired what this
meant and was told that Jesus of Nazareth was passing by.
On hearing this, he cries out to Jesus. However, he does not
address him as Jesus of Nazareth but as Jesus, Son of David.
He thus proclaims Jesus' royalty and asks that Jesus have
mercy on him (18:36-37). In effect, the blind man is asking
for the manifestation of messianic salvation (see 4:18; 7:21).
The multitude, however, stands in the way and tries to
silence him, but to no avail (18:38-39). When Jesus calls
for him and asks what he can do for him, the beggar addresses Jesus as Lord and asks to receive his sight (18:40-41).
It is thus as Lord, risen Lord that is, that Jesus is the Son
of David and the messianic king and not in any earthly
historical sense. The man's faith calls for the gift of sight.
In the same way, the apostles would have their eyes opened
by the risen Lord once they had responded to him in faith.
Having received his sight, the man follows Jesus on the

journey, glorifying God and moving all who saw the event to give praise to God (18:42-43).

Jesus' response to Zacchaeus, a chief tax collector in Jericho, prefigures the future course of christian history in which religious outcasts would repent, give to the poor and be saved, over the objections of those who deemed themselves righteous.

The story's literary structure helps us to discern the author's message. First we have an introduction, which situates the event geographically and presents the protagonist and the immediate social context (19:1-4). The body of the narrative is framed by an inclusion. In 19:5, Jesus states: "I must stay at your house today." In 19:9, he says: "Today salvation has come to this house." To have Jesus as one's guest is to be host to salvation. The conclusion draws an important generalization from the event: "The Son of man came to seek and to save the lost" (19:10; see 15:4-7, 8-10,24,32).

In 19:2, Luke emphasizes the fact that Zacchaeus was rich. The story thus shows how with God it is possible for a rich man to be saved (see 18:24-27). What is required is that he accept Jesus' offer of table fellowship, repent for any injustice he has done, give to the poor and welcome Jesus into his home. On these conditions he becomes a true son of Abraham (19:9b). Like the blind man in 18:35-43, Zacchaeus thus overcomes the difficulties presented by the crowd which surrounds Jesus, and Jesus reaches out to him in spite of their objections. So will it be among those who enter into the kingdom and are saved on the day of the Son of man.

v. Up to Jerusalem.
*To every one who has will more be given.*
19:11-27.

> [11]As they heard these things, he proceeded to tell a parable, because he was near to Jerusalem, and because

they supposed that the kingdom of God was to appear immediately. [12]He said therefore, "A nobleman went into a far country to receive a kingdom and then return. [13]Calling ten of his servants, he gave them ten pounds, and said to them, 'Trade with these till I come.' [14]But his citizens hated him and sent an embassy after him, saying, 'We do not want this man to reign over us.' [15]When he returned, having received the kingdom, he commanded these servants, to whom he had given the money, to be called to him, that he might know what they had gained by trading. [16]The first came before him, saying, 'Lord, your pound has made ten pounds more.' [17]And he said to him, 'Well done, good servant! Because you have been faithful in a very little, you shall have authority over ten cities.' [18]And the second came, saying, 'Lord, your pound has made five pounds.' [19]And he said to him, 'And you are to be over five cities.' [20]Then another came, saying, 'Lord, here is your pound, which I kept laid away in a napkin; [21]for I was afraid of you, because you are a severe man; you take up what you did not lay down, and reap what you did not sow.' [22]He said to him, 'I will condemn you out of your own mouth, you wicked servant! You knew that I was a severe man, taking up what I did not lay down and reaping what I did not sow? [23]Why then did you not put my money into the bank, and at my coming I should have collected it with interest?' [24]And he said to those who stood by, 'Take the pound from him, and give it to him who has the ten pounds.' [25](And they said to him, 'Lord, he has ten pounds!') [26]I tell you, that to every one who has will more be given; but from him who has not, even what he has will be taken away. [27]But as for these enemies of mine, who did not want me to reign over them, bring them here and slay them before me.'"

Jesus now tells a parable to those who have heard the things which took place as he neared Jericho (18:35-43) and passed through it (19:1-10). Jesus was near Jerusalem, the place where "everything that is written of the Son of man by the prophets will be accomplished" (18:31). Not understanding Jesus' prediction concerning the passion and resurrection (18:32-34), those who heard did not grasp that it is as risen Lord (18:41) that Jesus would be king (18:38-39). Like the Pharisees (17:20-21), they had a mistaken notion of the kingdom. Jesus tells them the parable because they believed that the kingdom as they understood it would appear immediately (19:11). As in 18:1,9, the parable is thus introduced by a statement concerning its purpose and general theme.

The parable concerns a nobleman, his servants and citizens. The nobleman goes to a far off country to receive his kingdom and to return with it (19:12). Historically, the story evokes events in the Herodian succession as rulers of Judaea. Theologically, it evokes Jesus' ascension to the Father (24:50-53) and his eventual return at history's fulfillment (Acts 3:20-26). The ten servants, who are commissioned to manage the nobleman's affairs during his absence (19:13), represent the Christians engaged in the christian mission between the ascension and the Lord's return. The citizens are those who hated the nobleman and did all to prevent his reigning over them (19:14). Their role is that of those who persecute the Church and reject the true kingdom which is in their midst.

After the introduction (19:11-14), the parable focuses on the nobleman's return after receiving the kingdom. It thus refers to the day of the Son of man, when the servants will be called to account for their stewardship (19:15-26) and the king's enemies will be slain (19:27). The author's concern is pastoral, and as such it deals especially with the role of the king's servants in leading the Church. The latter should not be overly preoccupied with the fate of their persecutors. The Lord himself will deal with them on his return.

The servants cannot remain passive during the Lord's absence. They have received a trust which must be developed each according to his ability. If they reject their responsibility, even out of fear, and leave matters in the same state in which they were at the Lord's departure, they are unfaithful in their mission and shall have no place in the full manifestation of the kingdom on the day of the Son of man. Their place will be given to those who had proven most faithful. The author's theme is thus similar to that developed in the parable of the lamp (8:16-18) and in Jesus' teaching on the right use of money (16:9-12). In the discourse at the last supper, we learn that those who have stood fast with Jesus in his temptations will receive a role as judges when the kingdom is fully manifested (22:30).

vi. Entry into Jerusalem.
*Blessed is the king who comes in the name of the Lord.*
19:28-48.

28 And when he had said this, he went on ahead, going up to Jerusalem. 29 When he drew near to Bethphage and Bethany, at the mount that is called Olivet, he sent two of the disciples, 30 saying, "Go into the village opposite, where on entering you will find a colt tied, on which no one has ever yet sat; untie it and bring it here. 31 If any one asks you, 'Why are you untying it?' you shall say this, 'The Lord has need of it.'" 32 So those who were sent went away and found it as he had told them. 33 And as they were untying the colt, its owners said to them, "Why are you untying the colt?" 34 And they said, "The Lord has need of it." 35 And they brought it to Jesus, and throwing their garments on the colt they set Jesus upon it. 36 And as he rode along, they spread their garments on the road. 37 As he was now drawing near, at the descent of the Mount of Olives, the whole multitude of the disciples began to rejoice and praise God with a loud voice for all the mighty works that they had seen, 38 saying, "Blessed is the King who comes in the name of the Lord! Peace in

heaven and glory in the highest!" [39]And some of the Pharisees in the multitude said to him, "Teacher, rebuke your disciples." [40]He answered, "I tell you, if these were silent, the very stones would cry out."

[41]And when he drew near and saw the city he wept over it, [42]saying, "Would that even today you knew the things that make for peace! But now they are hid from your eyes. [43]For the days shall come upon you, when your enemies will cast up a bank about you and surround you, and hem you in on every side, [44]and dash you to the ground, you and your children within you, and they will not leave one stone upon another in you; because you did not know the time of your visitation."

[45]And he entered the temple and began to drive out those who sold, [46]saying to them, "It is written, 'My house shall be a house of prayer'; but you have made it a den of robbers."

[47]And he was teaching daily in the temple. The chief priests and the scribes and the principal men of the people sought to destroy him; [48]but they did not find anything they could do, for all the people hung upon his words.

After telling them the parable on the servants' responsibility during the Lord's absence (19:11-27), Jesus "went on ahead, going up to Jerusalem"(19:28). Jesus is thus going up to receive the kingdom (see 19:12). The kingdom, however, is not to be Jerusalem's earthly kingdom, but the kingdom of God. Those who greet Jesus (19:38) proclaim this deeper reality, but some of the Pharisees, who remain on the human level, either fail to perceive this or, so perceiving it, view the greeting as blasphemous (19:39).

The unit includes a brief transitional summary (19:28), the three final stages of Jesus' journey (19:29-46), and a concluding summary (19:47-48). The transitional summary recalls the journey to Jerusalem and merely serves to bring Jesus from Jericho to its next significant stage which starts in the region of Bethphage and Bethany on the eastern slope of the Mount of Olives near the summit. The first stage brings Jesus from near Bethphage and Bethany to the descent on the western side of the Mount of Olives (19:29-40). In the second, Jesus is near the city at a point where he overlooks it (19:41-44). In the third, he enters the temple (19:45-46). The concluding summary focuses on Jesus' daily activities in the temple and the reaction to his teaching (19:47-48).

The descent of the Mount of Olives toward Jerusalem is carefully planned by Jesus. Presented as one who knows all, Jesus is firmly in control of the events. His detailed instructions to two of his disciples (19:30-34) parallel similar instructions for the preparations of the Passover (22:7-13). In both cases the disciples find things precisely as Jesus had indicated. Jesus' entry on a colt evokes Judah's rule over the twelve tribes of Israel (Gen 49:11), Solomon's arrival for his royal anointing (1 Kgs 1:38) and Zechariah's prophecy concerning the royal messiah's humble, peaceful and universal rule (Zech 9:9-10). The fact that the colt is one on which no one has ever sat (19:30) shows how Jesus' rule is a completely new phenomenon in salvation history. As king and leader of a new Israel, Jesus fulfills Old Testament expectations and transcends them.

As Jesus draws near and continues to descend, the whole multitude of disciples praises God for all the mighty works they had seen (19:37). The author thus recalls all the events which he had presented in the course of Jesus' mission and journey. The disciples of Emmaus would summarize these events as those of "a prophet mighty in deed and word before God and all the people" (24:19). Jesus is acclaimed as a blessed King "who comes in the name of the Lord" (19:38), as he had announced in 13:35. The announcement, however, had associated the greeting with Jesus' death (13:33-34) and Jerusalem's failure to respond to his efforts on her behalf (13:35). The greeting is thus an ominous reminder of how human expectations would be reversed and prepares the reader for Jesus' announcement that Jerusalem and its temple would be destroyed (21:5-28).

Some of the Pharisees, who were not privy to what Jesus had said in 13:33-35 asked that Jesus rebuke his disciples (19:39). Politically, they may have feared a messianic uprising and Roman reprisals. Religiously, they reacted against any claim that Jesus came as King in the Lord's name. In response, Jesus says that there is no silencing the truth. In the silence of the disciples, there would be no silencing the stones, which would acclaim Jesus' royal advent (19:40).

In the second stage, Jesus weeps over the city which cannot recognize the things that make for peace (19:41-42), a peace which is heavenly and not earthly (19:38b; see 2:14). He then announces Jerusalem's destruction (19:43-44a; see 21:20-28) and attributes it to her inability to recognize the time of her visitation (19:44b; see 1:68).

In the brief final stage, Jesus enters the temple and drives out the sellers (19:45). The meaning of the event is developed in Stephen's discourse in Acts 7:1-53. For the moment, Jesus merely indicates how Jerusalem has not been able to see "the things that make for peace" (19:42). The Lord's temple, which was meant to be a house of prayer (see Isa 56:7), has been transformed into a den of robbers (19:46).

The concluding summary (19:47-48) is closely related to this last theme. Rejecting the divine King of peace, the chief priests, scribes and principal men of the people seek a way to destroy Jesus. It also prepares the reader for 20:1-21:38, where we see how they did this on one of the days (20:1) when Jesus was teaching in the temple (19:47). The author also introduces "all the people" who "hung upon his words" as the principal human obstacle to the efforts of Jesus' enemies.

## C. 3. IN THE TEMPLE OF JERUSALEM.
## REJECTION AND VICTORY IN THE
## CHRISTIAN JOURNEY.
### 20:1-21:38

The third stage in Jesus' journey to God presents the events of one of the days when Jesus was teaching and preaching in the temple (20:1; see 19:47-48). A similar one-day schema would serve to unify all the events presented in chapter 24.

Like the two previous stages, this third stage is developed in two phases. The first is primarily concerned with Jesus' historical life and its implications for the life of the disciples (20:1-21:4). The second deals with historical and eschatological questions as Luke discusses the significance of the destruction of the temple and of Jerusalem in relation to the consummation of history on the final day (21:5-36). Like the second stage, it ends with a summary of Jesus' teaching activity in the temple.

The first phase includes two encounters, one with the chief priests and the scribes, with whom Luke has associated the elders (20:1-26), and one with the Sadducees and the scribes (20:27-44), as well as special teaching for the disciples (20:45-21:4).

In the first encounter, the chief priests and the scribes first try to trap Jesus directly (20:1-8). Unsuccessful in their attempt and on account of the people whom Jesus continues to teach (20:9-19), they then try to trap Jesus indirectly (20:20-26). By diverting responsibility away from themselves to the Roman authorities, they hope to achieve the destruction of Jesus without the risk that the people would turn against them.

In the second encounter, Jesus responds to a theological trap set by the Sadducees (20:27-36) and introduces a biblical proof that the dead do indeed rise again (20:37-38). Given the reality of resurrection, Jesus then shows the scribes that the special resurrection of the Christ or Messiah also is contained in the scriptures (20:39-44).

Speaking to the disciples in the hearing of the people, Jesus ends the first phase with a warning against assuming the attitudes and outward behavior of the scribes (20:45-47) and a positive teaching on the nature of genuine christian values (21:1-4). The latter is inspired by the contrast between the rich and the poor in giving to the temple treasury.

The second phase includes a long discourse (21:5-36) and a concluding summary (21:37-38), which recalls that of the journey's second stage (19:47-48) and the introductory summary given in 20:1.

This phase is divided into three units. In the first, Jesus discusses the destruction of the temple, separates this event from the end time, and presents the attitudes which must govern present behavior (21:5-19). In the second, he introduces the destruction of Jerusalem and contrasts the signs which precede it with those which announce the end and the coming of the Son of man (21:20-28). In the third, he addresses the end-time directly and shows how its inevitable coming should influence Christian attitudes at every moment of history (21:29-36).

### 3. a. Jesus and the Leaders of Israel.

#### i. The Authority of Jesus.
*As he was teaching the people in the temple.*
20:1-8.

**20** One day, as he was teaching the people in the temple and preaching the gospel, the chief priests and the scribes with the elders came up ²and said to him, "Tell us by what authority you do these things, or who it is that gave you this authority." ³He answered them, "I also will ask you a question; now tell me, ⁴Was the baptism of John from heaven or from men?" ⁵And they discussed it with one another, saying, "If we say, 'From heaven,' he will say, 'Why did you not believe him?' ⁶But if we say, 'From men,' all the people will stone us; for they are convinced that John was a prophet." ⁷So they answered that they did not know whence it was. [8] And Jesus said to them, "Neither will I tell you by what authority I do these things."

The journey's third major stage opens with an encounter between Jesus and the chief priests and the scribes with the elders (20:1). The context is the temple (see 19:47-48), whose destruction constitutes a major theme in 21:5-9. Hence Luke's mention of the chief priests, who were drawn mainly from the ranks of the Sadducees (see 20:27-38) and whose functions were associated with the temple. The Pharisees, on the other hand, were associated primarily with the synagogue. Although Luke's interest includes the synagogue (20:46), the temple setting does not call for their inclusion in the list of Jesus' opponents (20:1).

Luke's primary interest, however, is not with the chief priests but with the scribes, who are mentioned before the chief priests in 20:19, by themselves in 20:39, and as embodying the behavior which the disciples must avoid in 20:45. In 20:1-21:38, Jesus is presented as teaching the people (20:1; 21:37-38). In this function, he came into direct conflict with the scribes, who were Judaism's recognized teachers, and who like Jesus exercised their function in the temple as well as in the synagogue.

The chief priests, scribes and elders ask Jesus by what authority he does these things, or who gave him this authority (20:2). The question has to do with "these things," a summary reference to all the things that have been narrated in the previous chapters of the gospel. It bears on Jesus' authority and leaves open the possibility that it could be Jesus' own authority or one which had been given him by someone else.

Similar questioning had been presented in relation to the Pharisees and the scribes early in the account of Jesus' mission (5:12-6:11; see 5:21,24,30; 6:2,5). The Pharisees and the scribes had objected by referring to John the Baptist (5:33). In this new context, it is Jesus himself who refers to John. Sensing that his interrogators were not sincere but merely trying to trick him in their search for a way to destroy him (see 6:11; 19:47-48), Jesus asks whether John's baptism was from heaven or from men (20:4). Indirectly, he thus rephrases their own question concerning his authority. The real issue is whether Jesus' authority is divine or human.

In the circumstances, the Sadducees and scribes are unable to respond. Since they did not listen to John, they can hardly say that his baptism was from God. However, neither could they say that it was from men, since they would then be attacked by the people (see 19:47-48) who accepted John as a prophet. Jesus has thus placed the Sadducees and the scribes in the very position which they had planned for him. Trapped, they consequently answered that they did not know (20:5-7). Their response, however, is perceived not as an avowal of ignorance but as a refusal to answer, and this provides Jesus with the explicit grounds for refusing to answer them concerning the source of his own authority (20:8).

### ii. Jesus' Killers To Be Destroyed.
*The very stone which the builders rejected.*
20:9-18.

> 9And he began to tell the people this parable: "A man planted a vineyard, and let it out to tenants, and went into another country for a long while. 10When the time came, he sent a servant to the tenants, that they should give him some of the fruit of the vineyard; but the tenants beat him, and sent him away empty-handed. 11And he sent another servant; him also they beat and treated shamefully, and sent him away empty-handed. 12And he sent yet a third; this one they wounded and cast out. 13Then the owner of the vineyard said, 'What shall I do? I will send my beloved son; it may be they will respect him.' 14But when the tenants saw him, they said to

themselves, 'This is the heir; let us kill him, that the inheritance may be ours.' [15]And they cast him out of the vineyard and killed him. What then will the owner of the vineyard do to them? [16]He will come and destroy those tenants, and give the vineyard to others." When they heard this, they said, "God forbid!" [17]But he looked at them and said, "What then is this that is written:

'The very stone which the builders
   rejected
has become the head of the corner'?

[18]Every one who falls on that stone will be broken to pieces; but when it falls on any one it will crush him."

The encounter with the chief priests and the scribes together with the elders took place while Jesus was teaching the people (20:1). In 20:9-18, Jesus now continues to teach the people. His message includes a parable (20:9-16a), the people's reaction (20:16b) and Jesus' response to them (20:17-18). The entire passage presupposes the previous encounter and consists in a theological reflection on the involvement of the chief priests, the scribes and the elders in the events which climax in the killing of Jesus.

The parable concerns a man who planted a vineyard and left for a long sojourn in another country, tenants to whom he let it out during his absence, the owner's servants and his beloved son, the heir, whom he sent to claim some of the fruits of the vineyard. Since the "beloved son" who is to inherit the vineyard is a clear reference to Jesus (see 3:22,38; 4:3,9; 9:35), the owner of the vineyard is seen as God himself. The tenants are the leaders of Israel, and the scribes and the chief priests clearly understand that Jesus has them in mind (20:19). Given these symbolic identifications, the parable must be read as an allegory concerning the rejection of God's servants the prophets, and of Jesus himself (see 4:24; 13:33-35). As such it deals with the period of the Old Testament and of Jesus' historical life.

In the parable's conclusion, Jesus asks the people what the owner of the vineyard would do to those who killed his son (20:15b). Jesus himself provides the answer: the owner would come to destroy the tenants. Those who would destroy Jesus (19:47) would themselves be destroyed. After the destruction of the original tenants or stewards, the owner would then give the vineyard to others (20:16a). The parable consequently looks to the future as well as to the past. "The others" to whom Jesus refers point to the life of the Church in which Gentiles would replace Israel's leaders as tenants of God's vineyard.

The people are aghast at Jesus' announcement (20:16b), but Jesus emphasizes his conclusion by referring to the scriptures. First he asks about the meaning of Ps 118:22: "The very stone which the builders rejected has become the head of the corner." The stone in question was a traditional reference to Jesus, and its rejection to his passion and death (see 1 Pt 2:4-8; Mk 12:10). Luke understands it in the same way.

As in 20:15-16, Jesus' answers (20:18) his own question (20:17). His concern, however, is not with what happens to the stone itself but to those who rejected it. His answer includes two distinct statements, both of which are generalizations. First, he refers to those who fall on the stone and who will be broken to pieces (20:18a). It is not the stone but they who will be broken. The efforts to destroy the heir (20:15) are consequently frustrated and those who plot his destruction are destroyed by their own effort. As in Rom 11:11, the event is related to the place of Gentiles in the Church (20:16). Second, Jesus refers to the stone's crushing anyone on whom it falls (20:18b). He thus looks beyond the passion in which the stone is passive to Christ's active victory over his would-be destroyers. The entire passage is a warning to the people and to all who oppose the work of Christ and his Church as well as an assurance that Christ would be victorious.

iii. The Impartiality of Jesus.
*We know that you speak and teach rightly.*
20:19-26.

> [19]The scribes and the chief priests tried to lay hands
> on him at that very hour, but they feared the people; for
> they perceived that he had told this parable against them.
> [20]So they watched him, and sent spies, who pretended
> to be sincere, that they might take hold of what he said,
> so as to deliver him up to the authority and jurisdiction
> of the governor. [21]They asked him, "Teacher, we know
> that you speak and teach rightly, and show no partiality,
> but truly teach the way of God. [22]Is it lawful for us to give
> tribute to Caesar, or not?" [23]But he perceived their
> craftiness, and said to them, [24]"Show me a coin. Whose
> likeness and inscription has it?" They said, "Caesar's."
> [25]He said to them, "Then render to Caesar the things that
> are Caesar's, and to God the things that are God's." [26]And
> they were not able in the presence of the people to catch
> him by what he said; but marveling at his answer they
> were silent.

Jesus' encounter with the scribes and the chief priests
now enters into its second phase (20:19-26). The latter had
heard Jesus' parable and interpretation and "perceived
that he had told this parable against them," as indeed he
had done. These men who, like the Pharisees (6:11), already
were looking for a way to destroy Jesus (19:47) "tried to
lay hands on him at that very hour, but they feared the
people" (20:19). Now that Jesus was bringing their attitude
out into the open, the need to do something about him had
become even more pressing.

In the first phase of their encounter, they had already
tried to turn the people in their favor and against Jesus.
Not only had they failed at this, but there was danger that
Jesus would turn the people against them. Unable personally and directly to destroy Jesus, they consequently

sought a way "to deliver him up to the authority and juris-diction of the governor." By this indirect means, the people's wrath would be diverted from them and aimed at the non-jewish political authority and they would have nothing to fear from the people. For this to be effective, however, their role in the matter could not be obvious. They there-fore "sent spies, who pretended to be sincere." Since they had personally failed to trap Jesus in his words, they might well do so through others (20:20).

To the reader, the spies' opening statement is manifestly insincere. Affirming their acceptance of Jesus as a teacher who speaks and teaches rightly and shows no partiality in teaching the way of God (20:21), they try to force Jesus into a position where he would not be able to remain impartial while being true to the way of God. With a ques-tion which concerns the legality of giving tribute to Caesar, they hope that Jesus will speak out in favor of jewish law but against Roman law (20:22). Were they successful, they would then have grounds to deliver him to the governor.

Knowing the intention of the scribes and the chief priests (20:9-18) and perceiving their craftiness (20:23), Jesus reduces their spies to silence (20:26b). Requesting a coin, he asks that they identify whose inscription was on it, and on the basis of their answer he responds that they should give to Caesar what was his and to God what was his (20:24-25). Jesus thus demonstrates that their insincere charac-terization of him as impartial and as one who teaches the way of God was extremely well-grounded.

The scribes and the chief priests had failed in their first attempt to turn the people in their favor and against Jesus (20:1-8). Abandoning this dual effort, they had hoped at least to turn the people against either Jesus or the Roman authority, but even in this they had now failed (20:26a). Jesus' principle of allegiance to God and to Caesar, each within his own sphere, provided the Lukan communities with a claim to both jewish and Roman legality.

## iv. The Lordship of Jesus.
*How can they say that the Christ is David's son?*
20:27-44.

²⁷There came to him some Sadducees, those who
say that there is no resurrection, ²⁸and they asked him
a question, saying, "Teacher, Moses wrote for us that if a
man's brother dies, having a wife but no children, the
man must take the wife and raise up children for his
brother. ²⁹Now there were seven brothers; the first took
a wife, and died without children; ³⁰and the second ³¹and
the third took her, and likewise all seven left no children
and died. ³²Afterward the woman also died. ³³In the
resurrection, therefore, whose wife will the woman be?
For the seven had her as wife."

³⁴And Jesus said to them, "The sons of this age marry
and are given in marriage; ³⁵but those who are accounted
worthy to attain to that age and to the resurrection from
the dead neither marry nor are given in marriage, ³⁶for
they cannot die any more, because they are equal to
angels and are sons of God, being sons of the resurrection. ³⁷But that the dead are raised, even Moses
showed, in the passage about the bush, where he calls the
Lord the God of Abraham and the God of Isaac and the
God of Jacob. ³⁸Now he is not God of the dead, but of
the living; for all live to him." ³⁹And some of the scribes
answered, "Teacher, you have spoken well." ⁴⁰For they
no longer dared to ask him any question.

⁴¹But he said to them, "How can they say that the
Christ is David's son? ⁴²For David himself says in the
Book of Psalms,
'The Lord said to my Lord,
Sit at my right hand,
⁴³till I make thy enemies a stool for
thy feet.'
⁴⁴David thus calls him Lord; so how is he his son?"

Jesus' second encounter is with some Sadducees, a
jewish "sect" whose members were drawn largely from the

priestly class but which also included many aristocratic laymen (20:27-38). They are introduced at this point because of their position "that there is no resurrection" (20:27). What is begun as a theoretical discussion with Sadducees, however, is transformed into an incisive statement on Jesus' own resurrection and consequent lordship in a concluding dialogue with some of the scribes (20:39-44). Luke thus pursues his confrontation between Jesus, the teacher, and Judaism's recognized teaching class (20:1,19). In 20:1-26, this confrontation had focused mainly on Jesus' rejection, passion and death. In 20:27-44, it addresses his resurrection and ascension through which death was foiled and his apparent victors vanquished.

Like the scribes and the chief priests, the Sadducees address Jesus with the title "Teacher" (20:21,28). Their question concerns the levirate marriage as stipulated by Moses in Dt 25:5 and Gen 38:8. According to this law, a man was obliged to take his brother's wife and beget children who would receive his brother's name and inheritance when the latter died childless. The case brought forward involves seven brothers, each of whom tried to fulfill his legal obligation, but all of whom died without actually doing so before the wife also died. For the Sadducees, the situation showed the ridiculousness of the very notion of resurrection. To make their point, they ask Jesus whose wife the woman would be in the resurrection (20:28-33).

In his response, Jesus distinguishes two ages. In the first, which includes human history in this world, the question of marriage is pertinent. In the second, however, which follows the consummation of history, marriage is irrelevant. There are thus two modes of human existence. In the first, men and women live and act according to the conditions of physical birth. In the second, to which they are reborn in the resurrection, life and relationships are comparable to those of the angels. Accordingly, it is wrong to think of two ages in identical terms. Successive relationships in the first pose no problem in the second when all will be together (20:34-36).

Having answered their problem, Jesus proceeds to argue for the reality of resurrection. His stand is supported by the authority of Moses, whom the Sadducees themselves had cited. Does not Moses refer to the Lord as the God of Abraham and the God of Isaac and the God of Jacob? God, however, is the God of the living and not the God of the dead (20:37-38). Since Abraham, Isaac and Jacob had long ago died, they must consequently have risen to life, if Moses can refer to God in this way. Indirectly, Luke shows that resurrection cannot be viewed in material terms as though it were a resumption of historical life nor in temporal terms as though it would occur only at some future time. Since the patriarchs live to God, they must consequently have been raised, and resurrection is a biblically attested reality.

It is the scribes, teachers drawn largely from the "sect" of the Pharisees and who maintain belief in the resurrection, who answer. Once again silenced by Jesus and no longer daring to question him (20:40), they acknowledge that he has answered well (20:39). Jesus, however, does not let the matter rest. Others had tried to show that Jesus' views were contradictory. He now proceeds to show that his questioners are themselves contradictory. How can the scribes speak of the Christ as David's son when David himself speaks of him as his Lord. The reference is to Ps 110:1, which sees the Lord (Christ) at the Lord God's right hand until the Christ's enemies are vanquished (20:41-43). Does not this view of the risen and ascended Christ, who is Lord even of David, contradict the scribes' position that the Christ is merely human (20:44)?

v. A Message for the Disciples.
*Beware of the scribes.*
20:45-21:4.

45And in the hearing of all the people he said to his disciples, 46"Beware of the scribes, who like to go about in long robes, and love salutations in the market places and the best seats in the synagogues and the places of honor at feasts, [47]who devour widows' houses and for a pretense make long prayers. They will receive the greater condemnation."

**21** He looked up and saw the rich putting their gifts into the treasury; [2]and he saw a poor widow put in two copper coins. [3]And he said, "Truly I tell you, this poor widow has put in more than all of them; [4]for they all contributed out of their abundance, but she out of her poverty put in all the living that she had."

The first part (20:1-21:4) of the journey's third major stage (20:1-21:38) ends with a special message for the disciples (20:45-21:4). As in 20:1-44, Jesus continues to speak in the hearing of all the people (20:45). What is expected of the disciples is thus made a matter of public knowledge. First, proper christian behavior is contrasted with that of the scribes (20:46-47). Second it is contrasted with that of the rich and compared to that of a poor widow (21:1-4).

For the benefit of all the people as well as of his disciples, Jesus evokes the ostentatious behavior of scribes "who like to go about in long robes, and love salutations in the market places and the best seats in the synagogues and the places of honor at feasts" (20:46; see 14:7-11). While these men devour the houses or estates of widows, they maintain a pretense of justice by reciting long prayers. Their condemnation will be all the greater on account of such pretense (20:47).

In the context of 20:1-21:4, which deals with how Jesus responds to those who tried to trick and destroy him, the very presence of this brief warning presupposes that some of the christian leaders and teachers have assumed or tried to assume the way of the scribes. In the measure that they do so, Jesus' message to the scribes (20:1-44) has them in mind.

Mention of the widows in 20:47 calls to mind a story about a poor widow whose gift of two insignificant coins for the temple treasury contrasts with those of the rich (21:1-2). The gift is not measured by its amount but by the giver's generosity which depends not on the amount itself but on each one's relative means. When the rich give out of their abundance, they give little. When the poor widow gives out of her poverty, she gives all she has, which is more than all the gifts of the rich combined (21:3-4).

In 20:45-47, Jesus indicated what the disciples must avoid in their leadership of the christian community. In 21:1-4, he shows what these same leaders, who tended to be wealthy, must imitate, and he unveils the relative value of wealth. His message will be further illumined by the ideals presented in Acts 2:42-47; 4:32-5:11.

### 3. b. The Destruction of the Temple, of Jerusalem, and the End of Time.

#### i. The Destruction of the Temple.
*The end will not be at once.*
21:5-19.

> 5And as some spoke of the temple, how it was adorned with noble stones and offerings, he said, 6"As for these things which you see, the days will come when there shall not be left here one stone upon another that will not be thrown down." 7And they asked him, "Teacher, when will this be, and what will be the sign when this is about to take place?" 8And he said, "Take heed that you are not led astray; for many will come in my name, saying, 'I am he!' and, 'The time is at hand!' Do not go after them. 9And when you hear of wars and tumults, do not be terrified; for this must first take place, but the end will not be at once."
>
> 10Then he said to them, "Nation will rise against nation, and kingdom against kingdom; 11there will be

great earthquakes, and in various places famines and pestilences; and there will be terrors and great signs from heaven. [12]But before all this they will lay their hands on you and persecute you, delivering you up to the synagogues and prisons, and you will be brought before kings and governors for my name's sake. [13]This will be a time for you to bear testimony. [14]Settle it therefore in your minds, not to meditate beforehand how to answer; [15]for I will give you a mouth and wisdom, which none of your adversaries will be able to withstand or contradict. [16]You will be delivered up even by parents and brothers and kinsmen and friends, and some of you they will put to death; [17]you will be hated by all for my name's sake. [18]But not a hair of your head will perish. [19]By your endurance you will gain your lives.

Jesus' teaching to the disciples ended with a direct reference to the temple and observations on the rich who gave to its treasury. This context provided a springboard for Jesus' long discourse (21:5-36), which begins with reflections on the temple itself, its adornment and its wealth (21:5).

The first part of the discourse concerns the destruction of the temple and how this event is distinct from the end and the eventual return of Christ (21:5-19). For the historical Jesus and his immediate disciples, the temple's destruction still lay in the future. For Luke, however, it was already a fact of history. Mark had already indicated that the temple's destruction was not the beginning of the end (Mk 13:7,10). Luke emphasizes this view by establishing an even clearer distinction between what had happened and the end of time. We can only assume that some of Luke's intended readers viewed the internal difficulties and external persecutions from which they suffered as signs that the end was actually at hand and that the temple's destruction had constituted a first sign heralding its proximity.

As the discourse opens, Jesus announces the temple's destruction (21:6) and is asked when this will happen (21:7). He does not, however, answer this question directly. Instead he warns his hearers not to be misled by those who come in his name and claim to be the one who was to come at the end (21:8). Nor should they be terrified by wars and tumults. Such things are normal and must take place, but they do not indicate that the end is at hand (21:9).

The end will indeed come (21:10,11), but before it does the Christians will be persecuted by religious and political authorities (21:12), delivered up by close relatives, and some will even be put to death (21:16), all for the sake of Jesus' name (21:12,17). When that happens they must bear testimony with the sure knowledge that they will be provided with unassailable wisdom (21:13-15) and that they will not perish (21:18). To be put to death does not necessarily mean to perish. For those who stand firm and endure as Christians, it means to gain one's life (21:19). Luke's concern is thus to interpret the destruction of the temple in relation to the end as well as to help Christians to respond adequately to their present difficulties.

ii. The Destruction of Jerusalem.
   *Until the times of the Gentiles are fulfilled.*
   21:20-28.

> 20But when you see Jerusalem surrounded by armies, then know that its desolation has come near. 21Then let those who are in Judea flee to the mountains, and let those who are inside the city depart, and let not those who are out in the country enter it; 22for these are days of vengeance, to fulfill all that is written. 23Alas for those who are with child and for those who give suck in those days! For great distress shall be upon the earth and wrath upon this people; 24they will fall by the edge of the sword, and be led captive among all nations; and Jerusalem will be trodden down by the Gentiles, until the times of the Gentiles are fulfilled.

<sup>25</sup>"And there will be signs in sun and moon and stars, and upon the earth distress of nations in perplexity at the roaring of the sea and the waves, <sup>26</sup>men fainting with fear and with foreboding of what is coming on the world; for the powers of the heavens will be shaken. <sup>27</sup>And then they will see the Son of man coming in a cloud with power and great glory. <sup>28</sup>Now when these things begin to take place, look up and raise your heads, because your redemption is drawing near."

Having dealt with the temple's destruction and how this event was not to be directly related to the end (21:5-19), Luke does the same for the desolation of Jerusalem (21:20-28). As with the temple, the catastrophe looms in the future from Jesus' point of view but was already a fact of history for Luke and his disciples.

In the case of the temple, the author had concentrated on warning the disciples against false messiahs (21:5-9) and on showing them how to act when persecuted (21:10-19). He now concentrates on how to act when Jerusalem is actually destroyed (21:20-24) and when the Son of man does finally come (21:25-28; see 21:10-11). The two units thus complement one another as different aspects of a complete teaching on the christian response to the course of history.

Jerusalem will indeed be destroyed, and all will know that this is about to happen when they see the city surrounded by armies (21:20). At that moment, peoples will flee in all directions, and the situation will be terrible for those who look forward to new life in Israel. Some will be killed, others deported as captives and dispersed, and Jerusalem will succumb to the Gentiles (21:21-24a).

In Luke's day all this had already taken place, and Jerusalem was already desolate. Her desolate and downtrodden situation continued at the time of Luke's writing and so it would remain "until the times of the Gentiles are fulfilled" (21:24b). Luke thus defines this era as part of "the times of the Gentiles," a time which separates Jerusalem's destruction from the future day of the Son of man. Consequently, the city's desolation is not to be viewed as the beginning of the end, but as part of world conditions during christian history.

In 21:25-28, he describes the day of the Son of man in the traditional cosmological terms of apocalyptic literature. The signs in the heavens, on the earth and in the seas will overwhelm the human race with fear (21:25-26). At that moment, however, they will also "see the Son of man coming in a cloud with power and great glory" (21:27) as he returns from the heavens to which he has ascended (24:50-53). Such are the signs which herald the end and indicate that "redemption is drawing near" (21:28). They are not to be confused with the signs which announce Jerusalem's destruction (21:20) or with the actual destruction of the city (21:21-24), terrible as these might be.

### iii. The End of Time.
### *Watch at all times.*
### 21:29-38.

> [29]And he told them a parable: "Look at the fig tree, and all the trees; [30]as soon as they come out in leaf, the summer is already near. [31]So also, you see for yourselves and know that when you see these things taking place, you know that the kingdom of God is near. [32]Truly, I say to you, this generation will not pass away till all has taken place. [33]Heaven and earth will pass away, but my words will not pass away.
>
> [34]"But take heed to yourselves lest your hearts be weighed down with dissipation and drunkenness and cares of this life, and that day come upon you suddenly like a snare; [35]for it will come upon all who dwell upon the face of the whole earth. [36]But watch at all times, praying that you may have strength to escape all these things that will take place, and to stand before the Son of man."

[37] And every day he was teaching in the temple, but at night he went out and lodged on the mount called Olivet. [38] And early in the morning all the people came to him in the temple to hear him.

After situating the destruction of the temple (21:5-19) and the desolation of Jerusalem (21:20-28) with regard to the fulfillment of time, Luke addresses the end-time directly and calls for behavior which is appropriate in a history which is defined in large measure by the end and the Church's destiny (21:29-36).

First, Jesus draws an analogy with the annual cycle of the fig tree and other trees. When their leaves come out, all know that summer is near (21:29). In the same way, when the events described in 21:25-26 take place all should know that the kingdom of God, which was already hidden in their midst, is about to be fully manifested for Jesus' disciples (21:31).

At that time, heaven and earth will pass away (21:31a) but two realities will surely remain: this generation (21:32b), that is the human race, and the words of the Lord (21:33), which will then be fulfilled. The human race will consequently not be destroyed by present wars and tumults, nor by the final cataclysm. It will abide to meet the Son of man coming in a cloud (21:27) and only then, in the future age, will historical life and the sons of this age be transformed into the life of the resurrection (21:32b; see 20:34-36). Although at times it may appear that the words of Jesus are no longer relevant and have passed away, they too will abide. Such is Jesus' promise, which Luke now addresses to the Christians living in "the time of the Gentiles" (21:24).

Given these assurances, Christians must look to their present preoccupations. Dissipation, drunkenness, the cares of this life, indeed all escapist behavior, are altogether inappropriate and will not avert the reality of the end which will spring on those who indulge in these like a snare (21:34).

No one will escape the end (21:35). Christians should consequently watch at all times and pray for strength that they might not be destroyed by the universal cataclysm (21:36a; see 21:25-26) but survive to stand before the Son of man (21:36b; see 21:27). So ends Jesus' discourse.

Like the second stage in the journey (19:47-48), the third ends with a summary of Jesus' activities (21:37-38). In 20:1-21:36, Luke presented all the confrontations and Jesus' teaching as taking place on one of many days when he was teaching and preaching in the temple (19:47-48; 20:1). In this new summary, he recalls this general context: "Every day he was teaching in the temple" (21:37a).

As in 19:47-48, however, Luke also prepares the reader for the journey's next stage. In 19:47-48, he had introduced the chief priests, the scribes and the leaders of the people who were looking for a way to destroy Jesus. In 20:1-21:4, we saw how they went about doing this, but were frustrated by Jesus' responses and by the presence of the people. In 21:37b, Luke notes that Jesus used to go out at night and lodge on the mount of Olivet. It is there, away from the people that he would be apprehended and arrested (22:39, 47-53). Only in the day did the people come to hear him in the temple. We are thus given a clue as to how the dilemma of Jesus' enemies would be resolved and how they would seize him without fear of a popular uprising in Jesus' support.

C. 4. FROM JERUSALEM TO GOD.
     THE PASSION, RESURRECTION AND
     ASCENSION OF JESUS.
     22:1-24:53.

The fourth and final stage in Jesus' journey to Jerusalem shows how Jesus' journey to Jerusalem was actually a journey to God, something already suggested in 9:51. It includes an introduction and four major units, each of which is divided into three subunits.

The introduction (22:1-13) presents Jesus' passion from the point of view of those who conspired to have him betrayed (22:1-6) as well as from that of Jesus himself (22:7-13). The impending tragedy or passion is thus transformed into a personally initiated action.

The first major unit (21:14-53) presents Jesus' farewell meal and a discourse which interprets his passion and glorification, and it develops their implications for communities tempted to perpetuate the betrayal and denial which accompanied the original event (22:14-38). It continues with a new teaching on prayer, applying Jesus' earlier teaching (11:1-13; 18:1-17) to the context of the passion and persecution and emphasizing the petition that Christians be not subjected to the trial (22:39-46; see 11:4b). It concludes with Jesus' arrest and shows how Christians must respond to persecution when it does come (22:47-53).

The second major unit deals with Peter's denial of Jesus, the tendency for Christians to associate themselves with those who try to destroy him and the source of repentance and reconciliation when they do deny him (22:54-62). It then focuses on Jesus' two trials, that before the jewish council (22:63-71) and that before the Roman authorities (23:1-25). The question of Jesus' identity is clarified in a new synthesis which takes the end of his journey into consideration, and he is shown to be innocent of all religious and political charges.    The Christians need not hesitate concerning the legitimacy of their position as Jesus' followers.

The third unit first presents the crucifixion of Jesus, shows different reactions to him in his passion, and dwells on its invitation to reconciliation and salvation (23:26-43). Jesus' death marks the end of the Old Testament era (23:44-49). Unjustly condemned to death, the innocent Jesus is then given the burial of an innocent man in a new tomb, which marks the radical newness of what has taken place (23:50-56).

The fourth and final major unit first deals with the problem posed by Jesus' empty tomb. Christians must leave the tomb and seek the Living One among the living

(24:1-12). The author then shows how those who have lost track of the presence of the risen Lord in their lives may recognize him in the breaking of the bread and resume their christian mission (24:13-35). In this mission, which takes place during Jesus absence from history, they find and serve Jesus in the concreteness of human life. They must not seek escape into spiritual things. Blessed by Jesus with the fulfillment of God's promises to Abraham, they must reach out to all human beings, offering reconciliation to the ends of the earth. Jesus' ascension is consequently not a problem, but a source of blessing and a condition for the christian mission (24:36-53).

4. a. Introduction.
   Conspiracy, Betrayal and Preparation.
   *And they prepared the Passover.*
   22:1-13.

> **22** Now the feast of Unleavened Bread drew near, which is called the Passover. [2]And the chief priests and the scribes were seeking how to put him to death; for they feared the people.
>
> [3]Then Satan entered into Judas called Iscariot, who was of the number of the twelve; [4]he went away and conferred with the chief priests and officers how he might betray him to them. [5]And they were glad, and engaged to give him money. [6]So he agreed, and sought an opportunity to betray him to them in the absence of the multitude.
>
> [7]Then came the day of Unleavened Bread, on which the passover lamb had to be sacrificed. [8]So Jesus sent Peter and John, saying, "Go and prepare the passover for us, that we may eat it." [9]They said to him, "Where will you have us prepare it?" [10]He said to them, "Behold, when you have entered the city, a man carrying a jar of water will meet you; follow him into the house which he enters, [11]and tell the householder, 'The Teacher says

to you, Where is the guest room, where I am to eat the passover with my disciples?' [12]And he will show you a large upper room furnished; there make ready." [13]And they went, and found it as he had told them; and they prepared the passover.

The account of Jesus' passion-resurrection-ascension (22:1-24:53) begins with two complementary units (22:1-6, 7-13), which introduce the last supper (22:14-38) as well as the journey's entire fourth and final stage. As two units, the introduction follows a pattern established in 9:51-62; 10:1-37 and 13:22-30, 31-35.

The first unit (22:1-6) calls attention to the approaching feast of Unleavened Bread or Passover, which Luke views as one and the same feast (22:1). It presents the coming passion in terms of the efforts of Jerusalem's religious leadership to destroy Jesus. The second unit (22:7-13) describes an event which takes place on the actual day of Unleavened Bread, the day on which the passover lamb had to be sacrificed (22:7). It presents the coming passion in terms of Jesus' personal and active choice. Jesus' passion, an event in which he suffers as a victim at the hands of others, is thus reinterpreted as an action in which Jesus assumes the passion and willingly offers himself.

The first unit focuses on the efforts of the chief priests and scribes (22:2a) and on the complicity of Judas, one of the Twelve (22:3), without whose help the efforts of the former would have remained frustrated by fear of the people (22:2b). This initial emphasis on betrayal prepares a further development on betrayal in the last discourse (22:21-23). Its importance stems from the ongoing danger of betrayal in the life of the Christian community, and Judas' action stands as a warning to all future Christians.

The narrative is based on Mk 14:1-2, 10-11. Mark's intervening unit concerning the anointing of Jesus in view of his burial (14:3-9) is omitted. Since, as we shall see, Luke deemphasizes the importance of the empty tomb (24:1-12,

22-24), the inclusion of Mk 14:3-9 in Lk 22:1-6 would have been distracting and inappropriate. Luke had already presented a similar story in 7:36-50, where it dealt with an important aspect of the forgiveness of sins, rather than with the anointing of Jesus.

A major difference between Mk 14:1-2, 10-11 and Lk 22:1-6 appears in the mention of Satan in 22:3. Judas' part in the plot to destroy Jesus is credited to Satan's entry into him. The passion is thus presented as Jesus' confrontation with evil, a theme already elaborated in 4:1-13, where it interprets the meaning of Jesus' entire mission and journey. Following that unit, the narrator had indicated that the devil had finished all the tempting and had left Jesus to await another opportunity (4:13). That opportunity was now at hand, and evil comes to the fore in the figure of Satan who took possession of Judas and who had also asked for Simon and the other disciples (22:31-32). Jesus' passion is consequently no ordinary human confrontation with Jerusalem's religious leaders and the infidelity of an apostle, but a struggle with the forces of evil at work in those who try to destroy Jesus and his disciples.

The role of Satan also points forward to the life of Christians engaged in the history of salvation. In Luke, Satan figures in the journey narrative where he appears in relation to the mission of the apostolic community (10:18), as incompatible with the coming of the kingdom (11:18) or as enslaving those whom Jesus came to set free (13:16). In Acts, it is he who fills the heart of Ananias (5:3), who represents the basic challenge to the Pauline mission (26:18), and whose dominion (Acts 26:18) stands in direct opposition to the work of the Holy Spirit (Acts 5:3). By explicitly referring to Satan, rather than to the devil (Lk 4:1-13) in 22:3, Luke thus draws attention to the challenge of Christians who are called to withstand and overcome the forces of evil in the apostolic mission. Persecutions, resistance and internal struggles are consequently but the surface manifestations of Satan, the ultimate opponent.

Evil's conspiracy against Jesus took place as Passover was approaching. In noting this fact (22:1), Luke proved faithful to tradition (Mk 14:1). Within the context of his own gospel, however, he was also recalling another Passover, which Jesus celebrated together with those who first shared his history (2:41-51). On that occasion, Jesus had been lost by his parents to be found again after three days. The event had been fully in Jesus' control and reflected his acceptance of a divine necessity that he be with God. From the very start, Luke has thus started to evoke the positive aspect of the passion, which would provide the transition from the ancient Passover to its fulfillment in the kingdom of God (22:15-16). The hour of Jesus' enemies and the triumph of darkness (22:53) would be brief and illusory.

In 22:1-6, Luke outlined the Satanic plans and preparations of Jesus' enemies for his last Passover. The latter, however, were not alone in preparing the feast. In 22:7-13, Luke presents Jesus as firmly in control of the events, and as commissioning two of his disciples, Peter and John, to prepare the Passover supper. Jesus' initiative contrasts with Mark's presentation, where it is the disciples, rather than Jesus, who raise the matter of preparing the supper (Mk 14:12).

The narrative is closely patterned on the preparation for Jesus' entry into Jerusalem (19:28-34). The preparation for the supper thus points to the full implications of Jesus' triumphal entry into Jerusalem and associates it with the passion. From one point of view, the passion could be seen as the triumph of darkness (22:53). Unwittingly, however, the powers of darkness were working for the glorification of Jesus.

The events about to take place are endowed with the authority of Jesus and of God himself, whose overriding providence is reflected in the necessary unfolding of a historical plan of salvation. Thus it is that the unit begins by noting that the day had come when it was necessary to sacrifice the paschal lamb. The theme of necessity is not used lightly in Luke-Acts, where it appears in the context of the salvific mission of Jesus and his disciples. Within that context, it constitutes the dynamism which brings the promise of history to fulfillment. Given this general usage, the paschal lamb must be symbolic of Jesus himself, and its necessary sacrifice a symbol for the necessity of the passion.

Up to this point, we have presented the events in terms of the conflict between Satan and Jesus, both of whom work to prepare the Passover. Luke's account includes another important dimension. The Passover was not to be that of Jesus alone, but of Jesus together with his disciples: "Go and prepare the passover for us, that we may eat it" (22:8). The disciples, and by implication Luke's own readers, are thus associated with Jesus in the passion-resurrection. The sacrifice of the lamb prepares those who will share in Jesus' sacrificial meal to understand the nature of their persecutions.

## 4. b. Passover, Prayer and Arrest.

### i. The Last Supper.
*All that has to do with me approaches its climax.*
22:14-38.

> [14]And when the hour came, he sat at table, and the apostles with him. [15]And he said to them, "I have earnestly desired to eat this passover with you before I suffer; [16]for I tell you I shall not eat it until it is fulfilled in the kingdom of God." [17]And he took a cup, and when he had given thanks he said, "Take this and divide it among yourselves; [18]for I tell you that from now on I shall not drink of the fruit of the vine until the kingdom of God comes." [19]And he took bread, and when he had given thanks he broke it and give it to them, saying, "This is my body which is given for you. Do this in remembrance of me." [20]And likewise the cup after supper, saying,

"This cup which is poured out for you is the new covenant in my blood. ²¹But behold the hand of him who betrays me is with me on the table. ²²For the Son of man goes as it has been determined; but woe to that man by whom he is betrayed!" ²³And they began to question one another, which of them it was that would do this.

²⁴A dispute also arose among them, which of them was to be regarded as the greatest. ²⁵And he said to them, "The kings of the Gentiles exercise lordship over them; and those in authority over them are called benefactors. ²⁶But not so with you; rather let the greatest among you become as the youngest, and the leader as one who serves. ²⁷For which is the greater, one who sits at table, or one who serves? Is it not the one who sits at table? But I am among you as one who serves.

²⁸"You are those who have continued with me in my trials; ²⁹and I assign to you, as my Father assigned to me, a kingdom, ³⁰that you may eat and drink at my table in my kingdom, and sit on thrones judging the twelve tribes of Israel.

³¹"Simon, Simon, behold, Satan demanded to have you, that he might sift you like wheat, ³²but I have prayed for you that your faith may not fail; and when you have turned again, strengthen your brethren." ³³And he said to him, "Lord, I am ready to go with you to prison and to death." ³⁴He said, "I tell you, Peter, the cock will not crow this day, until you three times deny that you know me."

³⁵And he said to them, "When I sent you out with no purse or bag or sandals, did you lack anything?" They said, "Nothing." ³⁶He said to them, "But now, let him who has a purse take it, and likewise a bag. And let him who has no sword sell his mantle and buy one. ³⁷For I tell you that this scripture must be fulfilled in me, 'And he was reckoned with transgressors'; for what is written about me has its fulfilment." ³⁸And they said, "Look, Lord, here are two swords." And he said to them, "It is enough."

The passion narrative had begun with a general reference to the approaching feast (22:1). Its second pericope drew attention to a particular day (22:7). It now focuses on the hour (22:14), that is on the hour for the Passover meal in which Jesus would offer his life and interpret the coming events. Unlike Mark, who merely mentions the twelve (14:17), Luke emphasizes their presence and shows how they join Jesus in the meal. This would be their hour as well as that of Jesus. The apostles and Luke's readers are thus asked to associate themselves with the attitude and commitment which Jesus was about to demonstrate. Only in this way could they hopefully confront their enemies and the power of darkness which had permeated the hour of Jesus (22:53).

## A Farewell Banquet.
## 22:15-18.

As Jesus clearly indicates in 22:15-18, this Passover is Jesus' definitive meal, his final historical meal before the Passover's fulfillment in the kingdom of God. As such, it has the character of a farewell banquet, and Jesus' words at the meal (22:15-38) have all the characteristics of a farewell discourse.

In its opening verse, Jesus summarizes his previous attitude in relation to this meal. He has not tried to escape it and the realities it anticipates. Indeed he has earnestly desired them (22:15). Referring to the cup, he asks that the apostles take it as he had done and divide it among themselves (22:17).

Jesus' words also have a clear future orientation. In his last historical meal, Jesus looks to future meals when he would once again join his disciples at table in the kingdom (22:18). The text thus defines the present moment in relation to Jesus' past attitude and looks beyond the passion-resurrection to the future when the Christians would give living expression to the life and mission of Jesus. Jesus' farewell discourse to those who had joined him in the mission and journey is consequently a message to Luke's own readers. While its roots are in the life of the historical Jesus, the selection of its elements and the discourse's final shape were influenced by the situation and problems of the Lukan communities.

### The Breaking of the Bread.
*22:19-20.*

In keeping with the nature of a farewell discourse, Luke's concern is mainly with the implications of the events of Jesus' life and his message for his own readers. It was only appropriate then that Jesus' interpretation of the final Passover be followed by a liturgical text drawn from the lived experience of the Lukan communities (22:19-20).

This text, which had a long history, expressed the very core of the Christian commitment. The tradition found in Luke stands closest to that cited by Paul in 1 Cor 11:23-25. However, while Paul called this meal the Lord's Supper or the Table of the Lord, Luke referred to it as the breaking of bread (24:35; Acts 20:7), a designation which emphasizes the sharing aspect of the Lord's Supper or Table.

By associating the liturgical text with 22:15-18, Luke recalled its relationship to Jesus' definitive meal and enabled his readers to see their meal commitment as a response to the plotting and betrayal faced by Jesus. Like Jesus, it is they and not their enemies who dominate the situation and determine its meaning. In their gathering for the breaking of bread, they did what Jesus had done and gave historical expression to the attitude of the risen Lord.

### The Betrayal.
*22:21-23.*

Jesus now takes up the question of his betrayal (22:21-23), which the narrator had introduced in 22:1-6. Jesus not only knows that he will be betrayed but he knows that his betrayer is among those who have gathered with him and are celebrating the Passover and hearing his farewell message

(22:21). The events and Jesus' going away are being ful-filled precisely as it had been determined, that is according to the divine necessity which governs his passage through suffering to the kingdom (22:15-18; see 24:26). However, woe to the man by whom he is betrayed (22:22). Up to this point, the passage parallels 17:1-2, where Jesus spoke of the inevitability of scandal but of the woeful condition of those through whom it comes.

In Jesus' announcement, no name was given. From the point of view of the apostles, the betrayer could conse-quently have been any one of them. They therefore begin to question one another on who the betrayer might be (22:23).

### The On-Going Betrayal.
### 22:24-30.

The apostles' questioning concerning the identity of the betrayer (22:23) provided a transition to 22:24-30, where the apostles' behavior and Jesus' response furnish the answer. As he had done in 22:15-18, 19-20, Jesus thus moves from the historical context of the last supper to that of the Lukan communities.

Immediately after the betrayal statement (22:21-23), the apostles are disputing among themselves as to who is the greatest (22:24). Here was the betrayal! Jesus had already addressed this problem in the course of the gospel (9:46-48; see also 14:7-11; 18:9-17; 20:45-47). In his response, Jesus first points to the position and authority of earthly kings, who exercise lordship over their people, including Jesus' apostles. Such kings are called benefactors, a title frequently adopted by hellenistic rulers (22:25). The relationship of the christian leaders to the communities is quite other. The greater among them must become like the youngest and the leader like a servant (22:26). This is indeed a reversal from the worldly order of human relationships, but it is a reversal which has been authoritatively established by Jesus' own relationship to them (22:27). True greatness consists in the quality of their christian service. The latter, be it noted, does not consist in merely waiting on others at table, but in a life defined by service and which involves commitment and suffering.

In 22:28-30, Jesus refers to those who have continued with him in his trials (22:28), that is who have joined him in serving in spite of the attacks of those who tried to destroy both him and them. For this reason, Jesus assigns to them the kingdom which his Father had assigned to him (22:29). Through their service, the kingdom is thus made present in the world. As faithful servants, they accordingly will join Jesus, the faithful Servant, in the ultimate fulfillment of the passover in the kingdom (22:30a; 22:16,18). In Jesus' kingdom, they will one day sit on thrones judging the twelve tribes of the new Israel (22:30b). The struggles of the apostles mirror those of later christian leaders, and Jesus' teaching to them addresses all future leaders in the Church.

*The Denial.*
*22:31-34.*
In 22:28, Jesus had told the apostles that they had continued with him in his trials. This, however, was not immediately obvious. Had not Peter himself denied the Lord (22:54-62)? Jesus now addresses this situation and interprets it (22:31-34), just as he had done with Judas' betrayal (22:21-23). Satan, the one who entered into Judas (22:3), had desired to have the others and to shake them up violently as one sifts wheat (22:31), and this was indeed happening in the passion. Jesus, however has prayed for Simon, to whom the message is directly addressed (22:31a) that his faith might not fail (22:32a). Contrary to Simon's own expressed readiness to go with Jesus to prison and death, Peter will have denied knowing Jesus, and this three times before cockcrow (22:33-34). Violent as this test might be, however, his faith will bring him back. When he returns, he is to strengthen his brothers who will have been shaken by Satan (22:32b).

## The On-Going Denial.
### 22:35-38.

In 22:24-30, Jesus had reflected on how the Christians were in danger of betraying Jesus as Judas had done. In 22:35-38, he now shows how, like Peter, the Christian leaders continue to deny Jesus. Peter's denial (22:31-34) thus becomes a message to a later age.

At one time, Jesus had told the disciples to free themselves of all earthly supports in the exercise of their mission (22:35a; see 9:3; 10:4). So doing, they had lacked nothing (22:35b). However, they did need courage for their mission, if they wished to stand by Jesus in his trials (22:28). Jesus consequently alludes to his previous instructions and tells them that one who has a purse must take it, as well as a bag, and if he has no sword, let him sell his mantle and buy one (22:36).

Jesus' language is metaphorical and refers to the strength needed to join him in his fulfillment of scripture as God's suffering Servant (22:37). The Lukan communities, however, have failed to understand Jesus' statement as metaphorical. They have begun to rely on their goods and wealth, and their statement that they have two swords is indicative of their dependence on material means in the struggle with Satan (22:38a). In this way they are denying that they really know Jesus (22:34). Their minds are still closed to the meaning of the passion and the way they are to face it (9:44-45; see also 9:22-27).

Jesus' response, "It is enough" (22:38b), terminates the discourse. His rebuke to the apostles is also a rebuke and a warning to the leadership in the Lukan communities. Knowing of the passion and Peter's denial, are they not responding to persecution much like Simon had done? Are they too denying that they know Jesus? Are they unable to follow him on the way of suffering service? Why have they not been strengthened by Peter (22:32)? Are they still Peter's brothers?

## ii. At the Mount of Olives: Prayer.
*Rise and pray that you may not enter
into temptation.*
22:39-46.

<sup></sup>³⁹And he came out, and went, as was his custom,
to the Mount of Olives; and the disciples followed him.
⁴⁰And when he came to the place he said to them, "Pray
that you may not enter into temptation." ⁴¹And he withdrew from them about a stone's throw, and knelt down
and prayed, ⁴²"Father, if thou art willing, remove this
cup from me; nevertheless not my will, but thine, be
done." ⁴⁵And when he rose from prayer, he came to the
disciples and found them sleeping for sorrow, ⁴⁶and he
said to them, "Why do you sleep? Rise and pray that you
may not enter into temptation."

After the Passover meal and the farewell discourse
(22:14-38) in the upper room (22:12), the scene shifts to the
Mount of Olives. Coming out, Jesus went to the Mount
to spend the night as was his custom (22:39a; see 21:37).
The disciples, who had joined Jesus in the supper (22:11,14)
and who had accepted to divide his cup among themselves
(22:17), followed him (22:39b). Already, however, they
were proving weak in their commitment (22:24,31,38). Basic
loyalty to Jesus in his temptations was assured (22:28)
through Jesus' prayer for them (22:32), but it would not
be realized without their own prayer (22:40,46).

The unity and primary preoccupation in the account is
indicated in Jesus' command: "Pray that you may not enter
into temptation" (22:40,46). This twice-repeated command,
which in context constitutes a literary inclusion (see 19:5,9;
24:16,31), echoes the concluding petition in the Lord's
prayer (11:4). For Luke, that petition and the temptation
to which it refers coincide with the challenge of the passion,
first in the story of Jesus and second in that of the christian

communities, who must also face persecution and death in a life of service.

In his own passion, Jesus was only a stone's throw from the discipes, who were following him. He too prayed as his passion approached (22:41). Jesus' prayer is that his Father's will and not his own be done, but that if it should be his Father's will, let the cup of suffering be removed from him (22:42). Again we have echoes of the Lord's prayer, both in the address to God as Father (11:2) and in the prayer's petition for the Father's will according to the Matthean version (Mt 6:10). At the supper, Jesus had accepted that cup (22:17) and through the community's liturgical text had defined it as a new covenant in his blood which he would shed for his disciples (22:20). The disciples had been taught to pray as he prayed (11:1-4). He was now asking them to do so in relation to the passion. They too will want the cup, which they had accepted (22:17,20), to be removed from them. Praying as he did, however, they would accept the Father's will and not enter into temptation.

In many important manuscripts, verse 22:42 is followed by "And there appeared to him an angel from heaven, strengthening him. And being in an agony he prayed more earnestly; and his sweat became like great drops of blood falling down upon the ground" (22:43-44). Angels would not have kept Jesus from harm had he foolishly cast himself from the temple into the passion (4:9-11). Accepting the Father's will (22:42), however, was not the same as tempting God (4:12). Accordingly, an angel appears to strengthen him precisely as he sheds his blood (22:44; see 22:20). So must it be with the disciples. Weak and sleeping with sorrow (22:45), they too would be strengthened, provided they take up Jesus' prayer.

### iii. At the Mount of Olives: Healing.
*This is your hour.*
22:47-53.

⁴⁷While he was still speaking, there came a crowd, and the man called Judas, one of the twelve, was leading

them. He drew near to Jesus to kiss him; [48]but Jesus said to him, "Judas, would you betray the Son of man with a kiss?" [49]And when those who were about him saw what would follow, they said, "Lord, shall we strike with the sword?" [50]And one of them struck the slave of the high priest and cut off his right ear. [51]But Jesus said, "No more of this!" And he touched his ear and healed him. [52]Then Jesus said to the chief priests and officers of the temple and elders, who had come out against him, "Have you come out as against a robber, with swords and clubs? [53]When I was with you day after day in the temple, you did not lay hands on me. But this is your hour, and the power of darkness."

The first stage in the passion narrative now comes to its conclusion. At the very moment that Jesus is asking his disciples to pray that they might not enter into temptation (22:46), a crowd arrives led by "the man called Judas, one of the twelve" (22:47a). One of the disciples has entered into temptation and is about to fulfill his Satanic promise to betray Jesus. At night and at the Mount of Olives, there would be no danger of creating a disturbance (22:2-6). As Judas approaches to kiss Jesus, the latter holds him off by asking if he would betray the Son of man with a kiss (22:47-48). In their Lord's Supper, the Christians used to greet one another with a holy kiss (1 Cor 16:20b). The sign of fellowship must not become one of betrayal (22:24-27).

Those who had followed Jesus and were with him at the Mount of Olives (22:39) asked if they should strike with the sword and one of them proceeded to do so (22:49-50). Jesus had told them, however, that the sword they needed consisted in courage to face the passion's fulfillment of scripture, not a physical sword of war (22:36-38). Taking up the latter constituted a denial similar to that of Simon Peter (22:31-34). In 22:38, Jesus had exclaimed, "It is enough." His disciples had not understood how they should respond to persecution. He now repeats his rebuke, "No more of this!" and heals the stricken slave of the high priest (22:51).

In 22:52-53, Jesus addresses those who have come out against him, the chief priests, the officers of the temple and the elders and chides them about the way they have approached him. Why had they not taken him when he was with them "day after day in the temple" (see 19:47-48; 21:37-38). The reader knows the answer. Jesus was no robber or criminal. His enemies knew this. Otherwise they would have seized him in the open. The hour of Jesus' enemies had come, together with the power of darkness. Accepting the Father's will (22:42), Jesus continues his journey to God.

## 4. c. Denial, Jewish Trial and Trial before Pilate.

### i. Peter's Denial.
*And he went out and wept bitterly.*
22:54-62.

> [54] Then they seized him and led him away, bringing him into the high priest's house. Peter followed at a distance; [55] and when they had kindled a fire in the middle of the courtyard and sat down together, Peter sat among them. [56] Then a maid, seeing him as he sat in the light and gazing at him, said, "This man also was with him." [57] But he denied it, saying, "Woman, I do not know him." [58] And a little later some one else saw him and said, "You also are one of them." But Peter said, "Man, I am not." [59] And after an interval of about an hour still another insisted, saying, "Certainly this man also was with him; for he is a Galilean." [60] But Peter said, "Man, I do not know what you are saying." And immediately, while he was still speaking, the cock crowed. [61] And the Lord turned and looked at Peter. And Peter remembered the word of the Lord, how he had said to him, "Before the cock crows today, you will deny me three times." [62] And he went out and wept bitterly.

The second stage in the journey's concluding section opens with an introductory statement on how they seized Jesus and led him away into the high priest's house (22:54a). Peter, who had accepted to follow Jesus (5:11), that is to deny himself, take up his cross daily and follow in Jesus' steps (9:23) is indeed following, but at a distance (22:54b). Distanced from Jesus in the journey, he first denies any association with him or his followers (22:57-60). On Jesus' initiative, however, he later repents (22:61-62). In 5:8, Peter had asked Jesus to depart from him, a sinner. Now it is he who has departed, but Jesus reached out to him and drew him back.

The denial takes place in the middle of the courtyard of the high priest's house, where those who had led Jesus there were gathered by a fire which they themselves kindled. Luke notes pointedly that Peter was sitting among them (22:55). The one who followed at a distance was thus associated with those who were trying to destroy Jesus.

The fire is a physical reality, and as such it focuses attention within the narrative and positions its participants. However, it is also a symbolic reality. Jesus had come to kindle a fire on the earth (12:49), an event which would be described as his baptism or passion and which would occasion suffering and division (12:50-53). Christian baptism would be in that fire (3:16) as also the pentecostal birth of the universal Church (Acts 2:3). With this same fire, Jesus would be "a light for revelation to the Gentiles" (2:32). From one point of view, it is Jesus who kindled the fire. From another point of view, Jesus' enemies kindled the fire of the passion. Peter is now confronted by its challenge.

While Peter was sitting with the others in the light of the passion's fire, a maid saw him and gazed at him intently (22:56). She speaks to those gathered about the fire, and then two men address Peter directly. In turn, Peter denies that he had been with Jesus and knew him, that he was one of his followers, and that he even knew what the man was saying (2:57-60a).

While Peter was denying Jesus, his Lord, the latter was turned away from him. Unlike Peter, he had not desisted from the journey. At a given moment, however, a cock crowed, the Lord turned around and looked at Peter, who remembered how the Lord had foreseen this triple denial and tried to warn Peter about it (22:60b-61; see 22:34). Peter had faltered before the gaze of a maid. He sorrowfully repented under the Lord's gaze and left the company of those who arrested Jesus (22:62). Satan had not succeeded, and Peter's faith had not failed (22:31-32).

Peter had disowned Jesus in the presence of men, but he had not blasphemed the Holy Spirit. Accordingly, he was forgiven (12:8-10; 9:26).

   ii. Torture and Jewish Trial.
   *Are you the Son of God, then?*
   22:63-71.

> [63]Now the men who were holding Jesus mocked him and beat him; [64]they also blindfolded him and asked him, "Prophesy! Who is it that struck you?" [65]And they spoke many other words against him, reviling him.
>
> [66]When day came, the assembly of the elders of the people gathered together, both chief priests and scribes; and they led him away to their council, and they said, [67]"If you are the Christ, tell us." But he said to them, "If I tell you, you will not believe; [68]and if I ask you, you will not answer. [69]But from now on the Son of man shall be seated at the right hand of the power of God." [70]And they all said, "Are you the Son of God, then?" And he said to them, "You say that I am." [71]And they said, "What further testimony do we need? We have heard it ourselves from his own lips."

The night of farewell, prayer, betrayal and denial ends with the mockery and torture of Jesus (22:63-65), and the day of trials, crucifixion, forgiveness, death and burial begins with the whole assembly's gathering before the council (22:66-71). This double episode focuses on Jesus' identity as a prophet, the Christ, the Son of man and the Son of God. It thus recapitulates the question of Jesus' identity, a major concern in 1:5-2:52; 3:1-4:13 and 4:14-9:50, and relates it to his passion, death and glorification. At the same time, Jesus is shown to be innocent, a theme already introduced in Jesus' response to those who came after him at the Mount of Olives (22:52-53).

When the mockery and torture begin, Peter has already left the courtyard and the company of Jesus' enemies (22:62). Peter is consequently not a party to the mockery and the jewish trial which was itself a mockery. For readers who recalled Mark's presentation (Mk 14:53-72) in which the latter events were inserted (Mk 14:55-65) into Peter's story (14:54, 66-72), Luke's intention was obvious. Peter's denial could not be equated with the action of Judas and of those who were not Jesus' followers.

Jesus' enemies are obviously aware of the claim that he is a prophet, and so, having blindfolded him, they ask him to prophesy and to announce who it is that struck him (22:64). They are not aware, however, of Jesus' refusal to act as prophet in his native place (4:24) or of his apostrophe to Jerusalem that the latter was a slayer of prophets (13:34). Indeed, Jesus' enemies were actually God's instruments in the fulfillment of Jesus' prophetic role (13:33). Jesus was indeed a prophet, but not according to the simplistic and shallow understanding of those who were mocking him.

When day came, the chief priests and scribes, those who had been Jesus' principal opponents in 20:1-21:4 and whom Luke identifies as "the assembly of the elders of the people," gathered together and led Jesus to their council (22:66). The scene thus shifts from the courtyard to the council meeting place.

The assembly begins by asking that Jesus tell them if he is the Christ (22:67a). The point of their question is not whether Jesus is actually the Christ. In their minds, the answer to this was clearly negative. Rather, the point is whether Jesus claims to be the Christ. Were they to hear him make this explicit claim, they would have grounds to condemn him.

Jesus' response is double. First, he refuses to deal with the question as formulated. Were he to tell them that he is the Christ, they would not believe, and were he to ask them, they would not answer (22:67b-68). By his questions, Jesus had already reduced them to silence (20:7,26,40). Second, Jesus says that henceforth they would see the Son of man seated at the right hand of the power of God (22:69; see Acts 7:56). His answer thus looks beyond their question concerning Jesus' earthly role in history to the fulfillment of history, when as Son of man he would be associated with God in glory and power. The real issue is not the political liberation of Israel, but its ultimate deliverance, an event which transcends history (see 21:25-28; 24:19-27). Jesus is indeed the Christ. As such, however, his role is quite other than his interrogators' expectations.

Having heard Jesus' answer, the assembly then asks if Jesus is the Son of God (22:70a). They have understood Jesus' statement concerning the Son of man's transcendence and have perceived that the Son of man's association with God in power connotes divine sonship. As son of God, Jesus is fully Son of man, and he resists all temptations to act otherwise (4:1-13). It is precisely by accepting to be Son of man or Adam that Jesus manifests his divine sonship (3:38). Such is the mystery of the humanity and divinity of Jesus. Refusing to answer their question directly, Jesus simply says that it is they who affirm that he is Son of God (22:70b). It is through their action that the Son of man would proceed to the right hand of God and be manifested as the Son of God who pours out the Spirit he has received (see Acts 2:29-36).

For the reader, Jesus' response provided no grounds for accusing him. The assembly, however, judges otherwise, and it becomes publicly obvious that the elders have determined to condemn Jesus in spite of his innocence (22:71).

iii. Roman Trial.
*Are you the King of the Jews?*
23:1-25.

**23** Then the whole company of them arose, and brought him before Pilate. ²And they began to accuse him, saying, "We found this man perverting our nation, and forbidding us to give tribute to Caesar, and saying that he himself is Christ a king." ³And Pilate asked him, "Are you the King of the Jews?" And he answered him, "You have said so." ⁴And Pilate said to the chief priests and the multitudes, "I find no crime in this man." ⁵But they were urgent, saying, "He stirs up the people, teaching throughout all Judea, from Galilee even to this place."

⁶When Pilate heard this, he asked whether the man was a Galilean. ⁷And when he learned that he belonged to Herod's jurisdiction, he sent him over to Herod, who was himself in Jerusalem at that time. ⁸When Herod saw Jesus, he was very glad, for he had long desired to see him, and he was hoping to see some sign done by him. ⁹So he questioned him at some length; but he made no answer. ¹⁰The chief priests and the scribes stood by, vehemently accusing him. ¹¹And Herod with his soldiers treated him with contempt and mocked him; then, arraying him in gorgeous apparel, he sent him back to Pilate. ¹²And Herod and Pilate became friends with each other that very day, for before this they had been at enmity with each other.

¹³Pilate then called together the chief priests and the rulers and the people, ¹⁴and said to them, "You brought me this man as one who was perverting the people; and after examining him before you, behold, I did not find this man guilty of any of your charges against him; ¹⁵neither did Herod, for he sent him back to us. Behold,

nothing deserving death has been done by him; [16]I will therefore chastise him and release him."

[18]But they all cried out together, "Away with this man, and release to us Barabbas"—[19]a man who had been thrown into prison for an insurrection started in the city, and for murder. [20]Pilate addressed them once more, desiring to release Jesus; [21]but they shouted out, "Crucify, crucify him!" [22]A third time he said to them, "Why, what evil has he done? I have found in him no crime deserving death; I will therefore chastise him and release him." [23]But they were urgent, demanding with loud cries that he should be crucified. And their voices prevailed. [24]So Pilate gave sentence that their demand should be granted. [25]He released the man who had been thrown into prison for insurrection and murder, whom they asked for; but Jesus he delivered up to their will.

The whole assembly now brings Jesus to Pilate, the Roman governor of Judea (23:1). The purpose of the interrogation by the jewish council (22:66-71) had been precisely to find grounds to accuse Jesus before the political authorities. Their accusation, however, has little to do with their earlier questioning, in which they had not been able to draw Jesus into making politico-messianic claims. Determined to have Jesus condemned by the governor, they accuse him of forbidding the people to pay tribute to Caesar and of trying to subvert Roman rule by presenting himself as Christ a king (23:2). Since Jesus had already pointedly refused to forbid the paying of taxes to Caesar (20:20-26), their intention is transparent from the start.

Pilate ignores the question of Jesus' being the Christ, a title which was irrelevant to him as a Roman. For Pilate, the only accusation that matters is whether Jesus is actually presenting himself as an earthly king. He therefore asks whether Jesus is King of the Jews. Earthly kingship can be disassociated from Jesus' true messianic role. Refusing a direct answer, Jesus responds as he had done before the council (22:70), "You have said so" (23:3). Since Jesus makes no claims, Pilate declares him innocent of crime (23:4). Undaunted, the assembly points to Jesus' relationship to the people and to his teaching throughout all Judea, from Galilee to the very place where they have gathered (23:5). In their accusation, they use the Roman designation Judea to refer to the entire country, including Galilee (see 4:44). By specifically mentioning Galilee, however, they also provide Pilate with a reason to refer Jesus to Herod, the tetrarch who governed the Galilean region of Roman Judea (23:6-7).

The trial before Pilate (23:1-5; 13-25) is thus interrupted by an appearance before Herod (23:6-12). The event has a parallel in the trials of Paul at Caesarea. In that context, Paul was tried by Porcius Festus, the procurator (Acts 25:6-12; 26:24-32), but the latter brought King Agrippa into the case (Acts 25:13-26:23, 26-32). Like Jesus, Paul had previously been tried by the jewish council, the Sanhedrin (Acts 22:30-23:10). This had taken place during the governorship of Festus' predecessor, Felix. In both series of trials, the author is intent on showing the innocence of the accused.

In 13:31-33, Jesus had referred to Herod and strongly affirmed that the petty king would not prevent him from pursuing his journey to God. In 23:6-12, Jesus refuses to satisfy Herod's curiosity by performing an idle sign (see 4:1-13). One who casts out devils (13:32) does not do the work of the devil. That day, the jewish and Roman political leaders became friends, united by their involvement in the passion of Jesus (23:12).

Neither Pilate nor Herod was able to find Jesus guilty of the charges brought against him (23:13-17). Undaunted, the elders and council members ask for Jesus' condemnation and the release of Barabbas (23:18). Since the latter had been imprisoned for the very crime of which Jesus was being accused (23:19), the readers cannot miss the irony in their demand. Are not Jesus' accusers, rather than Jesus himself, guilty of fomenting insurrection? Shouts and loud cries drown out all reason. Contrary to the interest of Rome, Pilate releases a genuine insurrectionist and delivers an innocent man, a prophet, the Christ, the Son of man and the Son of God (22:63-71; 23:2), to be crucified according to the will of his accusers (23:18-25).

### 4. d. Crucifixion, Death and Burial.

#### i. Way to the Cross and Crucifixion.
*Father, forgive them.*
23:26-43.

26And as they led him away, they seized one Simon of Cyrene, who was coming in from the country, and laid on him the cross, to carry it behind Jesus. 27And there followed him a great multitude of the people, and of women who bewailed and lamented him. 28But Jesus turning to them said, "Daughters of Jerusalem, do not weep for me, but weep for yourselves and for your children. 29For behold, the days are coming when they will say, 'Blessed are the barren, and the wombs that never bore, and the breasts that never gave suck!' 30Then they will begin to say to the mountains, 'Fall on us'; and to the hills, 'Cover us.' 31For if they do this when the wood is green, what will happen when it is dry?"

32Two others also, who were criminals, were led away to be put to death with him. 33And when they came to the place which is called The Skull, there they crucified him, and the criminals, one on the right and one on the left. 34And Jesus said, "Father, forgive them; for they know not what they do." And they cast lots to divide his garments. 35And the people stood by, watching; but the rulers scoffed at him, saying, "He saved others; let him save himself, if he is the Christ of God, his Chosen One!" 36The soldiers also mocked him, coming up and offering him vinegar, 37and saying, "If you are the King of the

Jews, save yourself!" [38]There was also an inscription over him, "This is the King of the Jews."

[39]One of the criminals who were hanged railed at him, saying, "Are you not the Christ? Save yourself and us!" [40]But the other rebuked him, saying, "Do you not fear God, since you are under the same sentence of condemnation? [41]And we indeed justly; for we are receiving the due reward of our deeds; but this man has done nothing wrong." [42]And he said, "Jesus, remember me when you come into your kingdom." [43]And he said to him, "Truly, I say to you, today you will be with me in Paradise."

Unjustly condemned (23:25), Jesus was led away to be crucified (23:26). The narrative of the way to the cross and crucifixion (23:26-43) focuses on various participants in the story, Simon of Cyrene (23:26), a great multitude and women (23:27-31), two other criminals (23:32-33, 39-43), those who cast lots for his garments (23:34), the people (23:35a), the rulers (23:35b) and the soldiers (23:36-38). The crucifixion itself is briefly narrated (23:26a,33a). The main concern is with Jesus' response to the various participants. With deft use of irony, Luke uses the event to teach his readers the meaning of the crucifixion, and the principal vehicle for this teaching is the word of Jesus himself.

Simon of Cyrene carries the cross of Jesus and follows behind him (23:26). Very likely, Luke thinks of him as a type or human symbol of the Christians who were challenged to take up the cross of Christ. The story of Jesus' passion is also the story of Jesus' followers, who like Jesus are seized and persecuted. In his encounter with all the succeeding personages, Jesus thus models the attitude required of his followers.

The women of Jerusalem must not weep for Jesus. Their passion still lies in the future, when Jerusalem itself will be destroyed (23:27-30). Jesus message echoes his teaching in 21:20-24 and recalls his weeping over the city (19:41-44).

If Jesus' enemies can crucify one who is innocent, who is like green wood which is not meant for the fire, what will they do to a guilty Jerusalem, dry wood ready for burning (23:31)?

On his way to death, Jesus was accompanied by two criminals who were to be put to death with him (23:32). Crucified between the two criminals (23:33), the innocent Jesus asks that the Father forgive those who brought him to be crucified. They did not really know what they were doing (23:34). The narrator then goes on to tell us what they were actually doing. Casting lots to divide his garment (see Ps 22:19), they are fulfilling Psalm 22, which shows how Jesus' suffering and abjection is a passage to glory, an act of divine praise, and the opening of God's rule to all peoples on earth.

While the people are watching, the rulers scoff: let the one who saved others save himself if he is the Christ of God, his Chosen One (23:35). Ironically, as the reader knows, the Christ of God was to save others precisely by giving his own life, and in so doing, he himself would find life (see 9:23-24; 17:33). The soldiers also mock Jesus by offering him vinegar, a pain killer, and by asking that he save himself if he is King of the Jews (23:36-37). Like the rulers, they do not see that Jesus is saving himself on the cross and passing into the kingdom of God where he would drink of the fruit of the vine (see 22:17-18). The inscription over Jesus proclaims the truth concerning him: "This is the King of the Jews" (23:38).

The text now returns to the two criminals who were crucified beside Jesus (23:32-33). Jesus is one who forgives (23:34). The guilty, however, can either join those who mock Jesus and blindly ask for a limited earthly liberation (23:39) or they can acknowledge their guilt and ask that the Innocent One reconcile them to God (23:40-42). One of the criminals recognizes the nature of Christ's kingdom and asks that Jesus remember him when he comes into it (23:42). For this, he receives Jesus' assurance of salvation (23:43).

## ii. The Death of Jesus.
*Father, into thy hands I commit my spirit!*
23:44-49.

[44]It was now about the sixth hour, and there was darkness over the whole land until the ninth hour, [45]while the sun's light failed; and the curtain of the temple was torn in two. [46]Then Jesus, crying with a loud voice, said, "Father, into thy hands I commit my spirit!" And having said this he breathed his last. [47]Now when the centurion saw what had taken place, he praised God, and said, "Certainly this man was innocent!" [48]And all the multitudes who assembled to see the sight, when they saw what had taken place, returned home beating their breasts. [49]And all his acquaintances and the women who had followed him from Galilee stood at a distance and saw these things.

From the sixth to the ninth hour, there was darkness over the whole earth (23:44). Here was the hour of the triumph of darkness (22:53). At the ninth hour or three o'clock, when the people gathered in the temple for the afternoon prayer and sacrifice (Acts 3:1; Ex 29:38-42), the curtain of the temple was torn in two (23:45). The Holy of Holies was no more and the era of Israel's sacrifices gave way to the sacrifice of Christ. The destruction of the temple had begun (19:41-44; 21:20-24; 23:27-30).

Again Jesus prays to the Father. Fulfilling the Father's will and taking the cup (22:42), he had prayed that his enemies be forgiven (23:34), and he now commends his spirit into the Father's hands. With this word, Jesus breathed his last (23:46). Now that Jesus was exalted at the Father's right hand (22:69; Acts 7:56) as Lord, he himself would receive the spirit of those (Acts 7:59) who joined him in forgiving their enemies (Acts 7:60).

The account of Jesus' death ends with a number of reactions. The centurion, who was responsible for the execution, declared Jesus an innocent man (23:47; see 23:4, 14-15,22). The multitudes, who had stood watching (23:35a), returned home repentant and asking for forgiveness (23:48). All Jesus' acquaintances, however, and the Galilean women (see 8:2-3), who had followed Jesus from Galilee to Jerusalem, stood at a distance and saw all that was happening (23:49). Followers of Jesus, they had distanced themselves from Jesus' enemies. Since they were to observe the burial (23:55), find the tomb empty on the first day of the week (24:10a) and announce the resurrection in faith (24:10b-11), it was important that they be witnesses to the crucifixion as well. Those who did not abandon Jesus during the passion could appreciate his resurrection.

### iii. The Burial of Jesus.
*Looking for the kingdom of God.*
23:50-56.

> [50]Now there was a man named Joseph from the Jewish town of Arimathea. He was a member of the council, a good and righteous man, [51]who had not consented to their purpose and deed, and he was looking for the kingdom of God. [52]This man went to Pilate and asked for the body of Jesus. [53]Then he took it down and wrapped it in a linen shroud, and laid him in a rock-hewn tomb, where no one had ever yet been laid. [54]It was the day of Preparation, and the sabbath was beginning. [55]The women who had come with him from Galilee followed, and saw the tomb, and how his body was laid; [56]then they returned, and prepared spices and ointments.

Burial is part of the story of the Son of man (23:50-56). Jesus' entry into Paradise on the day of his death (23:43) does not preclude his burial or interrupt the normal course of a human being's life, death and burial.

In the trial accounts (22:66-23:25), the jewish council had been presented in a very bad light. Contrary to all the evidence it had succeeded in having Jesus condemned by one who recognized his innocence but was too weak to act in Rome's best interests. Jesus' salvation and the kingdom, however, were not for the Gentiles alone. Accordingly, Luke singles out a member of the council, a man named Joseph from the jewish town of Arimathea, a good and righteous man, who had not consented to the council's purpose and deed. This man was looking for the kingdom of God (23:50-51).

Unlike the council which had gone to Pilate to seek Jesus' death, Joseph went with a request for Jesus' body that he might provide it with the burial appropriate for a good Jew who had done nothing to subvert the rule of Caesar. Jesus is thus accorded the burial of an innocent man. Pilate's ready acquiescence mitigates his responsibility in Jesus' death and provided persecuted Christians with a precedent demonstrating Christianity's innocence before Roman law.

From Luke's account, we receive no indication that Jesus was buried in the criminals' graveyard near the place of execution where his remains would have been separated from those of his fellow Jews. Jesus was not given an insurrectionist's burial. Luke thus continues to affirm Jesus' innocence, and shows how it was recognized by both the Roman governor and a member of the jewish council.

Just as Jesus had entered Jerusalem on an ass on which no one had yet ridden (19:30), he was now placed in a tomb where no one had ever yet been laid (23:53). Jesus' entry into Jerusalem marked a totally new and unique event. His death and burial were also like that of no other.

The story of Jesus' journey from Jerusalem to God (22:1-24:53) has now reached the end of its first day. It had been a day of fulfillment. Symbolically, it had also been a day of Preparation (23:54a). The women remained faithful to their call to follow Jesus, even as he was being buried. They saw how he was laid and then returned to prepare spices and ointments in order to acknowledge Jesus as the

Anointed One or Messiah (23:55-56). The day of Preparation was thus oriented to the Sabbath (23:54b) as well as to the christian day of the Lord, the first day of the week (24:1).

## 4. e. Visits to the Tomb, Recognition and Mission.

### i. The Empty Tomb.
*Why do you seek the living among the dead?*
24:1-12.

> On the sabbath they rested according to the commandment.
> **24** But on the first day of the week, at early dawn, they went to the tomb, taking the spices which they had prepared. ²And they found the stone rolled away from the tomb, ³but when they went in they did not find the body. ⁴While they were perplexed about this, behold, two men stood by them in dazzling apparel; ⁵and as they were frightened and bowed their faces to the ground, the men said to them, "Why do you seek the living among the dead? ⁶Remember how he told you, while he was still in Galilee, ⁷that the Son of man must be delivered into the hands of sinful men, and be crucified, and on the third day rise." ⁸And they remembered his words, ⁹and returning from the tomb they told all this to the eleven and to all the rest. ¹⁰Now it was Mary Magdalene and Joanna and Mary the mother of James and the other women with them who told this to the apostles; ¹¹but these words seemed to them an idle tale, and they did not believe them.

The account of the women's visit to the tomb is closely connected with the story of Jesus' burial (23:50-56) as well as with the Emmaus journey narrative (24:13-35; see vv.22-24). Its source is Mk 16:1-8. This relationship, however, should not obscure its distinctive characteristics.

First the women, who remain unnamed until 24:10, are said to have actually taken the spices which they had prepared with them, and it is explicitly mentioned that when they went into the tomb they did not find the body and were perplexed about this (24:1-4a). Only then does the text introduce the two men who stood by them in dazzling apparel (24:4b). In Mark, on the other hand, no mention is made of actually bringing the spices to the tomb and attention focuses immediately on the young man. The absence of Jesus' body is not considered until later when it forms part of the young man's message. These observations enable us to perceive the Lukan problem and theological response. In Mark, the basic problem is the passion and death of Jesus. The young man responds to this problem by proclaiming the resurrection in the midst of the tomb and the symbols of death. In Luke, the basic problem is the absence of Jesus' body and the empty tomb itself. The two men respond to this problem by orienting the women away from the tomb toward the community of the living.

As in Mk 16:2, the event takes place on the first day of the week, a day associated with the assembly for the breaking of bread (Acts 20:7). All the other events in Lk 24, including the breaking of bread at Emmaus (24:13-35), the apostolic assembly in Jerusalem (24:36-49) and the ascension (24:50-53) occur on this same day.

In Mark, only one man, a young man, spoke to the women in the tomb and proclaimed the resurrection. In Luke, on the other hand, we find two men. They are disciples, two of the seventy or seventy-two elders whom Jesus had sent out in pairs (10:1). A similar pair had prepared Jesus' entry into Jerusalem (19:29-35) as well as the last supper (22:7-13). The story of Emmaus would tell how two of these had abandoned the way to Jerusalem but had been found by the risen Lord who explained the Scriptures to them and revealed himself in the breaking of the bread (24:13-35). In the present context, the two men fulfill the mission of christian elders to interpret events in light of the message which Jesus had spoken during his historical life and to help the Christians to orient their search for the Lord properly as they pursue their journey to God. Their function is thus both catechetical and prophetic.

Once the women have redirected their attention to the two men (24:4b), the latter begin by challenging the women's focus on the tomb: why were they seeking the living one among the dead? (24:5). They then reaffirm the resurrection by recalling Jesus' own words concerning the passion and resurrection of the Son of man (24:7). To do this effectively, however, Mark's reference to going into Galilee where Jesus precedes his disciples had to be transformed into a flashback to the Galilean context of Jesus' prediction (24:6). For Luke, this was also important in view of his symbolic use of Jerusalem as the city from which the gospel was to be preached, an event which was not possible until the apostolic community had been gifted with the Spirit.

Remembering Jesus' words, the women return from the tomb and tell everything to the eleven and the others (24:8-9). However, the apostles do not believe the women (24:11), and this prepares the way for a further visit to the tomb (24:12). Lk 24:12 is not found in a number of manuscripts and has been omitted from the Revised Standard Version of Luke. In keeping with the most recent study of the text, however, it should be inserted: "But Peter rose and ran to the tomb; stooping and looking in, he saw the linen cloths by themselves; and he went home wondering at what had happened." The empty tomb is consequently not seen as a proof of the resurrection, but only as a source of wonderment. Faith in the resurrection springs from the actual experience of the risen Lord, and such is the message of the following units (24:13-35).

ii. The Journey to Emmaus.
*He was known to them in the breaking of the bread.*
24:13-35.

¹³That very day two of them were going to a village named Emmaus, about seven miles from Jerusalem,

¹⁴and talking with each other about all these things that had happened. ¹⁵While they were talking and discussing together, Jesus himself drew near and went with them. ¹⁶But their eyes were kept from recognizing him. ¹⁷And he said to them, "What is this conversation which you are holding with each other as you walk?" And they stood still, looking sad. ¹⁸Then one of them, named Cleopas, answered him, "Are you the only visitor to Jerusalem who does not know the things that have happened there in these days?" ¹⁹And he said to them, "What things?" And they said to him, "Concerning Jesus of Nazareth, who was a prophet mighty in deed and word before God and all the people, ²⁰and how our chief priests and rulers delivered him up to be condemned to death, and crucified him. ²¹But we had hoped that he was the one to redeem Israel. Yes, and besides all this, it is now the third day since this happened. ²²Moreover, some women of our company amazed us. They were at the tomb early in the morning ²³and did not find his body; and they came back saying that they had even seen a vision of angels, who said that he was alive. ²⁴Some of those who were with us went to the tomb, and found it just as the women had said; but him they did not see." ²⁵And he said to them, "O foolish men, and slow of heart to believe all that the prophets have spoken! ²⁶Was it not necessary that the Christ should suffer these things and enter into his glory?" ²⁷And beginning with Moses and all the prophets, he interpreted to them in all the scriptures the things concerning himself.

²⁸So they drew near to the village to which they were going. He appeared to be going further, ²⁹but they constrained him, saying, "Stay with us, for it is toward evening and the day is now far spent." So he went in to stay with them. ³⁰When he was at table with them, he took the bread and blessed, and broke it, and gave it to them. ³¹And their eyes were opened and they recognized him; and he vanished out of their sight. ³²They said to

each other, "Did not our hearts burn within us while he talked to us on the road, while he opened to us the scriptures?" [33]And they rose that same hour and returned to Jerusalem; and they found the eleven gathered together and those who were with them, [34]who said, "The Lord has risen indeed, and has appeared to Simon!" [35]Then they told what had happened on the road, and how he was known to them in the breaking of the bread.

Luke's story now moves away from the tomb to the context where one might meet the Living One (24:5). The second episode in the resurrection narrative is situated on the same day that women and Peter visited the tomb, the first day of the week (24:1). The account involves two disciples (see 10:1; 19:29; 22:8; 24:4), one of whom was named Cleopas (24:18), who are abandoning the christian journey to God. Leaving Jerusalem, they are going to a village named Emmaus, which was seven miles distant from Jerusalem (24:13).

As the disciples are going their way, they are discussing everything that had happened (24:14). Later, they would spell out what these things were and how they perceived them (24:19b-24). During their discussion, a third personage drew near to them and went along with them. The narrator tells us that this third personage is Jesus. The disciples, however, do not recognize him. In fact their eyes were prevented from recognizing him (24:16). Ever deft at irony, Luke has the readers, who know Jesus' identity, listen to the disciples tell the Living One of their discouragement over his death (24:19b-24). Unable to share their knowledge with the two disciples, the readers identify with their grief and plight as they are told a story which parallels their own. Like the two disciples, the Lukan communities suffer from not being able to recognize the risen Lord in the midst of their difficulties and persecutions.

The body of the story is literarily framed by the theme of recognition. It tells how the disciples moved from not being able to recognize Jesus (24:16) to their recognition of him (24:31a) in his absence as a historical personage (24:31b). The narrative thus uses the inclusion technique (24:16,31) which had been used in the story of Zacchaeus (19:1-10; see 19:5,9) and in the prayer at the Mount of Olives (22:39-46; see 22:40,46).

The body includes two distinct subunits, a dialogue narrative, which is situated on the way to Emmaus (24:17-27) and a meal narrative, which is located at Emmaus itself in the home of the disciples (24:28-30). These two units reflect the general structure of the early christian assembly for the breaking of the bread, which included both a discussion and a meal (Acts 20:7-12).

The dialogue narrative is introduced by Jesus who inquires into the subject of the disciples' conversation (24:17; see 24:14-15), by the disciples' questioning response concerning the stranger's ignorance of the events (24:18), and by Jesus' request that they tell him about them (24:19a). Again Luke shows himself a master of irony. The disciples ask Jesus if he is the only visitor in Jerusalem who does not know what has happened to him. Since Jesus obviously knows, his role in the introductory dialogue is simply to draw out the disciples.

The disciples' response articulates the events of the good news with many of the expressions which had become traditional in early christian faith and reflection. Discouraged, however, they see the good news as bad news. Their statement proceeds in three stages, each of which focuses on how wonderful things had been, how hopeful they themselves had been, and how their hopes had been recently rekindled. This triple statement is balanced by a return to immediate reality as they now saw it, how Jesus' story ended in disaster, their former hopes were dashed, and their recent glimmer of hope was disappointed (24:19b-24).

Jesus of Nazareth was a prophet mighty in deed and word before God and all the people (24:19b). Their chief priests and rulers, however, had delivered him up to death and crucified him (24:20). The disciples thus summarize and recapitulate Jesus' entire story from his first manifestation as a prophet (4:14) to his death (23:49) at the hands of those who had found a way to circumvent Jesus' popularity with the people (19:48; 20:19; 22:1-6, 47-53) as well as his prophetic might before God (22:66-71) by making use of Rome's political authority (23:1-25).

The second stage in the disciples' response focuses on their own hopes. Jesus' prophetic might before God and all the people had led them to believe that he was the one who would redeem Israel (24:21a). For the disciples, Jesus had thus been like a new Moses (see Acts 7:22,25,35-37). They had understood Jesus' life according to the scriptures. The new Moses, however, was not expected to die, and their understanding of Jesus did not include suffering and death. Jesus' death was definitive. It was already three days since it had occurred (24:21b). Language of faith, associated with the vision of the risen Lord (see 1 Cor 15:3-5), is thus the vehicle for non-faith and blindness.

The third stage focuses on the visits to the tomb by the women and Peter (see 24:1-12). The women failed to find Jesus' body and claimed that they had seen a vision of angels who declared that Jesus was alive (24:22-23). However, while others of their company could verify the women's report, they did not see Jesus himself (24:24). The disciples' summary has thus brought us to Luke's main concern, the recognition of the risen Lord.

Jesus now responds. The men are foolish or ignorant. They are slow to believe all that the prophets have spoken (24:25). They may have understood things according to the scriptures, but their approach to the prophets was too narrow. They had failed to consider the many texts which referred to the suffering and death of God's Servant.

As he had done during his historical life (24:6-7), Jesus once again teaches them and shows them how the events concerning him were scripturally founded. Jesus' life, death and glorification are thus according to the word of Jesus as well as according to the scriptures. First Jesus draws out the biblical lesson which responds to their lack of faith and hopelessness: "Was it not necessary that the Christ should suffer these things and enter into his glory?" (24:26). The dialogue itself stops here, and Jesus' summary statement is not elaborated. Instead the narrator says that Jesus went on to interpret for the disciples the things concerning himself in all the scriptures beginning with Moses and continuing with all the prophets (24:27).

We now come to the second part, the meal narrative. Luke tells us that as they neared the village, Jesus acted as if he were going further and leaving the disciples behind at Emmaus (24:28). Again the readers are made privy to special information. The disciples, however, are unaware of the real intention of Jesus and they invite him to remain with them, since it is toward evening and the day is now far spent (24:29a). As in 24:17, 19a, Jesus thus draws the disciples out, and this time into inviting him, a stranger, into their house. The time is important. It is at sundown that the Christians gathered for their assembly and the breaking of the bread. Jesus accepts their invitation and goes in to stay with them (24:29b).

At this point, the guest assumes the role of the host, and Jesus takes bread, blesses, breaks it and gives it to them (24:30). The narrator thus evokes Jesus' last supper (22:19a). The words cited function like a title for the whole eucharistic formula. As such, they were sufficient to establish a relationship between the christian assembly for the breaking of the bread and Jesus' last supper. Jesus himself is a participant and the host at the christian meal.

In sharing Jesus' meal, the two disciples accept the attitude which was his as he entered into the passion. With this, their eyes are finally opened and they recognize him, even as he has vanished from their sight. Those who open their table to the stranger and share their possessions and who take on the self-giving attitude of Jesus recognize the risen Lord and are reestablished in hope. Such is Luke's message to those who suffer persecution and can no longer recognize the risen Lord as they have in the past.

Upon Jesus' disappearance, the disciples' reflect on what has occurred. They become aware that their exploration of the scriptures and their reflection with Jesus on his life and death had had its effect. Did not their hearts burn within them as he opened them to invite Jesus into their home and to recognize him. Having recognized him, they became conscious of the word's impact and significance (24:32).

The disciples' experience is the source of gospel proclamation. The good news they had received must be shared with the community, which they think is still struggling with the same discouragement which had been theirs. They consequently return immediately to Jerusalem (24:33), only to be greeted by the apostolic proclamation of Jesus' resurrection. The Lord had already appeared to Simon (24:34). Peter, the first one to be called (5:1-11) and the one who had denied Jesus (22:54-62) had returned to strengthen his brothers (22:32). Luke had thus outlined the necessary conditions for the christian mission and shown how it was grounded in the apostolic teaching and Peter's primary experience of the risen Lord. The narrator then summarizes the disciples' own story and the whole narrative in terms of "what had happened on the road and how he was known to them in the breaking of the bread" (24:35).

iii. Mission and Ascension.
*I send the promise of my Father upon you.*
24:36-53.

> [36]As they were saying this, Jesus himself stood among them. [37]But they were startled and frightened, and supposed that they saw a spirit. [38]And he said to them, "Why are you troubled, and why do questionings rise in your hearts? [39]See my hands and my feet, that it is I

myself; handle me, and see; for a spirit has not flesh and bones as you see that I have." [41]And while they still disbelieved for joy, and wondered, he said to them, "Have you anything here to eat?" [42]They gave him a piece of broiled fish, [43]and he took it and ate before them.

[44]Then he said to them, "These are my words which I spoke to you, while I was still with you, that everything written about me in the law of Moses and the prophets and the psalms must be fulfilled." [45]Then he opened their minds to understand the scriptures, [46]and said to them, "Thus it is written, that the Christ should suffer and on the third day rise from the dead, [47]and that repentance and forgiveness of sins should be preached in his name to all nations, beginning from Jerusalem. [48]You are witnesses of these things. [49]And behold, I send the promise of my Father upon you; but stay in the city, until you are clothed with power from on high."

[50]Then he led them out as far as Bethany, and lifting up his hands he blessed them. [51]While he blessed them, he parted from them, and was carried up into heaven. [52]And they returned to Jerusalem with great joy, [53]and were continually in the temple blessing God.


Luke's orderly account (1:3) of all that Jesus began to do and teach until the day when he was taken up (Acts 1:1) now reaches its final episode (24:36-53). His story of the human life and message of the Son of God (4:14-24:53), which had already been told in an account of Jesus' origins and destiny (1:5-2:52) and prepared in an account of Jesus' contexts in history and human life (3:1-4:13) reaches its conclusion. The journey to Jerusalem (9:51-24:53) and its final stage (22:1-24:53) climax with Jesus' ascension (24:50-51), an event prepared by the final manifestation and teaching of the risen Lord (24:36-49) and followed up by the community's joyful presence in the temple of Jerusalem (24:52-53).

The unit begins with Jesus' final self-manifestation before the ascension (24:36-43). The entire community, including the two who had returned from Emmaus, is assembled when Jesus himself stands in their midst (24:36). The assembly's reaction, however, reveals none of the joy and hope which pervaded the end of the Emmaus story (24:31-35). Startled and frightened, those assembled supposed that they saw a spirit (24:37). Luke thus means to deal with a further problem. Was the community's experience of the risen Lord in the breaking of the bread (24:35) an illusion or some spirit? Was this really the same person who had called them (5:1-6:11), constituted them as a new Israel (6:12-7:50), formed them (8:1-56) and sent them on mission (9:1-50)? Was this the same person whom they had accompanied on the journey to Jerusalem up to this point (9:51-24:35)?

Jesus calms their fears by showing them his hands and feet and by pointing out that a spirit does not have flesh and bones as they see he has (24:38-39). The stranger whom the disciples had met was a physical human being with all the tangible characteristics and needs of a human being. Jesus was not with them as a spirit but in the person of those who journeyed through life. For the disciples, this was too good to be true, but they joyfully knew that it was true. As they look on in wonderment, Jesus asks for something to eat. They give him a piece of broiled fish. He takes it and eats it (24:41-43). The disciples and Luke's readers are thus asked to extend nourishment to those in whom Jesus is really present. They are doing what he had done in memory of him, and through them others are associated in the breaking of the bread (22:19). The presence of the risen Lord in their midst requires a commitment to the earthly lives of people. It cannot be reduced to an uninvolved and purely spiritual reality.

Jesus' teaching (24:44-49) is closely related to the message of his self-manifestation (24:36-43). First he recalls his own words, spoken prior to his death and describes those words as a fulfillment of the law of Moses and the prophets and the psalms in his regard (24:44). The narrator thus achieves a synthesis of Jesus' teaching (24:7) and the scriptural word (24:25-27) by affirming that Jesus' teaching concerning the events of his life was actually according to the scriptures. Accordingly, he opens their minds to understanding those events (24:45-46). Heretofore, like his risen presence (24:16), their meaning had been concealed from them (9:44-45).

The word concerning Jesus (24:7) and Jesus' word, however, go further than on previous occasions. Those who have accepted to give bread to be taken and eaten (24:42-43) must preach repentance and forgiveness of sins in his name to all nations, beginning with Jerusalem (24:47). They must join Jesus in his universal mission of reconciliation, a mission which must begin with Jerusalem but which must reach out from Jerusalem to the ends of the earth (Acts 1:8).

Those assembled are witnesses to these things (24:48). Those who had eaten and drunk with him after he rose from the dead (Acts 10:41) and had associated themselves with the Lord of all (Acts 10:36) had a mission of reconciliation to all (Acts 10:42-43). The risen Lord now sends them the promise of his Father. For the present, however, they must remain in Jerusalem until they are empowered as missionary witnesses with power from on high (24:49). This they would receive on Pentecost (Acts 1:8; 2:14), but first they must follow him to the conclusion of his journey in the ascension.

Jesus then led his disciples out to Bethany (24:50a), the place from which he had entered Jerusalem (19:29) to be acclaimed as the one "who comes as king in the name of the Lord" (19:38). Once again Jesus would enter Jerusalem, the heavenly Jerusalem and the dwelling of his Father (2:49, 23:46). As he is carried up into heaven (24:51b), he blesses his followers while parting (24:50b-51a). The promises made to Abraham that all the families of the earth would be blessed (Acts 3:25) were being fulfilled in Jesus' blessing (Acts 3:26), which was associated with his ascension and presence in heaven (Acts 3:21).

Blessed by Jesus and heirs to the promises made to Abraham (1:72-73), Luke's gentile communities could continually bless God (24:53; 1:74-75). The concluding summary situates the community in Jerusalem and in the temple (24:52-53), joyfully faithful to Jesus' own practice before his death (19:47-48; 21:37-38): They would continue on earth the mission and the journey which Jesus had completed with his ascension.

# FOR FURTHER READING

Brown, Raymond E. *The Birth of the Messiah*. (Garden City: Doubleday & Company, Inc., 1977).

An excellent and exhaustive commentary on the infancy narratives in Matthew and Luke, rich in literary analyses and bibliography. Guided by the insight that as a prologue each infancy narrative constitutes its entire gospel in miniature.

Conzelmann, H. *The Theology of St. Luke*. (New York: Harper & Row, 1960).

An early contribution to the redaction criticism of the gospels and the point of departure for most contemporary study of Luke-Acts.

Creed, J.M. *The Gospel According to St. Luke*. (New York: St. Martin's Press, 1965).

The Greek text and a philological commentary with emphasis on Luke's relationship to his sources.

Danker, F.W. *Luke*. Proclamation Commentaries. (Philadelphia: Fortress, 1976).

A study of Luke's principal presuppositions, social context, solutions to problems, and literary modes of communication. Intended as a general orientation for those who wish to read and proclaim selected pericopes in the liturgy.

_____. *Jesus and the New Age according to St. Luke: A Commentary on the Third Gospel*. (St. Louis: Clayton, 1974).

An insightful commentary on Luke with numerous reflections on the problems of the Lukan communities and great awareness of the context in which the gospel is now read.

Fitzmyer, Joseph A. *The Gospel according to Luke I-IX*. Anchor
  Bible, Vol. 28. (Garden City: Doubleday & Company, Inc.,
  1981).
    The first volume of a highly authoritative commentary,
    which includes a lengthy introduction to Luke, a new
    translation, notes on the text and exhaustive bibliographies.
    Essential reading for historical critical and philological
    questions.
Jervell, Jacob. *Luke and the People of God*. (Minneapolis:
  Augsburg Publishing House, 1972).
    A provocative study of Luke-Acts with a strong emphasis
    on ecclesiology and the Church's continuity with Israel.
Johnson, Luke T. *Luke-Acts: A Story of Prophet and People*.
  Herald Biblical Booklets. (Chicago: Franciscan Herald Press,
  1981).
    A short and very readable introduction to Luke-Acts.
    Written for a popular audience from a literary and theo-
    logical point of view.
Karris, R. *Gospel of St. Luke*. Read and Pray. (Chicago: Fran-
  ciscan Herald, 1974).
    Comments, reflections and brief prayers on the text of the
    gospel. Ilumines the text in its ancient and modern settings
    in view of meditative prayer.
_____. *Invitation to Luke*. Image Books. (Garden City: Double-
  day, 1977).
    A sprightly and very readable commentary based on the
    *Jerusalem Bible* translation. Invites the reader to individual
    study, meditation and group discussion.
_____. *What Are They Saying about Luke and Acts?* (New
  York: Paulist, 1979).
    A brief synthesis of the theology of Luke-Acts with great
    sensitivity for its relevance to the modern world.
LaVerdiere, E. "The Presence of Christ in the Eucharist," in
  *Bread from Heaven*. (New York: Paulist, 1977) 87-101.
    An essay on Luke's view of Christ's eucharistic presence as
    participant and as nourishment, the interrelationship be-
    tween these two modes of presence and their implications
    for the life of the Church.

_____. "Give Us Each Day Our Daily Bread," in *Bread from Heaven*. (New York: Paulist, 1977) 19-33.

An analysis of the Lukan petition for bread in the Lord's prayer and its implications for pastoral life.

_____. *The Year of Luke*. (Kansas City: National Catholic Reporter, 1980).

Brief commentary on the Lukan texts included in Cycle C of the liturgy as well as on the texts which accompany them on Sundays and solemnities. Includes introductions to liturgical seasons. Intended as a guide for liturgical planning groups, lectors and homilists.

_____, and W.G. Thompson. "New Testament Communities in Transition: a Study of Matthew and Luke," *Theological Studies* 37(1976) 567-597.

A study of the historical and social contexts of the Matthean and Lukan communities and of the ecclesiologies which the two evangelists developed for them.

Marshall, I.H. *Commentary on Luke*. New International Greek Testament Commentary. (Grand Rapids: Eerdmans, 1978).

A comprehensive commentary on the Greek text of the gospel, with careful consideration of the state of scholarship on disputed questions and an effort to situate the gospel's units in their literary context.

*Perspectives on Luke-Acts*. Edited by Charles H. Talbert. Special Studies Series. (Macon, GA: Mercer Univ. Press, 1978).

An excellent collection of studies on introductory matters, literary forms, motifs and particular sections of Luke-Acts. Brings together the results of research conducted between 1972 and 1978 by the Luke-Acts Group of the Society of Biblical Literature.

*Studies in Luke-Acts*. Edited by Leander E. Keck and J. Louis Martyn. (Philadelphia: Fortress Press, 1966, 1980).

A collection of articles by international scholars of long-standing recognition, all of whom have contributed significantly to the advance of Lukan studies.

Stuhlmueller, C. "The Gospel according to Luke" in *The Jerome Biblical Commentary II*. (Englewood Cliffs, New Jersey: Prentice-Hall, 1968) 115-164.

A short commentary which is particularly insightful with regard to Luke's use of the Old Testament. Includes numerous references to helpful studies on particular passages.

Tiede, David L. *Prophecy and History in Luke-Acts.* (Philadelphia: Fortress Press, 1980).

Excellent study of Luke-Acts as a prophetic interpretation of history. Sensitive to literary and historical background as well as to the literary function of personages and events in Luke's story.

*NOTES*

*NOTES*

*NOTES*

*NOTES*

*NOTES*

*NOTES*